STRADDLING WORLDS

STRADDLING WORLDS

The Jewish-American Journey of Professor Richard W. Leopold

STEVEN J. HARPER

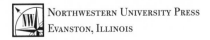

NORTHWESTERN UNIVERSITY PRESS
EVANSTON, ILLINOIS

Except as otherwise noted, photographs of Richard W. Leopold come from family collections maintained in the Northwestern University Archives; Leopold himself selected them for inclusion in this book. All of the William J. Loeb photographs come from his family's collection.

Northwestern University Press
www.nupress.northwestern.edu
Copyright © by Steven J. Harper
Published 2007 by Northwestern University Press.
All rights reserved.
Printed in the United States of America
10 9 8 7 6 5 4 3 2 1
ISBN-13: 978-0-8101-2444-8
ISBN-10: 0-8101-2444-0

Library of Congress Cataloging-in-Publication Data

Harper, Steven J., 1954-
  Straddling worlds : the Jewish-American journey of Professor Richard W. Leopold /
Steven J. Harper.
    p. cm.
  Includes bibliographical references and index.
  ISBN-13: 978-0-8101-2444-8 (cloth : alk. paper)
  ISBN-10: 0-8101-2444-0 (cloth : alk. paper)
  1. Leopold, Richard William. 2. Loeb, William Joseph, 1912- 3. Jews--United States--Biography.
4. College teachers--United States--Biography. 5. History teachers--United States--Biography.
6. Otolaryngologists--United States--Biography. I. Title.
  E184.37.L46H37 2007
  973'.049240092--dc22
  [B]
                          2007028661

  ∞ The paper used in this publication meets the minimum
requirements of the American National Standard for Information
Sciences—Permanence of Paper for Printed Library Materials,
ANSI Z39.48–1992

For Ben, Pete, and Emma—
The future belongs to those
who understand the past.

CONTENTS

ACKNOWLEDGMENTS

In many ways, this is Dick Leopold's final book. Without his active involvement at every step of the process, it would not exist. We conversed in his room every Sunday morning for almost a year before I gave him the first draft of my completed manuscript. Although he said it was "first rate," we thereafter together supplemented, edited, and revised it—page by page—until the last version was done. As we proceeded, I gained new insight into the high standards that prevented him from releasing more books to public scrutiny: In his endless search for perfection, he was always able to improve a sentence, paragraph, or chapter. His ability to add details seemed limitless. The final result is not a perfect biography, and I alone accept full responsibility for its failings. But Dick's tireless efforts made it far better than it otherwise would have been. Most importantly, this book tells his story as he wanted it told, and he was "grateful beyond words" for my participation in our collaborative effort. The feeling was mutual.

As with all of my successful endeavors, I owe the most to my wife, Kit, whose continuing support has made everything else possible and whose helpful suggestions have always improved my work.

Many others deserve special mention. Kevin Leonard has thoroughly mastered Dick's voluminous materials in the Northwestern University Archives. Kevin's assistance was indispensable, and I know that he sometimes called on Phillips Exeter Academy's Edouard L. Desrochers and Jacquelyn Thomas for specific information that I sought about Exeter. Scott Turow offered his time and insights in reviewing my initial manuscript, as did Yale's Sterling Professor of History (Emeritus) John Morton Blum, F. Sheppard Shanley, and Susan Sheehy. Dick's entire Northwestern community supported him and the project with enthusiasm. Dick was—and I am—especially grateful for the encouragement over many years from President Henry S. Bienen and his predecessor Arnold R. Weber, Provost Lawrence B. Dumas, Weinberg College of Arts and Sciences Dean Daniel Linzer and his predecessor Eric J. Sundquist, Northwestern University Press Director Donna A. Shear, the University Press board chaired by Professor Peter Hayes (whom Dick always described to me as "a good man"), Dick's

Northwestern faculty colleagues, and many loyal friends in the university's development and dean's offices, including Sarah Pearson, Matthew TerMolen, Kristen Williams, Eve Jeffers, and Stacia Kozlowski. Dick loved you all, and you returned his gift in kind.

AS HE SPOKE, IT WAS EASY TO FORGET THAT HE WOULD SOON CELEBRATE
HIS NINETY-THIRD BIRTHDAY. TODAY, HE WANTED TO DISCUSS HIS DEATH.

"I have one additional matter I would like to review with you, but we'll wait," Richard W. Leopold intoned from his motorized wheelchair. It was Labor Day 2004. Twenty-four years earlier, he had retired from Northwestern University as the William Smith Mason Professor of American History—the most distinguished chair in the department and one he held for more than seventeen years. Although he had been confined to a wheelchair since 1997, his limited mobility had not weakened a strong baritone voice that still retained the hint of his New York City origins. Nor had it diminished the razor-sharp mental acuity so dominating his persona. A few strands of thin white hair covered the top of his head, but he still had respectable coverage on the sides.

Before he had lost the ability to walk seven years earlier, he had stood over six feet tall. His gait was always brisk; he moved with efficiency and economy in all things. His physique had been solid—not slim, yet neither muscular nor over-weight. Simply solid. Now, from his electrically powered throne on wheels, his legs had atrophied, and a pesky tremor served as an additional and unnecessary re-minder of his mortality. His vision had been poor since graduate school in the 1930s, but shortly after his 1980 retirement, surgery removed cataracts from both eyes and clarified his sight in exchange for thick eyeglasses. Before the operations, he had worn thinner bifocals that had seemed less intrusive.

During the early years of his wheelchair life, he had confided in me when waves of depression wafted over him. At one point when doctors were still conducting tests, he told me that if an upcoming round of evaluations failed to hold promise for restoring his ability to walk, "That would be pretty much the end of the line for me."

As I pondered this latest analogy to the train travel he had so enjoyed during happier times, I responded that many people in wheelchairs led productive lives. I assured him that his then-eighty-five-year-old mind remained sharper than most, regardless of age. But adjusting to a new lifestyle as a handicapped octogenarian became understandably difficult for him. Because his beautifully appointed two-bedroom apartment overlooking Lake Michigan near downtown Evanston could not accommodate his new condition, he suffered a double blow when the rules of his residence required him to leave it. I had tried valiantly to persuade him that structural changes might be made to his eighth floor abode so he and his new wheels could remain there. At the conclusion of a long afternoon's discussion on the subject, he accused me of "grasping at straws" and announced that none of my schemes to move interior walls, eliminate carpeting, or widen doorways would work. As the president of the facility's residents' council, he had to set an example of how a person should respond when deteriorating health required relocating to a place where others could assist in the ordinary tasks of living.

He skipped what normally would have been the next step of the Mather progressive care organization he had joined a few years earlier and moved directly into the final stage, in which others tended to most of his physical needs. In exchange for his apartment, he received a single room on the top floor of the five-story nursing home called the Wagner Health Center. He had been assured that his was the best room in the house, but it was a far cry from the independent and satisfying life to which he had become accustomed during the first seventeen years of his retirement and the almost seven decades preceding it.

Exhibiting the strength of character that defined him, he persevered through this adversity and regained his equilibrium. Fortunately, the *New York Times* was always there to help. So long as he could look forward to the only newspaper that really mattered to him, along with books and manuscripts from friends and former students, his mind could remain fully engaged with the outside world. When his residential facility's unalterable evening meal schedule permanently collided with and displaced the PBS *MacNeil/Lehrer Report*—later just *The NewsHour with Jim Lehrer*—virtually nothing on television was worthy of his formidable intellect's time or attention.

As he yearned for the days of Edward R. Murrow, Walter Cronkite, and Eric Sevareid, he watched the news for an hour every evening at five o'clock, "but that was about it." He had observed painfully as vibrant colleagues retired from the life of the mind to adopt the life of a couch potato, waiting for the next episode of some inane daytime TV talk show and, it seemed, for the grim reaper. He was determined to avoid such an end, even as he spent day after day in what sometimes looked to me like God's waiting room.

He motioned with his eyes and a slight tilt of his head in the direction of the nurse's assistant who made up the bed in the single room he now called home. It was directly across from the dining room where he faced his most significant challenge thrice daily: seeking out a cogent mealtime conversation with one of his fellow "inmates," as he affectionately called them. His silent signal communicated that we would broach his designated subject—whatever it was—as soon as the nurse's assistant had departed.

When I had entered the room about an hour earlier, he was sitting where he always sat as we began our visits: at his desk facing the wall. His spread-open newspaper covered the top of his desk and everything on it, including the telephone. A stack of monthly railroad magazines rested on a small table to his right. Hanging on the wall above his desk was a former student's gift—a large framed print of the Northwestern University campus as it existed in the late 1800s. Just to its left was a map depicting Chicago's Columbian Exposition of 1893; then came several framed certificates marking important milestones in his life:

- "Lifetime Achievement in Teaching Award" from the Northwestern University College of Arts and Sciences.
- "Citation of Merit" from the United States Department of the Navy in 1983 for meritorious public service during 1969, when he single-handedly prevented the university from throwing the Naval Reserve Officer Training Corps off the campus. Similar programs died at all of the institutions "with which Northwestern likes to compare itself"—a phrase he often used.
- Another "Citation" the Navy awarded in 1984, recognizing his decades-long service on behalf of the committee determining the nature of historical source materials available to future generations in his profession.
- The "Distinguished Service Award" from the Organization of American Historians, noting in particular his role as its president during the 1976–1977 term.

Against the wall were a small chair with a leather seat for his all too infrequent guests, a television set, and a credenza on which approximately thirty books were piled in neat stacks of four or five each. All of the books had been published recently, and most were gifts from friends and former students. He had read and edited many when they were in manuscript form because their uniformly distinguished authors had requested his prepublication critique. Next to the credenza was a single floor-to-ceiling metal bookshelf holding the last remnants of his extensive private library. When someone asked him years earlier why he had so many books, he answered, "Some men have wives . . ." Opposite the bookshelves was a bathroom he could not use without assistance.

His bed projected from the wall opposite his desk; two large windows spanned the distance in between. He used a stick with a hook on the end to slide the windows open, but he needed help to close them. Between the bathroom and his bed was a dresser. Mounted above it was a framed photograph of the New York Giants baseball team's legendary pitcher, Christy Mathewson—a gift from Northwestern Assistant Archivist Kevin Leonard.

On the dresser top were several photographs of recent Richard W. Leopold Lecturers posing with him and several of his former students at the annual event of the lecture. Ten years after his retirement, I and other alumni had helped to establish the lectureship in an attempt to honor an educator who had positively shaped many lives. One photo included an invited lecturer who was a former graduate student and Democratic nominee for the presidency of the United States, Senator George McGovern. Another Leopold Lecturer and former student had also sought the presidency: Richard Gephardt ('62), who retired after a distinguished career including service as majority leader of the House of Representatives. Yet another lecturer and former student was Republican Congressman James T. Kolbe ('61) from Arizona, who once said he considered Dick Leopold "one of the two or three most important influences in my life." He later continued, "I used to say with great pride that I learned American diplomatic history from one of the greatest scholars in the United States—Dick Leopold. I knew that statement would not be challenged in or out of academic circles."

Thirty years after her college graduation, another lecturer, Georgie Anne Geyer ('56), began work on what would become an important biography of Fidel Castro. She credited her former professor, Richard W. Leopold, with giving her the confidence to pursue the project as it began. Also appearing in several of the photographs was a lectureship founder, Lee Huebner ('62), who was a former speechwriter for President Richard M. Nixon. Professor Leopold had friends on both sides of the aisle; what he had offered to the students he influenced to make the world a better place transcended politics.

Huebner was an interesting example of Dick's enduring impact at the most personal level. On graduation, Huebner received a doctorate from Harvard and then joined the Nixon administration. After tiring of politics, he eventually became the publisher of the *International Herald Tribune*. When he informed Dick in a Christmas card note that he was thinking about changing careers again, Dick suggested to Northwestern University President Arnold R. Weber and School of Speech Dean David Zarefsky (also a former Leopold student ['68]) that Huebner be given a joint appointment in the School of Speech and Medill School of Journalism. Respecting what he acknowledged as every "tribe's" deference to its ultimate elder, Weber concurred. Zarefsky endorsed the proposal, and Huebner got the job. As I was finishing this book in 2006, Huebner became director of George Washington University's School of Media and Public Affairs after consulting with Dick about the desirability of such a move at the age of sixty-five.

The most important of Dick's memorabilia was also on his dresser. The Northwestern University Medal of Merit acknowledged the creation of the Richard W. Leopold Professorship, which came about in an unprecedented way. Almost a decade after the lectureship was established, many of Dick's former students again banded together and contributed more than $1 million to endow the chair in his name. Once the $2 million mark was reached, the chair would become permanent—the ultimate tribute to a teacher and friend. He had never married; "no time for such folderol," he would say. His mistress was his profession; his offspring were the generations of students whom he nurtured and who, in turn, adored him.

Personal visitors and the telephone were his only interactive lifelines out of the room. A few years earlier, I had tried to persuade him that a computer might offer another link to the world through the Internet. With my two teenage sons in tow, I brought my laptop to his room and the three of us tried to demonstrate for him the remarkable capabilities of modern technology. Regrettably, my two well-meaning offspring spent most of the time explaining why each of their respective methods of Internet access was superior, while Professor Leopold smiled at the friendly intensity of their interaction. After politely allowing a reasonable period of time before calling the experiment to a halt, he said, "Maybe this works for your generation, but I don't think it's going to do much for me."

That had been quite a while ago. Now, as the nurse's assistant finished with the bed and left the room, I asked him about the matter to which he had alluded earlier. He was characteristically direct. With his head down, he began to speak.

"I have been thinking about this for some time now," he said, raising his chin from his chest and gazing into the distance. "As I contemplate the end—as we all must at some point—I've been trying to determine whether I should give any direction concerning a memorial service. I would hate to have former students feel as though they had to attend, particularly if it meant financial hardship for them. I would not want anyone to feel obligated. . . ."

He did not pose a question to me directly, but I knew I should answer him as if he had. This felt similar to the discussions dominating his legendary American foreign policy course I had taken thirty years earlier. It was, perhaps, the most famous undergraduate class on Northwestern's Evanston campus. The mere mention of its course number evoked a shudder in some, a knowing smile from others, and respect by all: C-13.

From 1948 to 1962, he had taught the subject matter in a large lecture format to as many as one hundred students at a time. For much of that period, he also taught an even larger survey course. One former student observed that Leopold "was the only professor I ever had who received an ovation after every lecture." As television and motion picture writer/producer/director Garry Marshall ('56) would later describe in a letter to his former professor, "On a cold, dreary wintry day in February, I was awoken from my half listening, half thinking about Tri Delts reverie, by you lecturing about a small, minor religious figure being killed in a long ago battle. You said, 'he was killed by a blast from a cannon. You might say he was canonized.' Your humor always made me listen more carefully."

With the publication of his seminal treatise *The Growth of American Foreign Policy: A History,* Dick could assign readings that included all of his diplomatic history lecture materials. That freed him to refashion the course into a discussion class of no more than forty students. It met all year on Monday, Wednesday, and Friday at eight o'clock in the morning. When a student brave enough to ask wondered why the course met at eight, he responded immediately: "Because the university will not allow me to teach it at seven." There was no undergraduate class like it at Northwestern and probably never will be.

Returning to the matter at hand—his concerns about the nature of a memorial service upon his death—I framed my response: "I have two thoughts on the subject. First, it will be very difficult for anyone—except, perhaps, you by some predeath decree—to prevent your former students, friends, and colleagues from gathering in your honor. And I am not sure that even your edict could stop us. I've known you for thirty years and I still feel like the new kid in town. You've had a profound impact on hundreds of lives over many decades. Appreciative friends and former students will want to find a way to give you a final farewell honoring your influence."

I thought this might lead to broader topics, so I established my willingness to pursue this as far as he wanted to take it. I continued without solicitation or interruption: "The recent deaths of my father and father-in-law have taught me a lot about this process. One thing I can say for certain is that a memorial service is far more important to the survivors than to the deceased. Those who have remained connected to you for many years will want closure that only a memorial service of some kind will give them. I think it would be a mistake for you to issue a directive taking such an opportunity away from them."

I detected a slight smile as I mentioned the "hundreds of lives" he had affected. Or maybe he was just proud to see my demonstration of a talent he had first nurtured in me as a student: to take another person's point on a subject, reverse it, make it my own, and maintain a friendly smile as I won the argument. My comments were certainly true, although a better estimate of the number of people this academic giant had influenced would have been "thousands." But if I had said so, he would have roundly dismissed my remarks as "hyperbolic nonsense."

"Second," I continued, "as to your concerns over those who might like to attend but really can't afford it, I wouldn't worry about that. Those people will know that you would understand their circumstances and that you'll take no offense—from wherever you preside after your death—at their absence from a formal service in Chicago. Moreover, those who had already planned a different trip elsewhere might adjust their plans and take a journey back to Evanston instead. Maybe they'll want to use a gathering in your honor as an opportunity to reconnect with people and places from another time in their lives. In short, I don't think you should let that factor affect your thinking about how you want things to proceed. You have friends and colleagues who will want to honor you, and you should let them do it."

I offered an example: "As my father's health failed, we discussed with him what he did and did not want done after his death. But he recognized that he had to leave the survivors sufficient flexibility to do what was necessary for their emotional needs, too. The result was a small service limited to immediate family and close friends."

He wasted no time in accepting my implicit offer to involve myself in these matters. "Maybe that is what I should do," he responded. "No speakers."

"No, I didn't say there were no speakers."

The pace was quickening, recalling to my mind the lively interactions in his classroom. As he guided those discussions, he rarely involved himself in their substance. In sharp contrast to those days, now he was deeply embroiled. "Each of my father's four children spoke," I continued. "Each said what he or she thought needed to be said."

"But," he countered, "that leads to a different problem for my situation: Who should speak?" Any answers to his questions always led to another question.

"I have a suggestion there, as well," I responded immediately. He smiled broadly, obviously enjoying the exchange. "I've been to several other funerals recently and, to this day, the one I found most fulfilling—if that's the right word—involved circumstances that were also the most tragic. The mother of my oldest son's best friend died at a very young age, leaving a husband and two small children. But she had enough time to plan exactly how she wanted her memorial to be conducted. She even wrote a letter she wanted read at the service. It ended with something like: 'This will be a wonderful party—with all of my friends and the people whom I love most gathered together. What a shame I will miss it!'" His eyes were now locked onto mine as he listened.

He subconsciously circled back to the description of my siblings and me speaking at my dad's memorial service and turned to his large group of former students; we both knew they were his children: "My students really fall into three generations: one from the Harvard period, which was prior to 1948—and there are not many of them around anymore; another group from what I would call the early Northwestern period extending to about 1965; and then what I would call the modern period, including your group from the mid-1960s through my retirement in 1980."

"You see," I interrupted, "I'm still the new kid."

"Yes, you are," he said as he pressed ahead. His grin revealed only slightly the toll that the combination of childhood orthodontia and age had taken on his teeth. "I would be concerned about selecting one person in each group and then having the others feel slighted."

"Actually, I think there may be a solution there as well," I responded. "Your constituents will respect your choices. You could select one person from each generation—or use some other criteria you think will best cover the needs of the audience. You know all of your family, friends, and former students better than we know each other. The people who care most about you will want you to have selected those who you think are most appropriate for the occasion."

"I am worried that there aren't many left in the Northwestern history department when I was there who would know enough about me to say much," he replied. "I certainly want anything said to be accurate."

Once a historian, always a historian, I thought.

I asked what biographical information on him might be available for our review: "You know, the *New York Times* does obituaries on famous people years in advance."

"And then they update and revise it as the person continues to live," he interrupted as he smiled.

"True," I said, "and there is nothing wrong with trying to gather basic information about you for the same purpose. We can always update it."

Noon arrived to stop our conversation. He now had to join his fellow residents for an unsatisfying lunch in the dining room. As always when that time approached, I helped him trade his thick reading glasses for a different pair, grabbed his terry-cloth bib that I secured with Velcro around his neck, and unfolded a bath towel that he kept in his lap as he ate. Noting the remnants from prior meals on the last two items, I asked him if anyone ever washed them.

"Only when absolutely necessary," he said, motoring himself toward the door I opened ahead of him. As we moved closer to his two-person table in the dining room, he surveyed the area and concluded, "This has been very productive. We'll continue this the next time you come."

"I look forward to it."

Riding the elevator down to the main floor, I resolved that I needed to see him more often than the bimonthly visits I had made in recent years. I mistakenly thought I had come to know him over the three decades we had maintained continuous contact since our first meeting when I was nineteen. Now it was becoming clear to me—at the age of fifty—that I had barely scratched the surface of the man. I wondered if he had ever allowed anyone to venture much deeper.

* * *

He wasted no time. Six days later, on the following Sunday evening, he called to ask if I had read the day's *New York Times.* Coincidentally, I had just started to open it.

"You'll enjoy page eight of the *Book Review,* on which Arthur's publisher has set forth endorsements of his book," he said. Arthur was Arthur M. Schlesinger Jr.—a fellow Harvard alumnus, longtime friend, former adviser to President John F. Kennedy, and, at age eighty-seven, one of the nation's leading American historians. He had also been the most recent Leopold Lecturer during the prior fall.

Schlesinger had just published a book describing why President George W. Bush's doctrine of preventive war had no place in the historical traditions of the United States and was doomed to failure that had already been its fate in Iraq. Dick and I had discussed the *Times'* lukewarm review of *War and the American Presidency* before we got to the matter he had really wanted to cover during my visit with him the previous Monday. He now directed my attention to the definitive rebuttal of the *Times* review. It was set forth in quotations he proudly read aloud as I found his referenced page and followed along. He started with Walter Cronkite: "Arthur Schlesinger again proves not just his astuteness but his brilliance in defining a major issue of our time."

Dick continued, quoting former Ambassador Richard Holbrooke: "When our nation's greatest living historian addresses one of our most important issues, Americans should listen carefully. Here, Arthur Schlesinger takes a fresh look at the nation's current crisis through the prism of history. His conclusions may annoy some and, hopefully, inform all."

He then read the praise of others, including former Secretary of Defense Robert McNamara: "In *War and the American Presidency,* Arthur Schlesinger, our leading historian, contrasts the Bush foreign policy with two centuries of American experience, revealing how we have strayed mightily from our historical course. Timely and urgently necessary, this is a book that must be read by all concerned American citizens, including the President himself."

The tone of Dick's readings reinforced the obvious: Each of these critics was far more distinguished than the unenthusiastic *Times* reviewer. Yet I knew this could not have been the sole reason for his call; he soon confirmed my suspicions.

"I enjoyed very much our conversation of Monday last," he continued.

"So did I. I was wondering if there were any printed biographical materials of you that I could review, so we could start working on the factual aspects of your life."

"Yes." He wasted no words, ever. "I worked with Kevin Leonard in the Northwestern Archives to prepare an index of the personal papers I donated to the university. I will have him send that index to you. Also, there are two articles reprinting speeches I gave some time ago. They contain some historical information that is somewhat biographical and may be of interest to you. I'll have him copy those for you as well. When you see the index of my papers, it will give you insight into the various persons who fall into the different generations I was talking about, as well as others with whom I have corresponded over the years. You know, at some point I'm going to have to let John know who Steve Harper is." John was his nephew and closest living relative. He was a state court judge in Denver.

"I'll leave that to you," I responded. "I met him for the first time at your ninetieth birthday party, but I have never really spoken with him at great length."

"I'll have Kevin send the index and articles to your home," he said, returning to the main purpose of his call. After additional conversation about an upcoming prospective-college trip to Ohio with my daughter, he wished me well. He asked me to check on one of his former Harvard students who had retired several years earlier from Denison University. I agreed and promised to continue our discussion of his life when I returned. I thought I detected a lilt in his voice that I had not heard in years. He was fully engaged in this project and he had fully engaged me as well. I had no idea where it would lead, but I knew the fun had just begun.

* * *

I could not believe my eyes. Two days after Dick's call, I received a thick envelope from the office of the Northwestern University Archives. In addition to the two articles he wanted me to read, the package included a nine-page summary containing a short biographical sketch and a descriptive index for each of the 182 boxes containing his personal papers. I laughed aloud when I read footnote five of the summary, which described how he had reported weather measurements in his "daily aides": "Temperature expressed in degrees Fahrenheit, time of day at which the temperature was recorded, relative humidity percentages, barometric pressure expressed in inches, and prevailing wind direction. Also commonly recorded are temperature readings reported from Chicago's Midway Field (MF), Grant Park (GP), and O'Hare Field (OH). The times of sunrise and sunset commonly are noted beside the date printed on each calendar page."

According to the index, his collection included student handbooks from Phillips Exeter Academy (1928–1929) and Princeton University (1929–1930). Diaries, engagement books, and daily aides spanning 1937 through 1997 (except for the notably omitted World War II period from 1942 to early 1946) alone filled seven boxes. I wondered if he had ever thrown anything away, other than his daily *New York Times*.

At least as far as the written record was concerned, the word *complete* now had new meaning for me. This was going to be a much larger project than I had imagined. After reading the summary, I began where he had suggested and read the two articles reprinting speeches he had given concerning his early years as a historian. But after reviewing them, I wanted to know more about the events that took him first to Phillips Exeter Academy, then to Princeton University for undergraduate work, then to Harvard University's graduate school as a doctoral student in American history, and, eventually, to Northwestern.

The biographical summary offered a useful start. But apart from disclosing his well-known love for baseball, there was little personal history about his formative years. That would be my first area of inquiry with him. The existing historical record was incomplete, and I hoped he would help me to fill the holes. That process began when I met with him the following Sunday and continued every Sunday thereafter for the next two years. Everyone has a story; I wanted to understand his.

PART ONE

"I have no religion myself . . ."

ONE

WINTER QUARTER 1974—
MY FIRST EXPERIENCE

As I prepared to dig deeper into Dick's life, I reflected on the earliest days of my own Leopold experience. In January 1974, I took his one-quarter course, "The Armed Forces in American History" (C-03). I knew the class was really a warm-up for the main event to follow the next fall and continue throughout the entire 1974–1975 academic year. During all of what Dick had described as his modern period that began in the mid-1960s, both C-03 and "The History of American Foreign Policy" (C-13) were taught by one of Northwestern's premier American historians in a unique and elegant room.

Before registering for either class, any interested student had to meet personally with Professor Leopold in his office, Harris Hall 208. I saw him in early December 1973 as the fall quarter of my sophomore year ended. We had a short conversation about the class and his expectations that each student be "fully prepared to discuss the materials assigned for that day." I suspected that the interview session was intended to apprise the unsuspecting of what lay ahead and that he rarely refused admittance. When our five-minute conversation was finished, he gave me the permission card I needed to sign up for his course at the university-wide registration in Parkes Hall a few days later.

Unlike the more daunting foreign policy class meeting at eight in the morning on Mondays, Wednesdays, and Fridays, "The Armed Forces in American History" met on those days at a more reasonable hour—ten o'clock—and only for the winter quarter. But the locale and essential format for both classes were the same. Harris 108 was the scene of the action. I assumed that its large wooden double doors remained locked at all times, except when Professor Leopold's classes met there. On my first entry into the room, which spanned the entire width of the history department building, I thought I had taken several steps backward in time. The doors opened into a meeting space with twenty-foot ceilings, ten-foot windows, and a large fireplace opposite the entrance. All of the furniture inside was movable. He had configured the area so his forty students sat around the perimeter of an open rectangular arrangement of tables. He sat at its head; a large Persian rug was in the middle. A chalkboard on a stand behind him contained three "Questions" for the next session—all of which he had handwritten onto the board before the class began.

He had explained to me during the screening interview that there were only three determinants of a student's grade: a book review, a two-hour final examination, and classroom participation. Insofar as his conduct of the course was concerned, I could see immediately that he had left nothing to chance. He had assigned each of us a place to sit, put a seating chart near each chair, and anchored attractive female students immediately to his right and left. I found my place: the third chair to his left. I felt a chill and turned around to see an open window behind me, even though the outside temperature in Chicago on that January 1974 morning was about thirty degrees. I wondered why he had opened that window, along with one at the other end of the room, but I assumed from the manner in which he had staged the entire scene that there must have been a reason.

Because it was the first day of class, he opened the session with an introductory overview of the subject matter and his teaching method. Two days later, I saw him in action. He began the discussion by restating one of the three questions he had written on the chalkboard during our prior session; those questions had guided our assigned readings for today. To participate, a student raised his or her hand and waited to be recognized as part of a sequential group: "We'll hear from John, Robert, and then Alexis," he would announce as all hands then came down. Although most students regarded his armed forces course as training for his yearlong class, it soon became clear that a few veterans from the prior year's more demanding American foreign policy class populated the room. In the early days of my first Leopold experience, the alumni of his other course had a distinct advantage over us newcomers. The pace was quick, and Professor Leopold guided the exchanges through a unique Socratic process. I pulled out my copy of the seating chart in an effort to associate faces with names.

When our first discussion session ended fifty minutes later, my head was spinning. I left the room thinking he had pursued precision in his pedagogy. He had controlled every condition; he had mastered every moment. That was the beginning of my relationship with Professor Leopold. Thirty years later, I now began a journey with him marking a time much closer to its end.

I already knew one fact that was especially interesting to me personally: Dick was born in the same year—1912—as my recently deceased father-in-law, Dr. William J. Loeb, whom I had called "Pop." Apart from outstanding personal character, excellence in their chosen fields, and the nominal "Leopold-Loeb" symmetry with the notorious 1924 Chicago murders, I wondered if they shared other attributes or experiences. I would soon learn far more than I could have imagined on that subject.

TWO

"The First Test: The Great Crusade"

"What is your earliest memory?" I asked him as we began the first of our regular Sunday morning sessions. I thought a chronological approach would be the easiest way to get him started.

He gazed thoughtfully at an imaginary spot on the wall above his desk for about thirty seconds before saying, "I was on a train. I have actually thought about this before, and, by putting together the various trips I took as a child, have concluded that I must have been two years old. I was lying in the lower berth of the sleeper, looking out the window, as the telegraph wires stretched from pole to pole. . . ." So began the Dick Leopold story as he himself would tell it.

* * *

I tried to place Dick's life in historical context as I learned it and, wherever possible, to use the chapter titles from his 1962 survey volume, *The Growth of American Foreign Policy,* to frame periods with reference to contemporaneous developments in international affairs. My goal was to use his words to illuminate his saga, even though they had been written more than forty years earlier. His earliest days coincided with the time he would call "The First Test: The Great Crusade, 1905–1921—in which the American people intervene reluctantly in a world war, rationalize their participation as a great crusade, but refuse to abandon isolationism."

As 1911 drew to a close, Sun Yat-sen's followers continued a rebellion leading eventually to the end of the Manchu dynasty and the beginning of the Republic of China. Germany's relationships with its neighboring nations remained precarious but of limited interest to Americans on the other side of the Atlantic. William Howard Taft occupied the White House as Theodore Roosevelt's chosen successor; however, Princeton University's former president, Woodrow Wilson, sat in the New Jersey governor's office with designs on Taft's job.

Closer to home, racing-car driver Louis Chevrolet had introduced his mass-produced automobile to compete with Henry Ford's Model T. In the most recent World Series, Connie Mack had managed the Philadelphia Athletics to victory over John McGraw's New York Giants, who lost two of the three games in which their ace Christy Mathewson pitched. In an apartment near West End Avenue and 97th Street in New York City, Ethel Kimmelstiel Leopold was pregnant with her second child.

On January 6, 1912, New Mexico became the forty-seventh state in the union, and Richard Leopold was born at home to Harry and Ethel Leopold, giving four-year old Harry Jr. a baby brother. Like his father and older brother, Dicky Leopold had no middle name—the "W" would come later. Two people of particular prominence in 1912 would eventually become important to Dick's life long afterward: Elihu Root, who had served as secretary of war under President McKinley and secretary of state under President Theodore Roosevelt, won the Nobel Peace Prize that year; Democrat Woodrow Wilson was elected president after Roosevelt's third-party candidacy undercut the Republican incumbent, Taft. None could have predicted that forty-two years later Dick would publish the best short interpretive biography of Root ever written, or that his closest professional collaborator by then would be the leading authority on Wilson.

"We were quite well off," Dick continued. "Our hired help included a private cook, a maid, and my nurse. All were white. The maid was a tall blonde woman named Agnes; my British nurse was Josie. When I was six, Mother acquired a Cadillac Town Car, a model that exposed our chauffeur to the elements as he drove us around, which wasn't very nice of her. He was the nephew of a famous Italian race-car driver.

"By the time I was ten, my father had traded his Stutz for a Cadillac he drove himself. After working in the family's textile importing business, he had initially taken a position in a Wall Street brokerage house and eventually acquired a partnership interest in a seat on the New York Stock Exchange with a man named Warner. As his finances improved, he joined a golf club and a bridge club, in addition to pursuing numerous other business and social activities taking him away from his wife and two sons." Dick was giving me the first clue about his father's role in his life; I would have to come back to that subject.

* * *

In the summer of 1914, a Serb nationalist assassinated Austria's Archduke Franz Ferdinand. After Serbia failed to satisfy the conditions of the resulting ultimatum, Austria-Hungary declared war on the tiny Balkan country. A complex tangle of treaties and alliances immediately triggered the involvement of every major European nation. When Russia mobilized to defend its small neighbor, Germany declared war on Russia and its ally France. When Germany failed to respect Belgian neutrality, Great Britain declared war on Germany and caused Foreign Secretary

Sir Edward Grey to lament: "The lamps are going out all over Europe; we shall not see them lit again in our lifetime." The United States openly reaffirmed its historical policy of neutrality as oceans on each side seemed to insulate North America from the conflagration.

As these momentous events were transforming America's role in the world, Ethel Leopold and her two sons boarded the Twentieth Century Limited for Chicago. As they rode the rails, Dick's journey became his earliest childhood memory and, along with similar trips, began his lifelong love affair with trains. They would remain a theme in his life as he traveled with his mother and older brother regularly from New York to Ethel's hometown.

Dick's maternal grandparents, whose original surnames were Kimmelstiel and Ballenberg, had been wed in 1878 at Sinai Temple on 21st Street and Indiana Avenue on Chicago's near south side. To Dick's knowledge, that marriage was the last such ceremony among his immediate relatives to occur in a Jewish temple. His mother was born in 1886 as the youngest of the three Kimmelstiel daughters. "A surprising number of years later," Dick told me, "a son arrived. The family lived in a Jewish community on Grand Boulevard—a street since renamed Martin Luther King Jr. Drive."

He continued to outline his family's history: "My parents were nonpracticing Jews. My Aunt Blanche's husband had changed his surname from Kirshberger to Churchill during World War I to eliminate any obvious Jewish and German connections to the family. Lots of Jews did that at the time. One of my mother's cousins made a similar change—from Ballenberg to Ballenger—for the same reasons. Although Blanche was the only Kimmelstiel sister who remained in the Chicago area as her siblings moved to New York, my closest cousins were Blanche's children—Alice, born in 1903, and William, born in 1905. My parents were probably married by a rabbi, but only because someone had to perform the task and the concept of a 'civil ceremony' would have made no sense to them. I do not think there was any real Jewish religious aspect to any of their lives, including the marriage ceremony." Having never broached any personal religious topic with him in our prior thirty years of conversations, I now knew I had another matter to which we would have to return: his perceived connection, or lack thereof, to his Jewish ancestry.

"The main purpose of our journey in 1914 was to join Aunt Blanche, who by then lived with her husband and two children near the University of Chicago on the city's south side. We all rented a house in Highland Park for the summer."

* * *

In 1916, President Wilson ordered Brigadier General John J. Pershing to pursue bandit Pancho Villa onto Mexican soil, Louis Brandeis became the first Jew appointed to the United States Supreme Court, and Dick celebrated his fourth birthday. Current events associated with the ongoing European war were producing what Dick would later call "The Breakdown of Neutrality" as America was being drawn into a conflict still on the periphery of his young life. But those events comprised another set of circumstances that, along with train travel, would create one of his lifelong fascinations: warfare.

"I remember playing with a small toy boat in our kitchen and telling our German cook that my ship would sink all of the German submarines," he said of a time less than a year after a torpedo had sunk the unarmed *Lusitania,* resulting in the deaths of 124 Americans among 1,198 fatalities. "She stuck her tongue out at me." When I smiled at his last comment, he continued with a lilt in his voice: "Well, these are the things one *remembers* as a child."

* * *

In November 1916, President Woodrow Wilson won reelection with the slogan "He kept us out of the war." Only five months later, he asked for Congress' declaration to enter "The Great Crusade" as he told a joint session, "The right is more precious than peace." With America officially taking sides, the conflict now engulfed the entire civilized world.

Wilson's task of keeping Russia in the war on the side of the Allied powers became more complicated when the Bolsheviks succeeded in their second bid for power on November 7, 1917. Nevertheless, what Dick would later call "Wartime Diplomacy" continued. After Germany spent the spring and summer of 1918 bending but never breaking the Allied lines on the Western Front, its leaders realized they could not win the war. The Kaiser's days were numbered, and the "Preparations for Peace" began.

In the United States, the ratification in 1919 of the eighteenth amendment to the Constitution banned the sale of alcohol. The Bolshevik Revolution led to the "Red scare," fueling Amerian anti-Semitism. The rising tide against Jewish immigrants, especially those from Eastern Europe, eventually culminated in restrictions set forth in the Immigration Act of 1921. The statute sought to preserve the predominance of white Anglo-Saxon Protestants without ever mentioning the word *Jew,* but everyone knew the intended targets.

Dick focused on more pressing pursuits as baseball entered his life: "I was seven years old when my grandfather took me to a New York Giants–Philadelphia Phillies game in 1919, and I was hooked." No rendition of "The Star-Spangled Banner" preceded the game, because Francis Scott Key's song would not become America's national anthem for another twelve years.

"The Giants won by a score of four to three," Dick told me eighty-five years later. He then added with a historian's precision, "However, I am not sure if my recollection of the players' fielding positions results from memory or from my subsequent study of *The Baseball Encyclopedia."*

The Cincinnati Reds won the pennant that year and faced the heavily favored Chicago White Sox in the World Series. Chicago's strange performance led to questions and scandal as the White Sox became the "Black Sox." Eventually, baseball's first commissioner decreed lifetime banishment for eight players, including Shoeless Joe Jackson and Buck Weaver, because of bribes some players had taken to throw the series in favor of the Reds.

As the second game of the series began on October 2, 1919, President Wilson's efforts to generate popular support for his League of Nations suffered a fatal blow when he had a massive stroke, paralyzing his left side and shattering his dreams of a lasting peace. Dick's 1962 book would subsequently describe these monumental international events as "A World in Turmoil," but his own life seemed perfectly calm at the time.

"Mother tried to give us the broadest possible view of people and the world, while herself becoming one of the boys," he said. However, I would soon discover one significant exception to his general point about the breadth of his childhood experiences: Aside from his older cousin Alice, he had no significant exposure as a child to any girls.

"Mother regularly took us to Broadway plays. I especially enjoyed Gilbert and Sullivan's *H.M.S. Pinafore.* At baseball games, she rooted for the Yankees because Harry and I cheered for the Giants. As my father remained more concerned with work and golf, she loved to travel, so we saw much of the American West. In addition to our frequent Chicago railroad journeys, the three of us visited the Grand Canyon and Lake Louise in 1922, and Yellowstone in 1927." He wrote seven decades later that Lake Louise remained etched in his memory as "the most beautiful single spot on the North American continent."

As for his brother, Harry, Dick said, "He was kind enough to put up with me." But it soon became clear to me that the connection between the Leopold children was much stronger than his lighthearted comment implied; it would remain an enduring element of his life. For their early school years, Harry and Dick attended an all-male predominantly Jewish private school, the Franklin School, which was the successor to the prestigious Sachs School for Boys.

"There were about twenty boys in each grade. All of my childhood friends, except one, attended that school. But he was Jewish, too," Dick remembered when I asked him about the presence of non-Jews in his early life. I found myself increasingly drawn to that topic in our regular Sunday discussions. Since he had opened it up with his self-description as "a nonpracticing Jew," it now became fair game for my biographical effort.

By the time he began at Franklin, the family had moved from Dick's original home to an apartment on West End Avenue near 83rd Street, a block from Riverside Park. When he was nine, the family moved into the first of many apartment hotels where they no longer needed private hired help, except for Mrs. Leopold's chauffeur. As he put it, "My father did not like to be pinned down to a timetable. At the apartment hotels where the staff took care of everything, the rest of the family could eat dinner at a regular time while my father could eat whenever and wherever was more convenient for him." As to his parents' respective household tasks: "My father must have regarded his role as providing the 'logistics' necessary for a family—money for housing, vacations, hired help, entertainment. Mother did everything else. For them, it was a perfect division of labor, responsibilities, and interests. Mother provided most of the parental emotional support. She was also a force of nature. When our teachers saw her heading their way, you could hear the whispers: 'Uh-oh, here comes Mrs. Leopold . . .'"

* * *

When Dick was ten, Harry Jr. enrolled at Phillips Exeter Academy, a college preparatory boarding school for boys in New Hampshire. Neither of his parents had attended college, and they were not sure if either son would attend an institution of higher education. Dick's brother could have remained at the Franklin School in New York, but Ethel and Blanche toured New England during the summer of 1921 and decided that Harry Jr. would join Blanche's son, Bill, at Exeter in the fall of 1922. The reasons for moving the boys out of their homes were never made clear: "The decision to send Bill to Exeter was especially puzzling," Dick said, "because I think he had completed his studies at the Harvard School on Chicago's south side. That was where wealthy Jewish families sent their sons to prepare for college." Among the Harvard School's students was Bobby Franks, whom Nathan Leopold and Richard Loeb would brutally murder in 1924—an event ultimately touching Dick and Harry, too.

Dick was later told that the Franklin School was the first step along a road eventually taking many of New York City's wealthier Jewish children to Columbia University; however, a few of Dick's classmates remained at Franklin through high school and went to Harvard or Yale. Dick's cousin Bill spent a single post–high school year at Exeter before entering Dartmouth College. Harry remained at Exeter for two years after Bill graduated; he then went on to the Wharton School at the University of Pennsylvania. Like other non-Jewish private schools throughout the country, Exeter was a much different place from Franklin and maintained informal quotas on the number of Jews admitted.

* * *

As we moved from Dick's early years and toward his adolescence, I decided it was time for me to consult the sixty-three-page, single-spaced autobiography my father-in-law, Pop, had prepared and given to his four daughters before he died in 2000. There he described his earliest recollections and, not surprisingly, they related to events generating lifelong interests: medicine and warfare. Pop's first memories were of weekly sessions with his great-grandfather Joseph Mellor, whose microscope led to Pop's fascination with things the naked eye could not see. Mellor used the microscope to conduct the first examinations of milk in the Cleveland area at a time when commercial pasteurization was still in its infancy.

Pop was an only child and his mother, Elsie, sent him to Mellor's house on the days she prepared articles for the *Film Daily, Motion Picture Daily,* and other national theatrical business publications. She had assumed those responsibilities from her father, Felix Rosenberg, who also served as a city editor for the *Plain Dealer* prior to his death in 1917. In those days, Cleveland was the nation's fifth-largest city.

"Great Grandpa Joseph Mellor was a physician born and educated in England," Pop wrote. Mellor emigrated to the United States—("How and why Cleveland I never learned")—after serving in the medical corps during the Crimean War. A leg injury limited Mellor's mobility, so he used a cane and ran a pharmacy that was really a "medical office in a store." His daughter, Rose, met Felix Rosenberg there; years later they married and had children who included Pop's mother, Elsie. She would eventually wed Joseph William Loeb, whose family traced their American origins to Charleston, West Virginia. At the age of five, Pop watched his mother wrapping bandages for the Red Cross during World War I. As he wrote long after his retirement, "I had been heading for medicine for as long as I can recall. Somehow Great Grandpa Mellor had left me feeling that medicine was the way to go."

* * *

Although the subject of childhood interests leading to adult professions is interesting, I found a more engaging point of comparison between Dick's family and Pop's: They systematically avoided cultural, religious, and ethnic aspects of their Jewish heritage. Both men were raised in homes maintaining an uncomfortable distance between themselves and their Semitic origins. In fact, Pop's family moved from their east side Cleveland home on 105th Street after "a conservative Jewish temple was built and many Jewish people moved into the area. . . . No real problem, but they lived differently." He reported that many "were immigrants from Eastern Europe and spoke English with a definite accent." He explained the "cultural difference between the Germanic Jewish families who had been oriented into national social structures for many generations and the Eastern European group who had been isolated and were forced to live apart from the rest of society." The latter group made his parents uncomfortable: "So, we moved." Their new home was in Cleveland Heights, which was becoming the suburb of choice for the area's German Jews seeking a more secular life.

I began to consider whether Dick and Pop straddled two worlds in ways uniquely defining their twentieth-century experiences. Like their parents, both were raised as nonpracticing Jews. I suspected that their respective families were not alone in continuing a route to success that prior generations had begun as a matter of survival. Pop's forebears had emigrated from an anti-Semitic Western Europe during what he described as "the German exodus of 1840" preceding the

Revolution of 1848. Fleeing persecution, they adopted as their approach, long before Pop or Dick was born, the unspoken creed of assimilation as essential to achievement. But throughout their lives, the Jewish label persisted because others still used it to classify them. For both men, I wondered if the dissonance between who they wanted to be—just like everybody else—and how society sometimes regarded them—Jewish—created a tension influencing their lives. In that respect, I was particularly eager to see how their stories developed.

The desire of Dick's family to persevere on its assimilation path offered one explanation for the mystery surrounding the decision of the Kimmelstiel sisters to send their sons to Exeter. As I reviewed background materials about American anti-Semitism, I was surprised to learn that Columbia University had been the birthplace of maximum quotas on Jewish enrollment. The growing number of Jews attending that university during the early 1900s caused the school's administrators to fret over their loss of men from America's wealthiest Anglo-Saxon Protestant families; Williams College and Amherst were identified as two of the white bastions benefiting from Columbia's perceived losses.

By the mid-1910s, about 40 percent of Columbia's undergraduates were Jewish, prompting its dean, Frederick P. Keppel, to ask rhetorically, "Isn't Columbia overrun with European Jews, who are most unpleasant persons socially?" It became the first major private college to implement limits on admission of Jews, using geographic quotas, personal interviews, photographs, required disclosure of an applicant's mother's maiden name, and tests for character; other premier institutions of higher education soon followed. It now seemed clear to me, albeit perhaps less obvious to Dick at the time, that an important early step in his life's journey was getting his older brother and, later, Dick himself derailed from what nonpracticing Jews regarded as the young Jewish man's track from the Franklin School to Columbia University.

Although Pop attended public school, I could begin to see his early life paralleling Dick's, perhaps in ways shared by other assimilating Jews who also achieved a level of unheralded American greatness by the end of the twentieth century. They comprised a subset of what some have more recently called the Greatest Generation. But I was realizing they confronted obstacles the non-Jewish world—with which I am identified—could not appreciate. Until Dick and I began our discussions about his life, I had never really focused on its close proximity to my own.

THREE

"The Interwar Compromise"

I entered the tunnel connecting Northwestern's modern library with "Old Deering" in search of the Archives I had never visited as a student. Assistant Archivist Kevin Leonard ushered me into the room where Dick had sat regularly for years after his retirement, organizing his materials. Fortunately, the 182 boxes containing his personal papers were smaller than I had feared. I had envisioned book boxes or moving cartons; these were more like folios, each containing several folders. I soon realized they held treasures telling large and small stories of a lifetime. Dick's earliest mementos included a note he had received from a summer camp counselor in 1923 when he was eleven. I had never thought of Professor Leopold as "Dicky," but once upon a time, he was:

> Here is to the boy with a thousand smiles, who lives in our midst at the Thousand Isles.
> With best wishes to my little friend, Dick.

Another message from the summer of 1924 read:

> To little Dicky Leopold, whose hand I often hold. Let this a small token he of the greater man to be.

* * *

Even for the person who survives to ninety-four, life's journey begins as somebody's child, and that status endures. When Harry began his studies at Exeter in 1922, ten-year-old Dick became the Leopold home's "only child." He worked mightily to fill the gap his older brother's departure created, especially in his mother's life. It would become a lifelong challenge.

25

As for then-current events, he had no awareness of what he would later call "The Battle in America" between President Wilson and the Senate over the League of Nations and the Versailles Treaty. Nor did he know that the requisite thirty-six states had ratified the nineteenth amendment to the Constitution; it gave women the right to vote in an election that produced Republican Warren G. Harding as Wilson's successor. But eighty years later, he did remember that film actor Wallace Reid left the world disgracefully in January 1923 from a combination of morphine addiction and alcohol abuse, although some publicists tried to pass it off as influenza. Reid had been one of Dick's childhood idols until the scandalous cause of the movie star's death became known.

Another event he recalled eighty years later was President Harding's death on August 2, 1923, when Dick was eleven. At the time, Dick was enjoying one of five childhood summers he spent at Camp Koenig, a predominantly Jewish summer retreat for boys located in the Thousand Islands area near Clayton, New York. It was run by the Franklin School's principal, and most of the summer campers attended Franklin during the academic year. Dick told me his main concern about President Harding's demise was to make sure that, as one of those singing patriotic songs to respect his passing, he had to "get the words right. Was it 'My country 'tis of thee, sweet land of liberty, of thee I sing' or 'to thee I sing'?" For all of his life, details mattered and should be correct.

"After camp one year, Harry, Mother, and I joined one of Mother's friends— who had two daughters about the same age as Harry and me—at the friend's summer home in Maine," he told me. "Those girls and another who lived nearby were the only ones my age with whom I had any real contact during my childhood. There were no girls at the Franklin School or at camp. I was quite insecure and lacking in self-confidence in that area."

* * *

In the same month of 1924 that Dick turned twelve, Vladimir Lenin died and Joseph Stalin began the purges that paved his way to power in the Soviet Union. Over the succeeding years, Russian and Eastern European Jews fled to America in increasing numbers as Stalin eventually became supreme dictator in 1929. Importantly, these immigrants' more conspicuous presentation of their religion and ethnicity diverged dramatically from that of assimilating Jewish families like the Leopolds. A secular existence was central for the nonpracticing German Jews, whose forebears had emigrated to the United States in the mid-1800s. The new wave of twentieth century settlers dressed and behaved in ways leaving no doubts about their Semitism. Over time, resentments sometimes intensifying to animosity eventually developed between these two Jewish groups.

In February 1924, Calvin Coolidge became the first president to deliver a radio broadcast from the White House, but it did little to create interest in what Dick's 1962 book would later describe as "a poorly read man [who] spent more than a fair share of most afternoons taking a nap." He would also quote Walter Lippmann on "Silent Cal": "There have been Presidents in our time who knew how to whip up popular enthusiasm. There has never been Mr. Coolidge's equal in the art of deflating interest." In April 1924, Adolf Hitler began to serve a nine-month jail term for the Beer Hall Putsch in which he had failed to gain control of the German government. While imprisoned, he wrote *Mein Kampf,* but Americans paid little attention to events in the country they had helped to vanquish only a few years earlier.

Meanwhile, Congress had passed new legislation restricting the influx of Jews. The Immigration Act of 1924 reduced the annual quota of immigrants from southern and Eastern European countries to fewer than 20,000—compared with an annual prewar average of 738,000. I was stunned to learn that Harvard University President A. Lawrence Lowell had followed Columbia's lead and even went a step further: As vice president of the Immigration Restriction League, Lowell was an outspoken leader of efforts to restrict Jewish emigration to America and the admission of Jews to its most prestigious institutions of higher education.

* * *

Dick had more important things than international affairs, immigration policy, and Ivy League college admissions policies to consider in 1924; he was visiting Harry Jr. at boarding school. For an entire week beginning on Memorial Day of that year—a few days after President Coolidge signed the Immigration Act of 1924—Dick felt privileged to be his brother's invited Exeter guest. By then he wore rubber bands attached to dental braces in an effort to bring forward his receding chin. Whatever else was accomplished, the result was a lifetime of cavities, because his orthodontia preceded the fluoridation of drinking water.

The special visit became a mixed blessing when Dick looked at the front pages of the Boston newspapers on display at Exeter's school post office. Headlines throughout the country covered the sensational murder of young Bobby Franks. The gruesome crime fueled anti-Semitism throughout the nation.

Franks had disappeared when nineteen-year-old Nathan Leopold, who had graduated from the University of Chicago and planned to attend Harvard Law School in the fall, and eighteen-year-old Richard Loeb, the youngest college graduate in the history of the University of Michigan, committed what they had plotted as the perfect crime. Both killers and their victim had come from prominent Jewish families living in the German-Jewish Kenwood neighborhood near the University of Chicago. Loeb's father was a retired vice-president of Sears, Roebuck and Company; Nathan Leopold's father owned a box manufacturing company.

Simply to prove it could be done, Leopold and Loeb intended to kidnap for ransom a boy whom they would select randomly on the afternoon of May 21, 1924. He would be promptly killed so he could not incriminate his captors. They had only two prerequisites for their target as they watched boys leaving the exclusive Harvard School after classes had ended for the day: He should come from a family able to pay their $10,000 ransom demand and he should be sufficiently familiar to Leopold or Loeb that he would willingly enter the car they had rented for the occasion. Franks, a fourteen-year-old boy from another of Chicago's most prominent Jewish families, met both requirements.

The plan proceeded and, after covering the naked corpse with hydrochloric acid so its later identification would be more difficult, the murderers dumped it into an open culvert near the Indiana border. The scheme went awry when a laborer discovered the body; Nathan Leopold's horn-rimmed glasses were soon found nearby. The unique hinges on the otherwise ordinary spectacles were traced to an optometrist who had made only three such pairs, one of them for Leopold. Loeb was the first to confess on May 31; his lover Nathan Leopold soon followed. As the heinous Leopold-Loeb murder monopolized the press's attention, Exeter's post office kept the daily issues of the Boston newspapers on display for students, faculty, and staff who used the facility regularly. Dick recounted to me what he saw there.

"Knowing that another 'Leopold'—my brother Harry—was among Exeter's student body, someone underlined every 'Leopold' reference in every article relating to the confessed killer. Someone decided that the Leopold at Exeter should be made to feel shame and embarrassment for the heinous acts of his Jewish namesake in Chicago. I was there. I saw it. I was visiting my brother at Exeter as public outrage over the murder surged." The resulting underlined newspaper references to a much different Leopold struck him and his brother in precisely their intended manner. As he told me eighty years later, "Can you imagine the uproar in 1924 if their victim, Bobby Franks, had not been Jewish?"

* * *

On completing his visit in early June, Dick rode alone on the late evening train from Exeter to Grand Central Station. Shortly after his return, Dick contracted "what people thought was scarlet fever" and was isolated at home for the duration of his recovery. "Somehow my cousin Bill, who by then had finished his first year at Dartmouth, was allowed to visit me. I did not know it was the last time I would see him." Then he told me the story.

"While I was away at camp during the summer of 1924, I opened one of the daily letters I received from Mother." I had noticed that throughout all the years of their correspondence, she always addressed him as "Sweetheart." "Mother's letter contained shocking news. My cousin Bill had been driving his car with friends in a northern suburb—Skokie, I think. It somehow left the road, overturned, and killed him. I had previously toyed with the idea of adopting an abbreviated version of Mother's maiden name, 'Kim' or 'Kimmie' for Kimmelstiel, as my own middle name because I had received none at birth. But when I learned the tragic news, I took the middle name of William."

Although no official action was ever taken to effect the change, from that moment he was Richard W. Leopold, and he always included the W. "You know," he said, "no one else knows that story because no one else has ever asked me about it." For all of his remaining days, Dick never drove a car; however, he insisted his cousin's accident had nothing to do with it: "A car in New York City made no sense. Besides, my father and older brother loved to drive. They got 'first dibs.'"

By the end of the summer, Leopold and Loeb again dominated the headlines, as their seventy-year-old defense lawyer, Clarence Darrow, brought one of his most famous trials to a close. Deciding to plead the young men guilty and rest their fate in the hands of a single sentencing judge rather than twelve jurors, Darrow persuaded the court to consider psychiatric evidence relating to the killers' mental state. After a monthlong hearing, the judge spared their lives and imposed life sentences. Ironically, Dick's distant cousin, who was a member of the previously renamed Ballenger family, maintained a close social acquaintance with Nathan Leopold's family. Some of the Ballengers remained among the convicted murderer's friends and welcomed him back to society when he was released from prison in 1958. Richard Loeb was killed by a fellow inmate in 1936.

* * *

In the fall of 1924, Dick wandered into the Republican Party headquarters on Madison Avenue: "I gathered up a number of 'Coolidge/Dawes' campaign buttons and gave them to my friends—just for the fun of it." Only twelve years old at the time, he could never have guessed that twenty-five years later he would have an extended personal discussion with Dawes, who would mostly repeat stories of his military service under General John J. Pershing. For Christmas 1924, he again traveled alone by train. This time, he rode from New York to Chicago for a visit with his Aunt Blanche to help offset the absence her household felt during the first holiday season following the tragic death of her son Bill: "By then, they were living at the Ambassador West, on the near north side."

As he entered adolescence, Dick began to realize that his dream of a professional baseball career seemed to be disappearing because his classmates, especially a fellow student named Harry Goldsmith, "hit the ball farther than I did." Fortunately, a substitute sports hero emerged as he watched his newest boyhood idol, tennis great "Big Bill" Tilden, defeat "Little Bill" Johnston in the United States Open at Forest Hills. Tilden beat Johnston in the championship matches of 1920, 1922, 1923, 1924, and 1925, thereby avenging in conclusive fashion Johnston's sole final-round victory over Tilden in 1919. In another vivid recollection from that period, Dick described how he watched thousands of fans standing for hours in long lines so they could enter a New York City funeral parlor displaying the corpse of silent film legend Rudolph Valentino during the summer of 1926. "We could see them all from our apartment window," he said.

A month later, Harry Jr. accompanied him, without their parents, as Dick began the next phase of his life at Exeter. Harry had graduated in 1925, and now fourteen-year-old Dick took his turn at the New Hampshire preparatory school that was helping to move the young Leopold men into the non-Jewish mainstream of America's elite. Usually, he had found himself at the top of his Franklin class and had enjoyed the respect accompanying his regular election to the class presidency: "You will see," he told me, "the sharp contrast between the status and resulting leadership positions I enjoyed at Franklin, compared to what awaited me at Exeter and Princeton."

* * *

Illuminating Dick's life through comparison with Pop's would offer insights into both men; contrast might light another equally revealing dimension. One difference between their families was financial. While the Leopolds owned two Cadillacs, Pop and his parents rode in a used Model T Ford touring car for most of his youth. Unlike Harry Leopold Sr., who achieved wealth as a member of the New York Stock Exchange, Pop's father sold building materials and earned a comfortable living, but little more. Pop told me his mother was quite stern and cold; Dick's mother seemed warmer and more deeply connected to her sons, although photographs of her depict a somewhat stern countenance. Dick's father placed a high priority on matters outside the home; Pop spent many hours with his dad and their woodworking tools. He also received loving and witty notes from his father throughout his life.

Their socialization with the opposite sex also differed, beginning at an early age. While Dick attended the all-male Franklin School, Pop sat in public school classrooms with girls. As he approached his teenage years, Pop was "introduced into the social graces, including dancing school." Those classes culminated in organized dances at the Excelsior Club. "This was THE social club of the community," Pop reported, "the members being exclusively of the 1840 German Jewish families. . . . [T]here was almost no pairing of boys and girls. The same ones attended all social functions because their parents were friends. Then we would ask some girl to go with us to the party. But always one from the group." Pop also loved to ice skate at the Elysium, the indoor rink at 107th Street and Euclid that was a "teen meeting place for everyone, regardless of school attended." Dick had no comparable childhood experiences with girls.

Nevertheless, striking similarities between Dick's life and Pop's were also emerging. Just as Dick had been "Dicky," my father-in-law had been "Willy" when he was young. At the same time Dick was spending his summers in the Thousand Isles, Pop was away at Boy Scout camp near Chagrin Falls, Ohio. Pop's first summer away from home lasted two weeks; the second lasted four; the third spanned eight. As Dick's father assimilated himself and his family into the New York world of high finance, Pop's father rose through the ranks of the Freemasons to become the Worshipful Master of his Cleveland-area lodge by 1934. Neither family celebrated Yom Kippur, Rosh Hashanah, or any other Jewish holidays, but they exchanged gifts at Christmas.

Both boys also personally experienced anti-Semitism at a young age, and it hurt. Pop reported seventy-five years later that he applied to the DeMolay–Sons of Masons, but was rejected "because they didn't take Jews," which seems curious to me in light of his father's significant involvement in the Masonic organization. He later wrote, "My interest in the Masonic order remained close to zero ever after in spite of many solicitations to join." He similarly thought his ethnicity had excluded him from the YMCA's "Hi-Y" boys' club. But the Boy Scouts accepted him, and he loved the experience he later said "was the beginning of leadership . . . most of the rest of my life, I was the leader of something, somewhere." That would describe Dick, too. Pop remained only one medal short of Eagle Scout because he could not swim well enough to pass the lifesaving test.

Pop must have endured some anti-Semitic backlash when the Leopold-Loeb murders dominated the headlines in every major newspaper during the summer he and Dick were only twelve years old. Unfortunately, it never occurred to me to inquire about the subject while he was alive.

FOUR

Exeter and Princeton

I had always assumed Dick performed at the highest levels throughout his schooling, but I was wrong. As I sat in Northwestern's Archives and reviewed his academic record at Exeter, I saw almost an equal number of B's and C's, and even a couple of D's in mathematics. It became easy to understand why, near the end of his first year there, Dick had written to Ethel: "If I get 'kicked' out of Exeter, will you still love me?" In his defense, he received A's in French, chemistry, and history, and the average grade at the rigorous school was a C+.

* * *

It did not help Dick's transition to the boarding school that he was young for his grade and, for the first time other than summer camps, living away from home: "Mother wrote daily; I did likewise; my father never wrote at all." Nor was the environment particularly welcoming for a Jew, albeit a nonpracticing one. Exeter possessed the strains of anti-Semitism pervading America at that time.

"The first time I set foot inside a religious building of any kind," Dick told me, "I was fourteen. It was when I walked into the campus chapel at Exeter. Chapel attendance was mandatory for all students. That was also when I held my first Bible, which Mother had given me as a parting gift on my way to school because she thought I should have one." He still had it and showed it to me: it was a King James Version, including both the Old and New Testaments.

Exeter reinforced Dick's assimilative impulse. Upon enrolling at the school, he knew that graduating seniors would cast ballots for their classmates in various categories, from "most likely to succeed" to "most athletic" to "best dancer" and numerous others. Dick focused on only one goal in that respect: "I did not want to be voted class 'heathen.' Harry and I thought the title always went to the student who had done the poorest job of masking his Jewish heritage during his years at

Exeter. Whether that was its true purpose, I cannot say. But that sure is what Harry and I believed at the time."

Exeter had fraternities, although they served neither residential nor eating functions. They were more like social clubs. Dick identified one he liked, but it never chose him, so he never joined it or any other. "To be in a fraternity at Exeter required one to be an outstanding athlete, or a star debater. I was not outstanding at anything. If my last name had been Johnson, would it have made a difference? I do not know, but it certainly did not help matters that I was identified as Jewish." I made a note to remember his phrase: "identified as Jewish."

Even so, Dick understandably embraced what he called the "new atmosphere" into which he had been thrust. During his first year as a "lower middler"—tenth grade—he met the person who would become his best childhood friend: William Ernest Gillespie, the son of the academy's overbearing and domineering Latin instructor. Perhaps his father's stern countenance accounted for Ernie's stutter, but it mattered not to Dick: "In his parents' apartment in Wentworth, Ernie and I played war games and created our own baseball contests with trading cards. I remained a Giants fan; I never understood Ernie's allegiance to the Cleveland Indians." Baseball, railroad trains, and warfare continued as themes in Dick's life.

"By the end of my first year, another good friend was a roly-poly kid named Stewart Cort from Pennsylvania," he recalled. "Like Ernie, he was not Jewish." In the spring of 1927, at about the time a group of New York City electrical and radio engineers first demonstrated a new invention called the television, Dick's parents visited Exeter.

"Mother and Father took Cort and me to lunch, where we all agreed that Cort and I would room together the following year. I viewed this as a crowning achievement in my efforts to assimilate myself completely into my new 'environment.' With this development, there would be no 'heathen' vote for Dick Leopold at the end of the senior year. As the fall term approached, I was a couple of days late arriving on campus because I had to stop at Princeton to take its college entrance examinations, one of which was in plane geometry that I flunked. There were no SATs in those days and nothing like what is now called the 'common application.' In any event, by the time I arrived at Exeter, I was dismayed to find no sign of Cort. Instead, my roommate was John P. Spiegel, whose Jewish family traveled in the same Chicago social circles as my Aunt Blanche. I think he was related to the Spiegels who owned the famous catalog merchandising company. I was profoundly disappointed that my effort to blend in with the non-Jewish culture of Exeter had been blown out of the water."

Dick later regretted the distance he maintained from his Jewish roommate during his second year. He eventually realized that he himself suffered the worst consequences of his own actions, because John P. Spiegel would have been a man worth knowing and friend worth having. Spiegel went on to Dartmouth College and, ironically, Northwestern University Medical School. He became a distinguished doctor, joined the Harvard Medical School faculty in 1954, and served as president of the American Psychiatric Association from 1974 to 1975.

In his third and final year at Exeter, Dick lived alone, again in a single room. He ate all of his meals at the same table in the dining hall for his final two years, but with a different group of four other boys for each year: "To the extent I had any choice, I would have gone out of my way to eat with non-Jews for all of my Exeter years. Only one of my dining companions during my final two years was Jewish."

As baseball receded from his athletic ambitions and basketball likewise remained beyond his grasp, he turned to tennis. A tournament at the beginning of the season determined the school's team membership for that year. "As a sophomore, I drew as my opponent in the first round a senior who was the team captain," he told me. "Predictably, I lost. The following year, I likewise drew the team's captain and lost. As a senior, I surprised everyone, including myself, by defeating an adversary whom everyone assumed to be far more skilled, but I promptly lost my ensuing match to a player whom I was expected to beat handily. As a result, my chances to make the school's varsity team vanished forever. I played well enough at the club level to win my Exeter numerals—class of 1929—through participation in the Exeter-Andover matches."

Socially, he had virtually no contacts with girls: "Unlike Andover, there was no 'sister school' for Exeter. There were occasional dances including some local girls along with others whom certain fellow students brought. And I remember we sometimes had to vacate our rooms for girls who remained overnight. But I never felt sufficiently competent as a dancer and, therefore, did not enjoy any of those events."

During his Exeter years, he learned that two of his New York cousins were gay: "One was a young woman; the other was a young man. Neither my parents nor theirs reacted particularly well to the revelations. I may have been the only person in our extended family who treated them with any level of understanding."

Dick graduated cum laude and received $10 for the Sherman Hoar Prize in American history. Some of his courses had been taught by Frederick R. Whitman, who would earn one of three dedications in Dick's 1962 book: In the preface, Dick would write that Whitman had "awakened my interest in history when I was a schoolboy at the Phillips Exeter Academy." Dick also succeeded in his quest to avoid being voted class heathen, but Ernie could not escape being named the "unluckiest student" in the class of 1929 because an accident of birth had made him the son of Exeter's "old-school" Latin teacher. "Guilt by association doomed him," Dick told me without an awareness of the remark's ironic applicability to his own background. "Who can control the family into which he or she is born?"

While Dick was still at Exeter, Harry Jr. left the Wharton School after two years and took a job in a New York City brokerage house. Dick never determined the reasons for his brother's departure from college, but three were always identified: "For one, Mother was unhappy that both of her sons were away. Harry's lack of enthusiasm for academic pursuits was another; and the Roaring Twenties lure of wealth persisting well into the decade was the third."

* * *

On graduation from Exeter, Dick enrolled at Princeton University. As he later wrote, he chose that school "because it was located neither in an urban setting, nor an isolated community, like Exeter." In our conversations, he later amplified on the selection process, which was his alone because secondary schools offered little college counseling in those days: "It never occurred to me that I could not attend whatever college I chose. I did not think of applying to Columbia, which would have been more of the New York City urban experience. I regarded Cambridge as being part of the Boston area and, therefore, also too urban, as were Yale and Penn. I thought Dartmouth and Cornell were too remote. I knew no one at Exeter who considered attending Brown. Princeton was a reasonable train ride away from home, but not like living in New York City itself. So a process of elimination led me to New Jersey. I certainly had no awareness of Princeton's attitudes toward Jews, but then again, I did not really regard myself as one anyway."

Like all of the other premier colleges and universities, Princeton had informal quotas limiting the admission of Jews. In fact, Princeton was far more restrictive than Harvard or Yale in that regard. As had been the case at Exeter, his nonpracticing status did not matter to the institution's classification of him. Although he was unaware of the statistics at the time, Dick was one of only seventeen Jews in his 1933 class of 615 students. The following year there were only eleven. The Catholics fared somewhat better with forty-six, and increased their numbers to fifty, sixty, and seventy-one over the succeeding three classes.

Dick's best friend, Ernie Gillespie, went to Princeton, too: "On the day we both headed for New Jersey, Ernie and I met coincidentally at Penn Station as we boarded the train. Ernie spent much of the trip telling me about all of the people he already knew at Princeton, including his older brother who was an upperclassman and an uncle who taught mathematics. I listened with great envy, hoping to encounter even a single familiar face as I began my new journey at an unknown place. I would have to establish myself anew in the eyes of faculty members who did not know anything about me. I certainly was excited to begin college but, at seventeen, I was possessed with much more fear, apprehension, and a general lack of self-confidence." Transitions would never be easy for him.

* * *

Politics had not been a featured subject in Leopold family discussions during Dick's earlier days at home. In 1928, his staunchly Republican father voted for his first and only Democratic presidential candidate, Al Smith, because of a single issue: Smith opposed Prohibition. Herbert Hoover still won the election in a landslide.

When the October 1929 stock market crash required cutbacks in the Leopold household, Dick became concerned that his schooling might be interrupted for financial reasons. As wealthy Americans across the country lost fortunes, the value of his father's assets plummeted. Both of his parents visited him at Princeton shortly after the crash and, together, they watched the Princeton-Navy football game. "The visit," Dick said, "was memorable to me seventy-five years later because it came immediately after Black Thursday. I think it was the only time my father ever saw me at college prior to my senior year."

During the summer of 1930, Dick worked as a "runner" on Wall Street. There he got a firsthand taste of his father's business life and did not much care for it. A few months later, his Aunt Blanche committed suicide.

"As Mother described it to me, her strife centered on frustrations growing from a hopeless extramarital affair. Apparently, she was involved with a married man. One of his children was close to Blanche's daughter, my cousin Alice. The man's wife was also one of Blanche's good friends. As I understand it, Blanche took poison one afternoon, lay on her chaise lounge, went to sleep, and never woke up. It was devastating to her husband and Alice. But Mother always responded well to crises and took care of all necessary arrangements."

* * *

Although both Exeter and Princeton maintained informal quotas on the admission of Jews, Princeton's living arrangements reflected more intensely America's unpleasant and discriminatory social realities. As a college freshman, Dick lived off campus in one of three bedrooms that a university employee rented out each year to a freshman; non-Jews occupied the other two bedrooms. To improve their prospects for campus housing the following year, he and a fellow Jewish Exeter alumnus, Bill Cahn, agreed to room together as sophomores in what Dick described to me as "a marriage of convenience." After a lack of initial success in the lottery, they were later assigned a room in Pyne Hall.

Anti-Semitism at Princeton was deeply embedded in the campus community. As at Exeter, minimum mandatory chapel attendance was an example. Dick wrote sixty years later, "I have no religion myself, but at Princeton I attended more than the required number of chapels, mostly to listen not only to the likes of Norman Thomas ('05), but also the irrepressible Chaplain Bobby Wicks."

Like fraternities popular elsewhere, Princeton's eating clubs were anti-Semitic. As a sophomore, Ernie was invited to join one; Dick and his Jewish roommate were not. Bids from Ernie's club finally came to Dick and Bill Cahn during their junior year, but Ernie warned that the offer had sprung from motives even more insulting than pity.

"Ernie told me the club was desperate for members who could pay for their meals there, just so it could survive. That was the only reason they were inviting two Jews to join."

"So, what did you do?" I asked.

"I said no."

Even seven decades later, his rendition of the story mixed bruised feelings with an air of defiance. It must have been the ultimate insult for a determined nonpracticing Jew to be regarded as a second-class citizen based on an ethnic identification he was working diligently to jettison, just as his own parents had.

During their junior year, Dick and Cahn roomed together in Witherspoon, but the best news was across the hall where Ernie Gillespie shared quarters with another Exeter classmate, Hank Breed: "Breed was on the swimming team and his father was headmaster at the Blair Academy, another top prep school." The four young men became even closer, especially Dick and Ernie.

Dick was surprised to find success outside the classroom during the fall of 1931 when he competed for a position as Princeton's basketball team manager: "From among the ten or so who tried out, I was amazed that they picked me, a person identified as Jewish, but I was equally stunned that they also chose another person, Al Newfield, who also was Jewish. The two of us were named assistant managers." Again, he described himself with the phrase, "a person identified as Jewish." He had carefully chosen those words.

His victory turned to defeat in the following year when he informed the team's manager that he could not drive a car: "He and I did not get along well, anyway. In some context, he asked me to do something involving an automobile and I told him I did not drive. So much for my career as assistant manager of the team."

* * *

As Dick continued in his senior year, the worldwide Great Depression deepened and the international workers' movement grew. The severe reparations burden that the Treaty of Versailles had imposed on Germany in favor of the Great War's victors created special problems for a country with six million unemployed workers. Charismatic nationalist Adolf Hitler was gaining prominence and power; Germans of wealth and property increasingly viewed him as a potential antidote to surging communism. In the Far East, a chain of events leading to World War II had begun in September 1931. The Japanese army manufactured a violent incident to justify its attacks on China. The impotence of the League of Nations to deal with the aggression set the stage for calamity to follow.

Meanwhile, Dick was still living with Bill Cahn in Witherspoon, across the hall from Ernie. He and Ethel were corresponding three times weekly. He was too young to vote in the November election, but he began to move away from his parents' lifelong Republican ideology. In the 1932 Princeton straw vote, which produced an overwhelming undergraduate majority for Herbert Hoover over Franklin Roosevelt (65 percent to 20 percent), Dick voted for the engaging and appealing Socialist Party candidate Norman Thomas, whose sermons regularly filled the Princeton chapel audiences with awe and wonder.

"I did not regard myself as a Socialist by any means," he explained. "It was just that I could not bring myself to vote for a Democrat and I knew Thomas had no chance of winning, so mine was a wasted vote anyway." In the faculty voting, Hoover won by a smaller margin—a 46 percent to 27 percent plurality over Thomas—with Roosevelt running third (26 percent).

Nevertheless, Roosevelt soon captured Dick's imagination and engendered his enthusiasm. It started with an unprecedented Chicago flight to accept in person the party nomination and continued with the vibrant style offering hope to a downtrodden populace. Meanwhile, shortly after Dick's twenty-first birthday—for which he received a letter from his father along with a check he "valued even more"—Adolf Hitler became chancellor of what was rapidly becoming Nazi Germany. Dick confronted the personal decision of what to do next, as he pondered undertaking a career in history rather than following his family's traditional track into business.

The very personal letter he wrote to Ethel on his twenty-first birthday is revealing. By his own account, he was "sensitive," "easily hurt," and "old in some respects, but a kid in most ways." At that particular time, he was also confused about his future and aware of the limitations confronting him as a Jew in America: "Where am I heading for? Am I doing the right thing? Am I suited for an academic life, will I be happy, can I make a success of it despite my racial handicap?" The letter also revealed a continuing emotional distance between Dick and his father: "Of course, I do not mean for you to answer these questions. I am merely thinking aloud and you are the only one except Harry to whom I can think aloud to. Father would like to help and listen, but he cannot—it isn't in his nature."

By June, Dick had resolved his doubts in favor of scholarship and teaching. His senior thesis examined the development of social thought in Russia from 1840 to 1890. He graduated with highest honors, Phi Beta Kappa, and received a $400 fellowship to attend Harvard for graduate study in history. In a Princeton alumni questionnaire sixty years later, he reported that he had enjoyed his four college years "primarily because of the excellent education I received," but he also mentioned the friendships he made: "I was not active outside the classroom; my only extracurricular achievement was Assistant Manager for basketball."

As at Exeter, he had virtually no involvement with any members of the opposite sex. "I simply had no confidence in that area," he told me.

His questionnaire response credited assistant professor in medieval history Gray C. Boyce with helping to guide his career. Also important to him was the second recipient of his 1962 book's dedications, Professor Raymond J. Sontag, "who did much to settle my choice of a profession while I was an undergraduate at Princeton University."

"Two other professors also deserve special mention," he said as we concluded our discussion of his Princeton years. "Walter P. Hall, known as 'Buzzer' because he wore an old-fashioned hearing aid, taught my required sophomore year survey course in European history; Clifton R. Hall, known as 'Beppo' for reasons I never knew, taught the second semester of the required junior year course in American history. Both heightened my interest in history." Dick also left Princeton with an amusing class tribute to the university chaplain:

Here's to the Reverend Bobby Wicks;
He knows the soul's most inward tricks.
He teaches socialistic knowledge
In this most capitalistic college.

*   *   *

Dick told me that he encountered his would-be Exeter roommate, Stewart Cort, only once again in his life. The men literally crossed paths on a Cambridge, Massachusetts, bridge over the Charles River in 1935. Apart from a knowing nod, there was no interaction between them, and Dick never learned what had become of Cort after his first year at Exeter. If he had asked, he would have discovered that Cort eventually graduated from Blair Academy in New Jersey before attending Yale for three of the years Pop was there. After receiving his degree in 1934, Cort received a master's degree in business administration from Harvard in 1936. In 1970, Stewart Cort became the president of his family's business, Bethlehem Steel. He died in 1980, but the two men never saw each other again after that fleeting encounter over the Charles.

Decades later, Dick learned of Exeter's policy whereby parents of withdrawing students provided the reasons for a son's departure. At last, he hoped, the mystery of the abrupt end to Stewart Cort's Exeter career would be revealed. But it was not to be. A source in Exeter's administration office reported that no such inquiry or response could be located in Cort's file. Dick would never know if his friend had left Exeter for academic or personal reasons or because of some impulse by others to block in the most definitive way Cort's attempt to room with a Jew.

*   *   *

Some similarities between Dick and Pop were now becoming remarkable to me. As Dick graduated with honors from Exeter in 1929 at age seventeen, Pop was graduating covaledictorian of his class at Cleveland Heights High School—also at seventeen. Both had been among the youngest pupils in their grades. "After one semester of kindergarten," Pop wrote, "I was promoted to first grade. After one semester of first grade, I was promoted to second grade. That made me a year younger than the rest of my schoolmates for all of the ensuing years."

The assimilation theme was likewise common to their lives. One of Pop's closest childhood friends was Clay Herrick Jr., whose forebears included the founders of Jamestown and whose then-current relatives included Myron T. Herrick, ambassador to France. Ambassador Herrick had an estate near Chagrin Falls, Ohio, where Pop met Charles Lindbergh shortly after his historic nonstop solo flight across the Atlantic Ocean in 1927. Pop put his latest hobby—photography—to good use and came away with a picture of "Lindy" that remained in his album for seventy-five years. He and Herrick also published a monthly newspaper in grammar school. During summers between his high school years, Pop worked with his mother as a local entertainment reporter.

Ivy League anti-Semitism was also an experience both men shared. Princeton's informal quota limited Jewish admissions, while exclusionary eating clubs reinforced the problem. Dick's experience with regard to the latter was typical for a Jew; that he was nonpracticing made little difference. In fact, Princeton's committee on admissions relied on eating club prejudices to deter Jewish secondary school students even from applying to the college. University Secretary Varnum Lansing Collins wrote in November 1922: "I hope the Alumni will tip us off to any Hebrew candidates. As a matter of fact, however, our strongest barrier is the club system. If the graduate members of the clubs will ram the idea home on the undergraduate bicker [invitation] committees and make the admission of a Hebrew to the club the rarest sort of thing, I do not think the Hebrew question will become serious."

Pop once told me that he attended Yale because Amherst, the other school he seriously considered, was reputedly too anti-Semitic for him. But Yale did not provide the welcoming environment for which he had hoped, either. In 1918, Yale College Dean Frederick S. Jones said of the Jews at the school: "We should do something to improve them. If we do not educate them, they will overrun us. . . . A few years ago every single scholarship of any value was won by a Jew. . . . We must put a ban on the Jews." Four years later Robert N. Corwin, chairman of Yale's admissions committee, wrote that he regarded Yale's typical Jewish student "as naked of all the attributes of refinement and honor as when born. . . . His wits have probably been sharpened but he has not gained wisdom, at least not the kind expected of college men." In May 1922, Roswell Angier, a psychologist and the freshman class dean, asserted that Jews were "more or less in the nature of a foreign body in the class organism. They contribute very little to class life."

Jewish enrollment at Yale reached its high point in 1923 at 13.3 percent of the entering freshman class. Harvard's President Lowell was already dealing with a worsening crisis in that regard because his school's Jewish enrollment had risen to more than 25 percent; Yale wanted to avoid Harvard's problems. In 1924, it followed Columbia's example in introducing subjective "tests of personality and character" as a basis for excluding applicants otherwise meeting Yale's admission criteria. That reduced the Jewish percentage to 10 percent of the class entering in 1924. In the fall of 1926, Yale Dean Clarence W. Mendell wrote that Lowell's similar anti-Semitic initiatives had taken hold: Harvard had limited its freshman class to one thousand and decided "to reduce their 25% Hebrew total to 15% or less by simply rejecting without detailed explanation. They are giving no details to any candidate any longer."

In a 1926 editorial entitled "Ellis Island for Yale," even the *Yale Daily News* student paper weighed in on the wrong side of the discrimination controversy. Only three years before Pop's arrival, it suggested that Yale "institute immigration laws more prohibitive than those of the United States government" and proposed that the college go beyond Columbia's requirement of personal photographs from freshman applicants and obtain pictures of their fathers, too. Admissions reflected those attitudes: by 1931, Jews accounted for only 8.2 percent of the entering freshman class. That was well below the 10 percent maximum quota the Yale Corporation's committee on educational policy had suggested in a 1922 memorandum. Jewish enrollment at Yale would not reach its record 1923 level of 13.3 percent again until the early 1950s.

Against this background, Pop described his life at the college: "Like any college, there were two ways to 'belong.' One was fraternities. In 1929–1930 they were still socially important. But the frats in Yale College were eating halls; members lived in dormitories. . . . Obviously, I was not fraternity material, except for the Jewish fraternity, which did not interest me."

Like Dick, Pop found himself living off campus as a freshman. In his sophomore year, he moved into a single room on the third floor of Yale's McClellan Hall. He once described it to me as "an oversized closet—and not very oversized at that." During his junior and senior years, he occupied a single "first-class second floor dormitory room" in the Memorial Quadrangle. The Yale residential college system came into existence after he graduated.

For all of their similarities, Pop and Dick continued to experience dramatically different social interactions with girls throughout high school and college. "The 'club' of teenagers," Pop wrote, "[was] a significant part of life in the 1920s, but the group started to break up when the college years began." At Yale, Pop had a steady girlfriend. I do not know anything about her, but current family speculation is that she attended college somewhere reasonably close to New Haven and was Jewish. No one knows the cause of the relationship's failure.

Also unlike Dick, Pop had no aversion to automobiles, so that helped his socialization with girls. During the summer between his junior and senior years, he acquired a 1924 Packard touring car from a friend of his mother. "Cost: $25.00," he later wrote. "Set off for New Haven that fall, driving three Cleveland students to school. . . . At $15.00 per passenger. . . . Returned to school at no cost to me and had a car." Although he could not afford the weekend journeys that his wealthier classmates took to New York City or New England, he made the best of the situation. Because only seniors were permitted to have cars on campus, he rented his out "some weekends to pay upkeep. Unfortunately, one weekend, the transmission went out. Sorry—no more car."

Pop was coxswain on the Yale crew team competing for a spot on the United States Olympic team in 1932, although he complained years later that despite his hard work, he "never made varsity in all that time." But he concluded it was just as well that the Olympics experience had eluded him because, as he later told me, competitors in those days had to pay their own way to the games and he "sure couldn't afford to do that." Another member of the Yale crew team was Donnald Devereaux Nimmo, who had been one of Dick's daily dining companions during their junior year at Exeter. Harry Goldsmith, one of Dick's Franklin School classmates whose continued growth as an adolescent had helped to dash Dick's dreams of professional baseball, was also in Pop's Yale class of 1933. So were two other Franklin schoolmates, Claude Sperling and Robert Wechsler. Another Yale student at the time was Dick's would-be Exeter roommate Stewart Cort, who graduated in 1934. I never had the opportunity to ask Pop whether he had known any of these men who had already crossed Dick's path, but it certainly seems likely that he did.

The man who would become Pop's most famous classmate was a Jew, Eugene V. D. Rostow. Named after socialist Eugene V. Debs, he had descended from Russian immigrants and was even younger than Pop when he started college at age sixteen. As an undergraduate, Rostow protested Yale's anti-Semitic policies. The last word was eventually his: In 1955, he began ten years of service as dean of the Yale Law School before leaving to join the Department of State as its undersecretary for political affairs. He served in Democratic and Republican administrations prior to his death in 2002. Eugene's younger brother Walt Whitman Rostow also attended Yale, graduated at age nineteen, completed his Ph.D in 1940, and served his country with distinction before he died in 2003. So few degrees separate all of us, but we do not know it.

FIVE

HARVARD

"In the fall of 1933," Dick said as he began our review of his life after Princeton, "I started graduate school. Ernie Gillespie arrived in Cambridge at the same time to study classics, but a last-minute change of heart that he never explained took him back to the familiar environs of Princeton. During my first two years, I lived in one of the business school dormitories because I could eat two meals a day there. After breakfast, I would trudge across the bridge to Cambridge, spend the entire day in classes and at the library, return to the dormitory for dinner, and then go back to the library. My only break during the day was to find lunch somewhere in Harvard Square. Even Sundays were no different, except the library was closed. So at the end of the day on Saturday, I had to check out the references I was using. All of this hard work paid off at the end of my first year when I received a master's degree and grades of A or A– in the required four courses. The following fall, I learned that my high grades excused me from taking the qualifying examination. This departmental policy, newly established, was intended to allow the best students to begin work immediately on their dissertations, which I did."

I had always marveled at the completeness of his expression. Words effortlessly became sentences flowing into paragraphs, pages, and chapters. As we spoke, he used only his memory to prompt him.

* * *

"My dissertation adviser at Harvard was the renowned American historian, Arthur M. Schlesinger," he said as he moved to the next critically formative period of his life. "That connection led to my friendship with his son Arthur Jr., who was five years younger but precocious enough to carry his side of conversations at the Schlesinger Sunday teas held weekly in the family home. I did not want to gild the lily by attending every week, so I went monthly.

"Schlesinger suggested that Robert Dale Owen would make a fruitful dissertation topic for someone interested, as I was, in American social and intellectual history. Owen was and remains a second-rank historical figure, but was quite prominent during the nineteenth century. He was born in 1801 and represented Indiana in the House of Representatives, where he supported the reannexation of Texas, the reoccupation of Oregon, and the Mexican War. Perhaps more importantly, he introduced a bill leading to the establishment of the Smithsonian Institution, and he became one of three congressional members of the Institution's Board of Regents. He was instrumental in determining the architecture of what is today the Castle. By the end of the Civil War, Owen had moved across the entire political spectrum—from war Democrat to radical Republican—and his letters on emancipation were thought to have influenced Lincoln's thinking."

With Schlesinger's encouragement, Dick decided to write a biography of Owen. He set about his task in the fall of 1934, but his first bump in the road came from an unexpected source when his father died suddenly at age fifty-three after what was supposed to be routine gall bladder surgery: "In retrospect, I began to wonder if he had been the victim of a bungled operation for which today's antibiotics and procedures might have prevented fatal results, and I never forgot our acrimonious automobile ride together during the prior summer."

Dick was referring to his defense of Roosevelt's domestic initiatives to bring America out of the Depression. It had evoked a stern response from his Republican father: "'You are a traitor to your class,' my father told me"—harsh words that still seemed to hurt when Dick repeated them to me seventy years later.

In his regular correspondence with his newly widowed mother, Dick began a process that continued for decades: He urged her to resist depression, look forward, and press on with the normal routines of life. Harry Sr.'s death left a gaping hole in Ethel's life, especially with her two sons now on their own. It also sparked a continuing family controversy for the next several years over whether and when to sell his father's interest in a seat on the New York Stock Exchange.

"The seat's value had already plummeted from its pre-crash 1929 highs, and I wanted Mother to sell it so she would retain sufficient financial independence. Harry and Mother resisted the suggestion, but I favored cutting the losses and selling the seat immediately." The family controversy over the issue continued for the next six years.

* * *

Through all of the personal and financial turmoil attending his father's sudden death and its aftermath, Dick was undeterred as he embarked on his biography of Owen. Part of the necessary process involved confirming that another graduate student had not preempted the topic. In the national register maintaining such information, Dick initially found no potentially competing entry.

"The problem," he later admitted to me, "is that I looked only at the prior year's listings. After I had already begun work, someone suggested I should review earlier registrations, too. When I did, my heart sank. I found a 1931 entry under the name of Maurice B. Cuba at Columbia University."

Dick reported his new discovery to Schlesinger, who immediately made inquiries with his friends in New York. The February 1935 response confirmed that the subject of Dick's proposed research—Robert Dale Owen's life—was "certainly open." But there was more.

"At about the same time someone at Columbia was assuring Schlesinger that my pursuit of Owen was fair game, I received a letter from Professor Elinor Pancoast of Goucher College. She told me she had been working for ten years on a publication about Owen. I went back to Schlesinger. He read Pancoast's letter and said, 'I think she is bluffing. Go ahead and call her bluff.' Schlesinger reasoned that someone who had already worked on a subject for ten years without publishing a single article on it posed no serious challenge to my effort."

With the added boost of a predoctoral Social Science Research Council field fellowship, Dick was on his way—literally and figuratively—to New Harmony, Indiana. As they would throughout his life, the trains carried him to his destiny.

"I took the train from Boston to the New York Historical Society. There I learned that someone—not identified by name—had recently sought material on Owen. At the Smithsonian in Washington, the trail got hotter when I received another report that a still unidentified researcher had reviewed the very Owen materials of interest to me. All of this recent activity relating to Owen was very disturbing, but what was I to do?

"From Washington, I took the Baltimore and Ohio Railroad to Vincennes, Indiana; then a bus to Evansville; and then an Illinois Central local from Evansville to Stewartsville where I found a driver who, curiously, was waiting to take me the final leg of the journey. When I arrived at the New Harmony Tavern, the owner surprisingly said he had been expecting me and wanted me to meet a friend who was already there. Puzzled by these remarks, I followed him into the dining room where he introduced me to a short, dark man with a mustache. It was Maurice B. Cuba.

"My dissertation topic and months of hard work appeared to be flying out the window before my eyes. Cuba insisted that his 1931 registration had reserved the topic for five years. He also said he had completed all of what he regarded as his necessary research on Owen in Indianapolis and Washington. I did not debate the matter with him; I merely listened. Cuba left the next day after spending only forty-eight hours in New Harmony, thanks to the use of a microfilm machine with which he copied large quantities of materials he took with him.

"Again, I turned to Schlesinger for advice. I wrote to him about Cuba's appearance on the scene. Schlesinger likewise responded by mail—there were not many phones around in those days, and the few existing required funds a struggling graduate student did not have. He told me to press ahead. Meanwhile, Cuba also wrote to Schlesinger, urging that he stop my work. Schlesinger responded that Cuba should not worry because, with his head start, he had nothing to fear from young Dick Leopold's newly initiated efforts.

"I pressed onward."

* * *

A year later, Dick could see the end of his Social Sciences Research Council fellowship on the horizon. "I am very anxious," he wrote in February 1936 to Exeter's principal, Dr. Lewis Perry, "to do active teaching next year." He sought Perry's "opinion of the present status of secondary school education as regards teaching careers for one in my position and the possibility of securing a position for the next year. I would be grateful for any suggestions that you might care to make concerning tactics to be pursued, institutions and men to which to apply. If there is to be any opening at Exeter in the near future, I should, of course, like to be considered an applicant."

Perry never responded.

* * *

Dick's impending financial crisis disappeared when Harvard unexpectedly provided funds for his research in England. The trip prevented him from voting in the 1936 election. In September of that year—six months after Germany occupied the Rhineland in another violation of the Versailles Treaty—Dick bought a third-class ticket on an ocean liner. Along the way, he wrote to Ethel that "the *Queen Mary* passed early Sunday morning" and, at 7:30, "the *Hindenberg* was visible upon the horizon." In February 1937, Ethel joined him in England. From London, they traveled to Scotland and Paris before returning to the United States in more pleasant second-class accommodations. Three months later, the *Hindenberg* exploded in flames while trying to dock at Lakehurst, New Jersey.

* * *

Hoping his most immediate obstacles to an academic career—in the forms of Cuba and Pancoast—were behind him, Dick pressed ahead with his dissertation. He was right in one sense: The biography of Owen now faced clear sailing to completion. But he was wrong if he thought the academy would embrace his quest. In that respect, he faced a problem he could not cure, even if he had been certain of its existence. He was Jewish, and it did not matter that he himself carried no such internal identification of his ethnicity, religion, or whatever other trappings the designation "Jew" carried with it. Perhaps that explains why Exeter's Dr. Perry did not answer Dick's thoughtful letter soliciting advice on a teaching career. Dick did not realize he was inadvertently seeking Perry's assistance in becoming what would have been Exeter's first Jewish faculty member in a particularly problematic field. As I would soon discover, Jews who wanted to teach American history confronted an especially daunting path.

* * *

In 1995, Dick would write, "I have no religion myself. . . ." But sometimes a man is what others make him, not what he believes himself to be. It was true in medicine, too. While Dick was in graduate school, Pop attended Western Reserve Medical School in Cleveland. He was one of eight Jewish students in his medical school class of eighty-three that graduated in 1937.

"By some decision it had a limit of 10 percent Jewish students," Pop later wrote. "Somehow or other it was felt that this represented the population proportion, and that the Jewish physicians would take care of the Jewish population."

I think I now understand why my mother, who descended from a long line of Lutheran ministers, always remarked to me as a young child growing up in Minnesota during the 1950s and 1960s that "the best doctors are Jewish." They had to be; otherwise, they would not have been accepted for the very few medical school openings available to a Jew in the 1930s and 1940s. "We graduated 68 of the 83 admitted students," Pop wrote, "and of course the 8 Jewish men."

Four of Pop's classmates were women; the only female graduate students in Dick's department were not his contemporaries, but were "mostly older teachers who had returned for graduate study and lived at home." Pop's rigorous schedule left little leisure time, but on the occasions when he did socialize, the eight Jewish students were together, "with proper female companionship, of course." During the summer preceding his final year of medical school, he was the doctor for a camp near Chagrin Falls. His senior-year rotation included obstetrics. "This required wheels," he noted, so he acquired a 1926 Chevy one-seater coupe, which "permitted me to move around socially on those infrequent times when I was able to. That social life was important, as will be seen later."

SIX

"Annus Mirabilis"

After about six weeks of our regular Sunday morning sessions, Dick realized that I was determined to compile the historical record of important events in his life while he himself was still around to elaborate on them. He knew I would not rely exclusively on his recollections—that would be folly for any historian—and I think he was surprised when I told him I had spent an entire day reviewing his papers in the Northwestern Archives. Even more surprising to him, I suspect, was my assertion that I hungered for more.

We were proceeding chronologically and then occasionally circling back for more depth as a particular matter might warrant, as my additional research might prompt, and as his penchant for privacy might permit. Every Sunday, I knew I had to arrive armed with a specific agenda of questions, topics, and discussion items. He did not suffer fools gladly or the ill-prepared at all. In that important respect, things had not changed very much from thirty years earlier, when a student attended class at his peril if he had not read the assigned materials and considered carefully the day's questions in C-13.

The difference now was that I was the only student in this tutorial, and it had become my task to frame the questions for discussion. Often he would suggest for my review particular materials from the remnants of his library or his papers in the Northwestern Archives. And once in a while he would give me a big clue: For example, he had thought sufficiently about his own autobiography to give the 1937–1938 academic year a chapter title: "Annus Mirabilis"—his "Miracle Year." He then proceeded to tell me why.

* * *

In the fall of 1937, Hitler's Nazi Germany aggressively supported Generalissimo Francisco Franco's fascist forces in the Spanish Civil War while Stalin sold arms to those defending the Republic. On the other side of the world, the Japanese battled the Chinese in the Far East. President Roosevelt's plan to reform the United States Supreme Court by first enlarging it failed as a hostile Congress resisted him. In Belfast, the Irish Republican Army detonated bombs directed at the new King of England, who had assumed the position after his predecessor Edward VIII abdicated the throne a year earlier so he could marry an American divorcée, Wallis Warford Simpson. In New York, Ethel Leopold moved into the Wyndham Hotel, where she would live for the next twenty-five years. In January 1937, she had been proud to learn that while her younger son was still finishing his dissertation, he had been appointed to a one-year term as an instructor and tutor at Harvard. He would meet his first class of students in September.

"As the fall term began in 1937, Schlesinger, who was an associate of Adams House, invited me to join his 'fist-ball' group. Among the players was Raphael Demos, acting master of Adams House, whose friendship changed the course of my life. The importance of fortuity in the unfolding of history—whether personal or of nations—cannot be overstated. Schlesinger's fist-ball group is a splendid example. But to understand why, you need to know something about Harvard's undergraduate housing system."

* * *

One of Dick's illustrious professors on the Harvard faculty was Samuel Eliot Morison, whose history of the university, *Three Centuries of Harvard: 1636–1936*, described how the "house" system had begun as an experiment in 1930. In the nineteenth century, the college had been small enough to house all undergraduates in the intimate setting of Harvard Yard. That became impossible as the student population grew. By 1900, Harvard student housing arrangements reflected America's social stratifications: Most of those from wealthy families lived in privately owned residences along Mt. Auburn Street, called the "gold coast." Such rooming houses lacked dining facilities because those living in the gold coast dormitories ate in the even more exclusive "final clubs."

Almost anyone whose family could afford it lived in a gold coast dormitory; final club admittance was by invitation only. "Their members often had prominent New England surnames, like Adams and Winslow," Dick told me, "and could trace their familial lineages to the Mayflower and Plymouth Rock. More recently, they had attended the especially exclusive private boarding schools of Groton, St. Paul's, Middlesex, and St. Mark's." Unfortunately, the search for the top of the pyramid never ended for them, because the final clubs, too, had a social hierarchy.

"Mason Hammond was one of my faculty colleagues and had been a Harvard undergraduate," Dick said. "He told me his father had been a member of 'Porcellian' and practically disowned him when Mason was not invited to join. Porcellian was regarded as one of the top final clubs."

Hammond was in good company: Years earlier, the same club had rejected an undergraduate who later became president, Franklin D. Roosevelt. Even decades later, Roosevelt would describe the event as the "greatest disappointment of his life"; his wife, Eleanor, suggested the incident gave him an "inferiority complex" that "had helped him to identify with life's outcasts." Needless to say, Jews were not welcome, either.

Although Harvard's President Lowell was likewise anti-Semitic, he thought university life should bring together the desirable students. He believed that men from different backgrounds and diverse geographic regions might learn from each other over the shared experience of a college education. The gold coast dormitories and related final clubs worked in the opposite way: Like-minded men of wealth and privilege banded together to live and eat separately from their less affluent classmates. As a consequence, life at Harvard outside the classroom increasingly mirrored, perpetuated, and even exacerbated America's socioeconomic differences. Lowell sought to restore the climate of intimacy and personal growth he had associated with a time many decades earlier, when all Harvard men had lived and studied together in the Yard.

Lowell gained an initial opening to change the housing system as the 1910 academic year ended. In an unprecedented act, most of the juniors in the class of 1911 used their housing preferences to locate themselves in four newly renovated buildings at the north end of Harvard Yard—Hollis, Stoughton, Holworthy, and Thayer. As seniors, these students lived together in the type of cross-sectional solidarity Lowell seemed to want. His task became to capitalize on this development and push it down to the lower classes. That began to happen when, shortly thereafter, a new freshman dormitory opened in the Yard.

Most freshmen, along with all sophomores and juniors, still had to fend for themselves while the self-defined social elite among them remained in the gold coast dormitories and related final clubs. By the mid-1920s, the undergraduate population had grown to more than 3,500. Freshmen and most seniors lived in the Yard, but the two classes in between were still scattered throughout the campus area. Although privately owned gold coast housing began to disappear as Harvard quietly bought those residences, final clubs remained, and the "clubmen" kept to themselves.

In 1928, Yale alumnus Edward Stephen Harkness offered three million dollars to fund a Harvard experiment combining several dormitory buildings into a single "house." It would have a master and resident tutors who would pick the house members from the ranks of freshman applicants completing their first year. Harkness promptly increased his gift to ten million dollars—enough for a total of seven houses—when he saw the enthusiasm with which Lowell and the Harvard Corporation greeted his plan. Ironically, he had made a similar offer to his alma mater, but Yale had been unable to reach a decision before the deadline Harkness had set for a response to his proposal.

Most Harvard faculty members opposed the project because, they claimed, the decision-making process had "railroaded" them; undergraduate clubmen resisted because it challenged their social domination of the campus; the *Harvard Crimson* student newspaper echoed concerns of non-clubmen who feared that a dreaded boarding school type of discipline would accompany the house system. Lowell prevailed over all objectors. The result was Harvard's new residential program, putting all freshmen in buildings around the perimeter of Harvard Yard and clustering most other students into unitary complexes called houses that actually included several different dormitories.

The first two houses, Dunster and Lowell, opened in the fall of 1930. Among the other five opening the following year was Adams House, combining two former gold coast dormitories with a new building; it was the only house with a swimming pool. Members of the three upper classes were eligible to live in one of the seven houses, each of which had its own identity and place in the social pecking order. "Adams House was in the middle of that social pack when I was at Harvard," Dick told me, "but the rankings changed over time."

The Harvard house system flourished. The master was typically a very senior faculty member who lived with his wife and children among the approximately 250–300 students in the house. Each house reflected its master's attitude because he selected a staff including a distinguished group of professors (called associates), a senior tutor, an assistant senior tutor, and the resident and nonresident tutors. The staff selected the students who were invited to become members. No student was assured entry into the house of his choice. Rather, as the freshman year ended, each expressed a preference for one of the houses. The students seeking admission did not know that Harvard had already categorized them in ways that would play an important role in determining their ultimate house assignments.

"There were five groups," Dick explained to me. "They were, first, the 'SPS'—students from select private schools, of which there were four—Groton, St. Paul's, Middlesex, and St. Mark's. We referred to them collectively as 'St. Grottlesex.' The second group included only Exeter and Andover. Their students enrolling at Harvard were so numerous they received their own category. The third group was 'OP'—other private schools. Fourth was 'PS,' public schools—a group whose membership was expanding dramatically as a result of the national scholarship campaign to diversify Harvard that James Bryant Conant had begun." After taking over from Lowell in December 1932, President Conant increased financial access and support for public high school graduates and thereby transformed the undergraduate population of the college.

"So you had SPS, Exeter/Andover, OP, and PS. That accounts for four of the five groups into which all freshmen were divided. The fifth group consisted of the 'stars,'" Dick said with a knowing smile. My facial expression revealed bewilderment about his last descriptive category. I initially thought he was talking about particularly distinguished students, but he immediately set me straight.

"The Jews. Whether practicing or nonpracticing, Harvard placed all of them under the 'Star of David' for purposes of determining their allocation among the seven houses. All houses were supposed to 'share the wealth,' shall we say, as to the 'stars.'"

"Spreading the burden" more accurately described the process as those making the decisions perceived it, reflecting an attitude emanating from the very top of the institution during Lowell's domination of the university. Ironically, the same Harvard president who had made bold and dramatic changes to the housing system in promoting diversification did not extend his benevolence to the Jews. In 1922, Lowell, who also served as vice president of the Immigration Restriction League promoting legislation that would eventually become the Immigration Act of 1924, had specifically proposed restricting Jewish enrollment. He disingenuously claimed such limits to be in the Jews' best interest locally: Limits would counter rising anti-Semitism produced by the increasing Jewish presence in Cambridge. In fact, Lowell actually believed Jews lacked the proper "character" for Harvard and could not be true Americans until they gave up their "peculiar practices." In 1926, chairman of Harvard's admissions committee Henry Pennypacker stated his concern for applicants with "extreme racial characteristics" who lacked the necessary "character, personality, and promise." Until his retirement in November 1932, Lowell worked assiduously to reduce Jewish enrollment at Harvard, and he succeeded.

Thereafter, President Conant tried somewhat to reverse the anti-Semitic tide, but his was an equivocal effort: His national scholarship program was available only to "western applicants," excluding automatically the large number of prospective Jewish students from New York and Boston. Even so, Conant moved his institution away from the more strident anti-Semitism characterizing Lowell's reign. By 1937, Conant's admissions officers also relied increasingly on a new examination the College Entrance Examination Board had developed. During the morning, the Scholastic Aptitude Tests (SATs) assessed capabilities; the afternoon was devoted to Achievement Tests measuring proficiency. Many colleges followed Harvard's lead in using the two tests as quantitative tools in reviewing applicants, thereby hoping to make admissions decisions less subjective.

Meanwhile, Lowell's undergraduate housing experiment became a great success as far as it went. Unfortunately, any particular sophomore class would find among its number those who had unsuccessfully sought admission into a house at the end of their freshman year. Some of those sophomores entered later, as students departed for various reasons and openings occurred. Some remained on the outside for their entire Harvard undergraduate careers. Yet Dick became convinced that, even with all of its shortcomings, the Harvard house system at that time embodied the best in undergraduate living options. "If the house system had existed in 1929, I would have spent my undergraduate years at Harvard, rather than Princeton," he said, a point that pervaded his later correspondence on the subject.

Only those tutors invited to become members of the houses to which they were assigned lived "in residence," receiving free room and board and the use of all facilities (such as the Adams House swimming pool). Dick's initial appointment as an instructor and tutor carried no automatic membership to any house. He began the academic year living in a rooming house on Hilliard Street.

The title "tutor" grossly understated the duties and responsibilities of the position. During his first year, Dick's charges included seven seniors who were writing honors theses, a junior who was preparing for examinations to determine his prospects for honors at graduation, and eight to ten sophomores. The tutor served as critic, supporter, adviser, teacher, confidant, and friend to each of the students assigned to him. In that role, he began a lifetime of mentoring. At the time, he was only twenty-five years old.

Dick started the 1937 academic year filled with anxiety and trepidation that he reiterated in my discussions with him: "Would I perform sufficiently well as a tutor to gain the respect and friendship of the students for whom I was responsible? Dare I think that I might even somehow become an invited member of any house?" But he held equally serious concerns about his teaching and scholarship: "Would my teaching meet my own high standards and, at the same time, be sufficiently popular among the undergraduates that I had some chance for reappointment the following year?" The answers to these questions ultimately produced what he called his Annus Mirabilis—the Miracle Year.

* * *

In the fall of 1937, Professor James Phinney Baxter left Harvard to become the president of Williams College. It is some measure of Baxter's stature that he had been instrumental in Conant's selection to replace Lowell as Harvard's president five years earlier. Baxter had served as the original master of Adams House since its founding in 1931. When he left, assistant professor of philosophy Raphael Demos, who had been the senior tutor, became the acting master. He held that position when he first met Dick at a fateful fist-ball game in September 1937.

Fist-ball resembled volleyball as teams of contestants stood on opposite sides of a net and smashed a ball with their fists rather than their open palms. At age forty-nine, Schlesinger was among the older members of a group he asked Dick to join for regular games at the Sargent Gymnasium on the law school campus. Others included the law school's dean, Erwin N. Griswold ("litigious—a poor loser"); distinguished law professor Austin W. Scott ("a delightful man"); history instructors John K. Fairbank ("a friend and colleague") and Myron P. Gilmore (whom he had met the prior May and who would become "one of the closest professional colleagues I would ever have"); physicist Percy Williams Bridgman ("quiet and unassuming, but a terror on the fist-ball court; he also went on to receive the Nobel Prize in Physics in 1946"); and Dick ("I was the youngster"). He later wrote that, although future Nobel laureate Bridgman (age fifty-three) was the eldest member of the group and "quiet and taciturn before and after the game," he "played the game with a zest and abandon that belied his years." Even Fairbank's autobiography commented on an episode that Dick, too, would remember for the rest of his life—when Bridgman slid across the floor on his chest to make a play. But forty years after their last game, Scott would remember Dick as "the best of all the players at fist-ball."

For Dick, the most important of his new fist-ball colleagues was the acting master of Adams House, Raphael Demos. Shortly after they first met, Demos invited him to dinner where they listened to economist John Henry Williams, an Adams House associate, discuss the growing economic recession. After passing the inspection to which he had been subjected, Dick was invited to become a resident tutor. He suspected Raphael's wife, Jean, was at least as important to the approval process as her husband. On a late November day in 1937 when the Harvard football team played Yale in New Haven, he moved into Adams House, apartment B-38.

*   *   *

Although Dick had completed all requirements for his doctorate by September 1937, he had to wait until February 1938 before Harvard formally conferred his degree. Maurice Cuba never resurfaced with any publication relating to Owen. In the preface of his published manuscript, Dick acknowledged "the assistance rendered by my colleagues at Harvard University," including history department chairman Frederick Merk and assistant professor of history Paul H. Buck. But he reserved his "greatest debt of gratitude" for "Professor Arthur M. Schlesinger, who first suggested the subject to me and who, over a period of years, has given unsparingly of his time. Without his genial humor, constant encouragement, and stimulating criticism, this work would not have been possible." Merk would be thanked again, as the third and final teacher to whom Dick would dedicate his 1962 book because he had "revealed to me the delights of scholarship when I was a graduate student at Harvard University."

On September 10, 1937, Dick was invited by James G. Randall, chairman of the program committee for the 1938 Indianapolis meeting of the Mississippi Valley Historical Association, to present a paper on Owen. "The invitation resulted from my research contacts in Indiana," he explained to me. "It was unusual for a Harvard person to attend such a meeting in the Midwest and also unusual for so junior a person to be invited. Flattered by this unexpected bid and seeing an opportunity to discuss possible publication of my dissertation with the Bobbs-Merrill firm in Indianapolis, I agreed and read a paper entitled, 'Was Robert Dale

Owen a Reformer?' Because I knew Maurice Cuba and Elinor Pancoast were also working on biographies of Owen, I had to strike a balance—trying to say something new, while not giving away too much of my findings and conclusions. So I played it pretty close to the vest."

Twenty years after attending the Indianapolis gathering, Dick himself would be the program chairman for the association's annual meeting in Pittsburgh. Twenty years after that, when it had been renamed the Organization of American Historians, he would become its president.

* * *

By spring 1938—as the Anschluss began with Hitler's annexation of Austria—Dick's success as a teacher had earned him reappointment for another year as an instructor, but he was about to confront a dilemma. Again, James Phinney Baxter's departure from Harvard was the triggering event.

"I was swimming in the Adams House pool when Paul Buck approached. He had been an instructor from 1926 to 1936 and had procrastinated so long in completing his dissertation that Schlesinger finally imposed a requirement that Buck submit one new chapter each week. He eventually finished, and it was published in 1937. Buck told me that if I changed my field from social and intellectual history to diplomatic history, I would likely receive a five-year appointment to become effective upon the completion of my three existing one-year terms. The new position would include not only a semester-long lecture course on the subject matter previously taught by Baxter, but also a one-semester graduate seminar. If what Buck was telling me was true, I could remain gainfully and continuously employed at Harvard until May 1945.

"Shortly thereafter, I conferred with department chairman Merk and he confirmed what Buck had told me. With Baxter gone, the tenured professors in American history at that time were Merk, Schlesinger, and Samuel Eliot Morison. Buck had just won the Pulitzer Prize for his book, thanks in large part to publicity from his friend Benny DeVoto, who was a prolific and flamboyant writer for *Harper's*. Winning the Pulitzer forced Harvard's hand with respect to Buck. They really had to give him the tenured position that had been Baxter's, even though I was being asked to teach Baxter's diplomatic history course—a subject, by the way, about which I had little knowledge and no particular interest.

"Merk also reiterated what I already knew: a tenured spot would not become available for me because the department's demographics precluded it. One of the assistant deans—a mathematics professor named William Graustein—had developed a university-wide table showing all anticipated tenure openings for each department. History had none, other than the Baxter slot now reserved for Buck. No retirements were foreseen because Morison and Merk were only fifty years old and Schlesinger was forty-nine. Even worse for me, Conant had decreed that Harvard would no longer allow assistant professors to stay on indefinitely without any hope of promotion. He decided that a person could be an instructor for no more than three years and an assistant professor no more than five. That is what they were offering me, along with my own lecture course and a graduate seminar.

"My older friends and fellow fist-ball players, Myron Gilmore in Renaissance history and John Fairbank in Chinese history, had previously received similar appointments and their own courses. However, those opportunities had come in their chosen fields of specialty, so their subsequent research and writing continued without interruption. I would have to start over."

Harvard's invitation was a great compliment to Dick, but it changed the course of his scholarly life. Fellow graduate student Elting E. Morison, whom Dick had first met in Merk's seminar in February 1934 and who was Samuel Eliot Morison's second cousin, expressed concern. He worried that this dramatic change in Dick's field of specialization would reduce his near-term ability to write the scholarly works necessary for further professional advancement. As Dick told me when we discussed the topic, "When friends like Elting later criticized me for taking this apparent step backward in my development, I asked a very simple question in response, 'What would you have done in response to such an offer from Harvard?' I have yet to hear a satisfactory answer to that one."

In a letter almost sixty years later, Dick explained, "The choice was between bringing in Sam Bemis or Dexter Perkins [pre-eminent diplomatic historians at Yale and the University of Rochester, respectively] and thus losing Buck, or promoting Paul and being obliged to scrape the bottom of the barrel to handle Baxter's courses. As the only instructor in United States history with a Ph.D, I was the bottom of the barrel." Summarizing President Conant's new limits on nontenured faculty, he observed, "Simple arithmetic indicated that I could not hope for more than eight years, no matter how effective my teaching or brilliant my scholarship." He was offered the best deal he could ever expect from Harvard, and he accepted it. Dick Leopold—a social and intellectual historian—now found himself in diplomatic history.

Dick's maiden performance in his new field was a lecture Baxter had previously given in the survey course. In April 1938, Elting Morison sat through a rehearsal and "suffered through my preliminary reading of my first lecture in old History 5—the one Jim Baxter had formerly given on 1914–1917. I had enough material in that lecture to occupy at least two."

When Baxter periodically returned from Williamstown to monitor the progress of his former domain, he came to admire Adams House's newest tutor. As Dick told me, "Baxter was greatly suspicious that I, as a young upstart, could somehow be teaching his course. But we eventually developed a close friendship, and he regularly told colleagues I was 'the best diplomatic historian in the field'— which, of course, wasn't true. But it was nice of him to say so."

* * *

Dick was on his way, but he was still "identified as Jewish," which meant that wholly apart from the stated departmental demographic obstacles, it was hard to imagine how a tenured position for him at Harvard would ever exist. But the issue never presented itself to him in that way. He had not been told that his Jewish background played any role in the decision and could never be sure it did. Rather, when Harvard offered him the five-year appointment to follow his three one-year terms, the department's position had been simply that there would not be any tenured openings in American history. As Dick saw it, the absence of any likely retirements in the near future meant an impossible blockage to his advancement in Cambridge.

Still, the prospect of a strong Harvard foundation for his career made it easy to rebuff Amherst College's expression of interest in April 1938 when he wrote to Professor E. D. Salmon, "[R]ightly or wrongly, I have decided that my position here for the next year is too extraordinary to give up. I am quite overwhelmed by the opportunity to teach a course of my own and direct graduate work in a seminar." A remote place like Amherst would also have required him to drive a car.

*   *   *

Fortuity struck again when new permanent master of Adams House, David M. Little, arrived and Demos returned to his senior tutor post—albeit as a nonresident. In the spring of 1938, assistant senior tutor S. Everett Gleason accepted a position at Amherst College. On June 15, Little and Demos tapped Dick as a replacement, even though he was the house's newest resident tutor.

"It meant a much more comfortable suite in Adams House. My new room, I–11, came with an extra bedroom, a kitchen, and a refrigerator. Raphael's office was next door." With Demos as a new master and the senior tutor living outside Adams House, Dick found himself with "unprecedented responsibility in the years ahead. My proximity to Dave Little enabled him to ask my advice on countless issues that normally would have been referred to the senior tutor. It was a remarkable climax to a miraculous year."

Dick's second family in Cambridge grew every year: Myron and Sheila Gilmore, Arthur and Elizabeth Schlesinger (and their son, Arthur Jr.), Paul and Sally Buck, and Elting and Anne Morison. The Miracle Year added Raphael and Jean Demos, followed by Dave and Henge Little. Another addition was Payson S. Wild, who taught political science and was tutor for a not particularly distinguished undergraduate named John Fitzgerald Kennedy.

Dick capped the year with an unpleasant event when he attended the fifth-year reunion of his Princeton class of 1933. Some of his classmates were married by then, causing him to feel somewhat alienated because, as he later wrote, he had "no wife for support." Many more engaged in "excessive drinking" he found distasteful. "So did the sneers at FDR," he added when we spoke about it. That Princeton reunion would be his last.

*   *   *

In Dick's favorite language—the words and phrases of baseball—he had gone three-for-three during his academic Miracle Year of 1937–1938. He had been invited to join the Adams House staff. He had reason to expect a five-year appointment beginning in the fall of 1940, assuring him a solid Harvard base from which to launch his academic career. He was selected over all other resident tutors to become the assistant senior tutor of Adams House, although he actually wielded even more power and influence than the title suggested. Fortuity had played its hand in Dick's favor, although the decision to change his specialty from social and intellectual history to diplomatic history caused some concern because its implications were not clear.

Dick's achievements were especially significant for that time. Selig Perlman, a labor economist at the University of Wisconsin, advised Jewish graduate students in history to change their fields because, as he put it, "history belongs to the Anglo-Saxons." American history was an especially daunting career path because major universities hesitated to allow Jews, many of whom were regarded as uncultured radicals, to educate the nation's youth about the nation's past. A 1937 report of the American Jewish Committee found it "very difficult these days for Jews to become full professors in the leading universities." Throughout the 1930s, Harvard's only Jewish faculty members were Harry A. Wolfson, who taught Hebrew as part of what was called Semitic studies; Associate Professor of Fine Arts Paul J. Sachs; and Honorary Professor of Medicine Milton J. Rosenau.

So it was in the training of physicians. Pop wrote that when the time came for his medical internship, "Cleveland's University Hospital did not accept Jewish interns then nor did St. Luke's. They went to City Hospital or Mt. Sinai." He went to Mt. Sinai where "many of the staff patients—those admitted to wards because they could not afford private care—were of the recently immigrated Jewish group from Poland and Russia. I heard a lot of Yiddish."

Pop received a reserve commission in the Army Medical Corps as a second lieutenant and, in June 1938, married a Cleveland woman, Sue Goldsmith. She was a direct descendant of Simson Thorman, a Bavarian immigrant who became Cleveland's first Jewish settler in 1837 and whose success as a fur trader on Lake Erie prompted nineteen of his fellow European townsmen in Unsleben to join him two years later. By the time the first era of Jewish immigration ended around 1880, Cleveland's Jews were primarily Germanic and numbered 3,500. They were highly Americanized, but not universally accepted in the larger community. To help care for their own, they founded the Hebrew Relief Society in 1875. In 1892, the Young Women's Hospital Society began to raise funds for what would eventually become Mt. Sinai Hospital.

Sue's maternal grandfather had made his fortune as one of John D. Rockefeller's bankers in the early twentieth century. By then, the next major wave of Jewish immigration to Cleveland was under way as Eastern European Jews fled persecution in Russia and Poland. In contrast to these more conservative and orthodox Jews who adhered to their religious traditions, Sue's family identified itself as Reform, for which Pop offered one of his characteristically succinct summaries: "Cleveland and New York had the first Reform temples about which we have any knowledge. This means there was a Rabbi. Services were held on Sunday, almost entirely in English, totally in English in some temples. They were a continuity of Judaism mostly because the members were socially Jewish . . . No Jewish holidays at home; we had Christmas trees, Easter bunnies and baskets, and such, because that was a way of life. . . . The truth is, we were in no way truly Jewish, but were always Jews to the rest of the world. The Reform Jews were considered totally unacceptable by the conservative and orthodox groups. The latter lived in closed circles because their way of life demanded it."

A Cleveland rabbi who headed one of the nation's largest Reform congregations and would later lead the Zionist movement in America, Abba Hillel Silver, performed the ceremony that wed Pop and Sue at her parents' Cleveland Heights home before they boarded the sleeper train to Chicago. There Pop had obtained a first-rate medical residency with a prominent eye, ear, nose, and throat surgeon. He had been recommended by a Cleveland physician whose own father's medical career owed its origins to Pop's grandfather, Felix Rosenberg: Rosenberg had sponsored that man when he had emigrated from Germany during the late nineteenth century. So, it seems, one of Dick's favorite themes—the circularity of history—would pervade Pop's life, too.

After eight months in a small furnished Oak Park apartment, Pop and Sue found what he described as "a nice furnished one-room apartment in a big building at the corner of 55th and Hyde Park Blvd. . . . Somehow, unknown to me, social relationships developed. . . . That's where people of our age group lived, with whom we could be friends." They were living a few blocks away from the former residence of Dick's Aunt Blanche in an area of assimilating Jews.

After a year of study, Pop's mentor surprised him with an invitation to remain in Chicago as his senior resident, providing a perfect symmetry to Dick's promotion to assistant senior tutor. It was Pop's Miracle Year, too.

SEVEN

"Groping for a Policy"

At the end of September 1938, British Prime Minister Neville Chamberlain hailed as "peace with honour . . . peace for our time" the Munich Agreement dismembering Czechoslovakia and giving Hitler control of the Sudetenland. In November, what many would mark as the official public commencement of the Holocaust came with Kristallnacht—the Night of the Broken Glass—when Nazi troops and sympathizers attacked Jewish businesses, destroyed one hundred synagogues, and arrested thousands of men. In March 1939, Hitler violated the Munich Agreement, annexed the rest of Czechoslovakia, and announced that Poland and Lithuania were next on his list. In June, more than nine hundred Jewish refugees on the *S.S. St. Louis* were on what would be described decades later as the Voyage of the Damned. The ship was denied permission to dock in Florida after Cuba had rejected a similar request. It was forced to return to Europe, and most of its passengers would eventually die in Nazi concentration camps.

On September 1, Hitler invaded Poland. France, Australia, and the United Kingdom immediately declared war on Germany. By the end of May 1940, Germany had secretly established a new concentration camp at Auschwitz and had conquered Poland, Denmark, Norway, Belgium, Luxembourg, and the Netherlands. On June 14, the Germans occupied Paris.

* * *

It was a time of strife in the Leopold household as well. The continuing controversy over the disposition of Harry Leopold Sr.'s seat on the stock exchange eventually came to a head in 1940. Ethel asked Dick for a loan to cover the annual dues associated with maintaining the seat. He refused, affirming in a letter that "if you needed money to live, I would gladly *give* it to you, not lend it. I would consider such a gift as part of my filial obligations, and it would be cheerfully made." But this was not a situation of need for her. Dick had developed a frugal lifestyle consistent with his limited means as a young academic in a difficult economy; however, Ethel had not reduced her expenditures to accommodate the loss of her husband's income. In his view, she could and should cut her extravagant expenses and/or sell the seat as needed to pay those expenses. Because he did not favor maintaining the stock exchange seat anyway, he would not contribute financial support "to a policy and practice which I have steadily opposed since 1934." At the end of each strong letter reiterating his position, he was always careful to close with a request that she call or write to discuss any aspect with which she disagreed. He always left open all doors to dialogue.

"The seat was eventually sold and the proceeds allowed Mother to live at a very comfortable level," he assured me. Through it all, he and Ethel remained close, even as she acknowledged the antagonism between their competing views without agreeing to Dick's position on the matter. However intense the words that followed might be, the salutations in her letters to him always began "Sweetheart," just as they had during his childhood summers at Camp Koenig.

* * *

"In the classroom, I enjoyed the lecture course that I began offering in the fall of 1938. Although Harvard alumnus Samuel Flagg Bemis had written the authoritative text on American diplomatic history, it did not lend itself to use in an undergraduate class. Like most of my Harvard colleagues, I assumed it was beneath my dignity to use a textbook for instruction of any kind. Therefore, I assigned readings in various primary sources and secondary works to supplement my lectures."

He prepared a typewritten narrative of each lecture; his students had the added organizational tool that his detailed handwritten outline on the chalkboard behind him provided. After observing an early lecture, Dick's mentor had only one suggestion that Dick carried forward for the rest of his teaching days: "Schlesinger said that, to make sure students did not become drowsy during my lectures, I should always keep a window open—even during the coldest days of a Cambridge winter." When I heard this for the first time almost seventy years later, I understood why the windows were always open on frigid Chicago mornings during my tenure in his classes throughout 1974 and 1975.

After his first year, Dick rewrote all of his lectures. An important teaching aid arrived in 1940 when Thomas A. Bailey's new textbook, *A Diplomatic History of the American People*, received critical and popular acclaim. Bailey's book was good enough for Dick to eschew the history department's traditional hostility to such works; he used it with his lecture class. Bailey's treatment of the topic, unlike Bemis's dense treatment, had made the subject matter accessible while providing sufficient depth. It was Dick's first and highly indirect contact with Stanford University's Bailey, but it would not be his last. "Wait until you see how Bailey keeps circling back to my life," he said with a smile.

By 1940, Dick was giving lectures twice each day: first at Emerson Hall to the Harvard men; immediately thereafter, he crossed the Cambridge Common and delivered the same remarks at Longfellow Hall to the Radcliffe women.

* * *

At Adams House, Dick found himself at the vanguard of the house system's racial integration: "In the spring of 1939, Lucien V. Alexis, whose father had graduated from Harvard and was a prominent New Orleans physician, applied for admission to Adams House. The staff and I understood that, if accepted, Alexis would become the first African American member of Harvard's house system. Although there were a few African Americans in the freshman dorms, none was in any of the houses. Dave and Raphael favored Alexis' admission and assigned to me the difficult task of sounding out the members of the House Committee, which included eight students. Apart from the issue of student attitudes at the time, there were very practical matters to consider. For example, people asked, 'What problems might we have later at a house dance or other social function?'" In the end, Dick guided the house toward the right result and Alexis was accepted; the racial barrier to Harvard's house system had been breached. As he wrote five decades later, "'Lucky' proved to be an excellent member."

Dick's dedication to his students manifested itself in an approach to a particularly troubled undergraduate. During the same month his book on Robert Dale Owen was receiving a generally favorable review from the *New York Times,* he had to deal with one of his greatest challenges as Adams House's assistant senior tutor. As he described the incident to me, I gained a new insight into the origins and depths of his concern for students.

"My worst Thanksgiving ever occurred in 1940," he told me during my visit over the Thanksgiving weekend of 2004. "A few days earlier, an Adams House student who had received a scholarship and was regarded as among the brightest at Harvard had mysteriously disappeared. The boy's father traveled from the family's home in Cleveland to search for him. Normally, the master or senior tutor would have dined with the father, but the Littles had arranged a dinner party and Raphael Demos was tending to his hospitalized wife. That made me—as the next highest ranking staff member—the odd man out and alone with the father as we sat at an Adams House dining room table. Any effort to engage in conversation was hopeless. We both feared the worst.

"The next Sunday morning, another Adams House student informed me that the missing student had been spotted in Boston's motion picture theater district. Upon hearing the news, I caught a ride downtown with a student who had a car. I spent the afternoon pacing the sidewalk in the area of Boston's largest movie house, but the young man was nowhere to be found. So I returned to Cambridge."

As he described the episode in a letter to Ethel, three days later the boy was again sighted. That evening, Dick was "reading and restless" in preparing a lecture he was to give the following day when he finally decided to take a "'flyer,' make another wild goose chase," and travel back downtown by subway. "By quirk of fate," he wrote, "I spotted him, one chance in a hundred, walking the streets on a bitter cold night. I followed him and he disappeared into a cheap lodging place."

Dick found a telephone and called assistant dean Sargent Kennedy. A few minutes later, Kennedy arrived by car, intercepted the student, put him in the rear seat with Dick, and drove all of them back to the campus. Dick eventually learned that what he had described to Ethel as "one hellish week" over the missing student resulted because the boy had bought a large number of used books on credit. Lacking the means to pay his debt and fearing the consequences, he simply ran away. Dick persuaded the editor of the *Harvard Crimson,* fellow Adams House resident Spencer Klaw, to defer any publication about the incident until the Boston papers reported it. "I do not know when anything has hit me harder," he wrote to Ethel.

The young man was hospitalized and did not resume his studies during that academic year. Dick visited him in the hospital and spoke to the boy extensively over the phone. Both Dick and his Adams House charge were relieved when the student's father went back to Cleveland. "If anything, his father's reaction made things worse," Dick said. "He was too harsh."

However dubious the contributions of the boy's father may have been to his recovery, there can be no doubt that Dick had a very real role in rescuing a depressed young man. He had responded with a combination of determination and compassion, and then followed through with continuing friendship and genuine concern.

* * *

Although Dick had received his Ph.D in early 1938, the final chapter in the saga surrounding his biography of Owen was not yet written. Shortly after he completed his dissertation, a woman who claimed to be researching spiritualism asked Harvard's Widener Library for permission to read it. Dick availed himself of Harvard's policy allowing the author to deny such permission for the first five years after a dissertation was finished, but he said he would gladly meet with her, which he did. Her name was Anne E. Lincoln.

Sometime thereafter, he learned Lincoln's true mission: She was collaborating with Goucher College professor Elinor Pancoast, who had tried at the outset to dissuade him from pursuing an Owen biography. As Dick was reviewing the galleys of his manuscript prior to formal publication, Pancoast and Lincoln published their own work on Owen. But he was relieved to learn their volume was only 109 pages long, "lacked an index, and tried to fit Owen's varied career into a single mold." It could not rival as a serious treatment his 470-page thesis, of which more than 400 pages were text.

On its publication in 1940, Dick's biography of Owen earned him the American Historical Association's John H. Dunning Prize for the best book on any subject pertaining to United States history. "At the December awards ceremony in New York," he told me with a smile, "I observed two Harvard mentors, Charles Howard McIlwain in medieval constitutional history and Sidney B. Fay in European diplomatic history, behaving as if they were proud fathers of a favored son, which, of course, they were." Shortly thereafter, Indiana University expressed interest in recruiting Dick to its history department, but it did not make a formal offer.

Schlesinger's earlier advice notwithstanding, there seemed little danger that sleep would disrupt the efforts of Dick's students to learn from a gifted teacher. G. Wallace Chessman ('41) told me more than sixty years later: "Dick Leopold was a great teacher, outstanding lecturer, accomplished scholar, and, perhaps more than all of these, a person who connected well with others. You knew that he genuinely cared about you." Chessman credited Dick, who was in his mid-twenties when they first met during Chessman's interview to enter Adams House, as one of the people whose professional and personal influence moved his own career toward history and teaching. After receiving his doctorate from Harvard, Chessman went on to chair the history department at Denison University. He retired after a distinguished career that started with a focus on Theodore Roosevelt's papers and spanned more than three decades of teaching and scholarship.

Chessman was in distinguished company among the early beneficiaries of the Leopold experience. Bradford Perkins was in Dick's graduate seminar and eventually became a history professor at the University of Michigan. Dick encouraged another student, Robert Osgood, to follow up on an article Walter Lippmann had written on America's entry into World War I. That project eventually led to a book receiving much acclaim when Osgood was at the University of Chicago studying political science with Hans Morgenthau. Dick reviewed Osgood's manuscript prior to its publication.

"I also served as an informal counselor to Princeton graduates entering Harvard's history program after me. The first were Rod Davison and Robert Lansing Edwards, both from the Princeton class of '36. Edwards' grandfather had replaced William Jennings Bryan as President Wilson's secretary of state. A few years later, George Elsey from the class of '39 began graduate study at Harvard, but he left after a year, joined the Army, and moved to Washington where he was assigned, of all places, to the White House map room. Talk about fortuity; what a job he had during the war!"

Another noteworthy Harvard graduate student in history was also making his way through the program at the time: John Hope Franklin. He was the department's first African American Ph.D and went on to become the first African American full professor at a white institution, Brooklyn College. In May 1941, Dick sat with Paul Buck and Arthur Schlesinger Sr. on Franklin's three-man dissertation committee. Although he was the most junior faculty member, Dick had been enlisted to serve on such committees and agreed to do so, provided that he not be asked to sit for any candidates who were his contemporaries. Franklin had been two years behind Dick in his studies—far enough back to satisfy Dick's criterion.

As Franklin later described in his autobiography, Dick kept the entire group occupied with a series of questions requiring the earnest doctoral student to explain what he would do if, hypothetically, he were asked to give a series of lectures at Oxford on labor history. According to Franklin, Dick asked him, "What would be the subjects of the lectures, how would they be organized, and what would be the principal sources on which I would rely in writing them? Since I regarded that as a playful question, I saw no reason why I should not 'play' with it. This was the beginning of a delightful conversation between Leopold and me that must have lasted for the better part of an hour and in which the other members of the committee joined."

Yet another student destined for success, undergraduate John Morton Blum ('43), sat through Dick's classes during the 1942 summer term. Blum later described Dick's lectures as delivered "in high style." He said Dick "had the good sense to realize that we were all fixated on the war" and "gave special attention to Woodrow Wilson and the prospect for peace after the current war ended." Dick became his tutor and "was later for many years my close friend." Blum credited Dick with helping to shape the senior essay on Guam that became Blum's "intellectual preoccupation" for the rest of his undergraduate days.

* * *

John Morton Blum was in the Harvard class that Dick would single out as the best collection of undergraduates he had ever taught. In addition to Blum, it included future *Washington Post* executive editor Benjamin C. Bradlee, author Norman Mailer, Roger D. Fisher (Adams House resident and future Harvard Law School professor), and future scholars Eric Larrabee, James W. Morley, Robert E. Osgood, and Adam Yarmolinsky.

Blum was also a nonpracticing Jew. When I studied his autobiography that Dick recommended for my review as our project began, it seemed to me that Blum followed a path similar to Dick's and Pop's, making his way through the anti-Semitism pervading America's elite educational institutions during the first half of the twentieth century. As Blum observed about his days at Andover that followed by a decade Dick's similar experience at Exeter, "Jews were admitted, but were not yet first-class citizens." He was subjected to aggressive anti-Semitic attacks from two fellow students. It "began with verbal abuse, which soon escalated to physical attacks," and, on one occasion when he tried to resist, Blum was "blamed by a proctor for creating a disturbance. Of course the unwritten student code ruled out reporting the matter to any master."

There were no Jews or Catholics on the Andover faculty. There were no religious services for Jews at Andover and, "though it was a matter of indifference to me," Blum recounted, "it offended some other Jewish students and was another example of the prejudice that made Jews uneasy at Andover." Like Dick, Blum became keenly aware that, except for Semitic studies, there were no tenured Jews on the arts and sciences faculty of Harvard, Yale, Princeton, or Dartmouth.

John Hope Franklin's 2005 autobiography was more direct in discussing Ivy League anti-Semitism. As an African American working his way through the challenges of racism in the middle of the twentieth century, it was among other Harvard students of United States history that he "witnessed anti-Semitism for the first time." It occurred when Franklin served on the Henry Adams Club's nominating committee in the spring of 1936. He proposed a second-year graduate student, Oscar Handlin, as an officer for the upcoming year.

"After I made the nomination," Franklin later reported, "there was dead silence in the room. Eventually, one of the members spoke up and said that although Oscar did not have some of the more objectionable Jewish traits, he was still a Jew. I was appalled. I regarded my nominee as merely a white man who was brilliant, active, and deserving. Growing up, I had necessarily spent time and energy dealing with racial bigots, and I had learned to identify them by their skin color and degree of ignorance. I had never heard any educated white person speak of another in such terms, and I lost respect not only for the individual who made the statement but for the entire group that tolerated such views." Dick was not present for the session and told me that he had never heard about the incident before it was reported in Franklin's book.

Medicine presented similar challenges. After completing his second-year residency in Chicago, Pop was invited to join the prestigious private practice of his mentor, but there was a religious catch. Pop was told that to obtain the hospital privileges essential to his future success, he would have to "convert." As Dick later put it, the response to such a question for Jews like him—just as for Pop, Blum, and many others—would have been: "Convert from what?" The subject became academic in October 1940 when Pop received his notice to report for active duty in the Army Medical Corps.

RICHARD LEOPOLD PHOTOS

Ethel Kimmelstiel Leopold holding her infant son, Richard (1912).

Harry Leopold Sr. (1932).

Harry Jr., Ethel, and Richard Leopold (1913).

Richard Leopold in what became his favorite childhood photograph (1914).

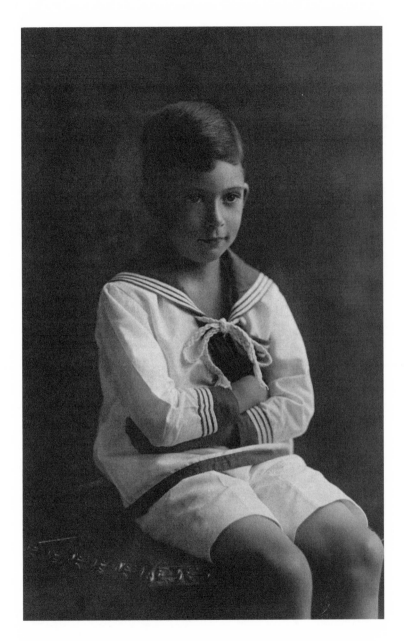

Richard Leopold in his sailor suit (circa 1919).

Harry Jr., Richard, and Ethel Leopold on Mt. Rainier (1922).

Richard Leopold at the Banff Springs Hotel swimming pool (1922).

Richard Leopold at Camp Koenig (circa 1924).

Richard W. Leopold as a Princeton freshman (1929).

Richard W. Leopold as a Harvard instructor and assistant senior tutor at Adams House (1940).

Richard W. Leopold as a naval officer (1942) (Photograph by Fabian Bachrach).

Richard W. Leopold and his fellow workers in the Office of Naval Records and Library. Walter Muir Whitehill is seated in the center and holding his pipe. Ruth Delano is seated to Whitehill's immediate right. Commander Percy Wright is seated up and to Whitehill's immediate left. Leopold is standing at the end of the back row (to Whitehill's right). (1944).

Richard W. Leopold at the time he published his second book, Elihu Root and the Conservative Tradition *(Boston: Little, Brown and Company, 1954) (Photograph by E. L. Ray).*

Richard W. Leopold attending the Northwestern University NROTC formal dinner (1967).

Harris Hall 108 during one of Professor Leopold's legendary class discussion sessions (1980) (Courtesy: The Daily Northwestern).

Professor Leopold umpiring the annual C-13 softball game (1977).

Richard W. Leopold and Arthur S. Link at the OAH Convention in 1985.

Professor (emeritus) Richard W. Leopold among the more than 180 boxes of his personal papers in the Northwestern University Archives (1990) (Courtesy: The Daily Northwestern).

Portrait of Professor Richard W. Leopold that hangs in Harris Hall 108 (Copyright: Evanston Photographic Studios, 1980).

William J. Loeb Photos

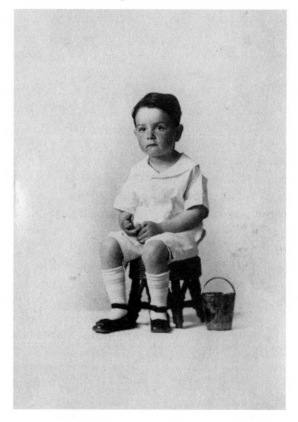

William J. Loeb at age three (1915).

Joseph Loeb with his son, William (1917).

William J. Loeb as a Boy Scout (circa 1924).

Major William J. Loeb (1943).

William J. Loeb's photograph of Mt. Vesuvius erupting (March 1944).

Major William J. Loeb with present and future Israeli military and political leaders (Moshe Dayan stands at the center; Loeb is to Dayan's immediate right) (1956).

Colonel William J. Loeb (1957).

PART TWO

"It was, perhaps, the most exciting period of my life."

"THE SECOND TEST:
THE STRUGGLE FOR SURVIVAL"

Dick cast his first vote in an American presidential election when he was twenty-eight years old. In November 1940—five months after the fall of France and eight months after Mussolini, Stalin, and Hitler formally became the Axis powers aligned against France and Great Britain—he joined a large majority in electing Roosevelt to an unprecedented third term over Wendell Wilkie. Part of Roosevelt's appeal had been success in keeping the country out of the expanding war, but that was becoming more difficult as Hitler continued his rampage across Europe—conquering Crete, Yugoslavia, and Greece before turning his sights on his former ally, the Soviet Union. In the Pacific, Japan occupied French Indochina and continued its drive to dominate that side of the globe while maintaining its alliance with Nazi Germany.

Most Americans still preferred neutrality and, in a Des Moines speech on September 11, 1941, one of the isolationists' most popular figures linked American Jews to Roosevelt's effort to push the United States into war. Charles Lindbergh, whom Pop had met at ambassador Myron Herrick's Ohio estate in 1927, gave lip-service opposition to anti-Semitism, while cautioning that "no person of honesty and vision can look on [the Jews'] pro-war policy here today without seeing the dangers involved in such a policy, both for us and for them." He railed against Jewish ownership and influence "in our motion pictures, our press, our radio, and our government." Lindbergh and the isolationists lost any hope that America could avoid what was becoming the Second World War when, three months later, the Japanese bombed Pearl Harbor.

* * *

Dick was at his regular Sunday dinner with the Demoses, listening to the New York Philharmonic on the radio, when an announcer interrupted the music to report the attack on America's Pacific fleet. He wrote to Ethel the following day: "The most significant challenge that can come to my generation has come, and it remains to be seen what we will do about it." For the first and only time in his teaching career, he canceled his noon lecture at Radcliffe because, he told me, he "thought it important to listen to President Roosevelt's comments on the situation." He spent the rest of the month supervising air raid warnings and preparing Adams House's defense against attacks from incendiary bombs. The campus was in a complete uproar and would never be the same.

"In the midst of these momentous events, I attended the American Historical Association's annual meeting in December," Dick told me. "There, I met for the first time Stanford's Tom Bailey, whose new text on diplomatic history I had been using. He was eagerly seeking information from me about Harvard because he was scheduled to teach my course—History 64—during the 1942 summer session, but it never happened. The war disrupted everything."

War created both serious complications and remarkable opportunities. Dick realized it was only a matter of time until all able-bodied men, even those of his relatively advanced age of thirty, were destined for service in the armed forces. In January 1942, he explored briefly the possibility of a teaching position at Amherst, writing of his hope for a position permitting "some security for the future . . . some assurance that I might be allowed a reasonable time to prove my worth." But he later told me that he had no real chance for any permanent teaching job anywhere because of his overarching vulnerability to the draft. "The main benefit of the Amherst visit," Dick later told me, "was my opportunity to meet Amherst's interesting president, Stanley King."

Dick made several attempts to enlist in the Navy where he could gain a commission without the officers' training the Army required. But each time, his poor eyesight prevented him from passing the physical examination: "My eyes stopped me cold."

* * *

In late January 1942, the top-secret Wannsee Conference in Berlin adopted "relocation" as the "final solution" to the Jewish overpopulation problem resulting from Germany's conquest of Poland and other countries with sizable Semitic constituencies. During that summer, Anne Frank's father gave her a diary, and the entire family went into hiding above his Amsterdam warehouse. As the German killing machine made surreptitious plans to turn even more aggressively inward on its own people, the United States draft board called Dick in February 1942 for a physical examination. His poor eyesight led to a rejection for active duty.

"I considered pursuing Harvard's Japanese language program, where I hoped the Navy would overlook my eyesight and commission me upon completing the program. I sat in on a few of Eddie Reischauer's Japanese language classes but decided against continuing on that potential path to a commission because, in the end, there were no guarantees I would get one if I did. Meanwhile, I became one of two Harvard faculty members, along with English historian and Lowell House master Elliot Perkins, appointed as the War Service Information Bureau to advise undergraduates on their military service options. I favored the Air Corps because I thought it needed strengthening."

Among those who accepted his advice was a student who would become an especially close friend among the undergraduates, Dana Reed. He was a nonresident member of Adams House and in the extraordinary class of 1943.

"It became something of a joke that the adviser might himself be drafted," Dick said in describing that, by August 1942, it became clear he would have to report for active duty in September or October—bad eyesight and all. A *New Yorker* article explained that the Army had lowered the minimum physical requirements for service: "They felt the body, and if it was warm. . . ." It did not report—because most of the world did not know—that the Germans had opened a new Polish death camp near Treblinka on July 23.

"Once again, fortuity shaped my life," Dick said as he related the story of his entry into World War II. "One of Perkins' friends and professional acquaintances was Walter Muir Whitehill, who was the director of the Peabody Museum in Salem. Whitehill's work put him in regular contact with Dudley W. Knox, who had served on Admiral Sims' staff during the First World War. Knox was widely regarded as 'Mr. History of the Navy' and headed the Office of Naval Records and Library, which was the closest approximation to a history department in that branch of the service. Because of President Roosevelt's special interest in the Navy—as you know, he had served as its assistant secretary—Knox and FDR were personal friends. Sims, by the way, was Elting Morison's father-in-law.

"Knox encouraged Whitehill to apply for a commissioned position in his office. By the summer of 1942, both men knew Whitehill's commission was on its way, so Knox dispatched him to recruit another qualified scholar, Bernard Brodie, to join the team. Brodie taught political science at Dartmouth and had written two books on the importance of sea power. On his way to New Hampshire, Whitehill stopped at Lowell House to have a drink with his friend, Elliot Perkins. 'Perk' had known me for some time and had actually been the person responsible for getting me the position on the War Service Information Bureau. When Whitehill explained the mission on which Knox had sent him, Perk immediately suggested there was no reason to continue the journey to Dartmouth because the man he really wanted and needed was in Cambridge: Dick Leopold."

Dick paused to emphasize one of his consistent themes: "You see how fortuity plays into a person's life?"

He then resumed without waiting for my response: "Shortly before the Labor Day weekend of 1942, Whitehill knocked on my Adams House door and we met for the first time. He urged me to complete the necessary paperwork for a commission and submit it at once. I knew working with Whitehill in Washington would be far preferable to any job I would have as an enlisted man, so I used the Harvard history department's special wide-angle typewriter to complete the oversized commission form. At the end of the holiday weekend, I took it to the Navy's downtown Boston facility."

He was racing the clock, because the government's 1-A classification for regular Army service was already on its way to him. On September 22, 1942, Dick received a notice to report for induction at Phillips Brooks House on the campus. In his last days as a civilian, several undergraduates, including John Blum and Dana Reed, helped him pack his books for long-term storage. On the afternoon of Saturday, October 3, Raphael and Jean Demos held a farewell party in his honor. That evening, he wrote to Ethel what he melodramatically called his "final letter as a civilian." On Sunday evening, Dave and Henge Little hosted a goodbye dinner including the Demoses, the Perkinses, and the Bucks. On Monday, he reported for duty and was promptly sent to Fort Devens, about thirty miles west of Boston. On his daily calendar, he made the last entry he would write for almost four years: "Off to war."

"After reaching Fort Devens," he continued, "I was asked if I wanted to remain there to classify recruits. I said no, for reasons I still cannot explain sixty years later. I do not know what I was thinking. My best guess is I thought my experience as an enlisted man would somehow help me in understanding history." It never occurred to him that he would have little influence over his destiny from that point, or that he might become a combat soldier.

He shipped out of Fort Devens by the end of the week. The train made its way west toward Greenfield: "I knew from my knowledge of the railroad lines that if the train went west from Greenfield, I was headed for Denver and the Air Corps. But the train turned south and arrived at Atlantic City around eight in the evening. There I saw things I had never seen before. I was especially impressed by the regular citywide blackouts resulting from the Nazi submarine menace along the eastern seaboard."

After three weeks of testing, Dick boarded the train again. He traveled west around the modern engineering marvel known as "Horseshoe Curve" to Pittsburgh and then to Chicago, where record cold temperatures held the city in an icy grip. From Chicago, he went south to Rantoul, the site of the Chanute Army Base. He was not prepared to find himself sleeping with three hundred to four hundred recruits in the "brick barracks" structure. His simple comment to me years later: "Talk about privacy. Forget it." At Chanute, he learned basic codes and ciphers.

"I was working KP duty on Thanksgiving of 1942 when I received a letter from the officer in charge of processing my application for a commission. Its tone was pessimistic and I feared I had made a very big mistake in failing to accept the assignment clerk position at Fort Devens."

On December 2, 1942, he and his comrades left Chanute for Jefferson Barracks in St. Louis. In describing the scene to me, Dick mimicked the lilting tone of residents who advised him as he entered the facility: "'You won't like it here,' they told me. But in fact, the experience turned out better than I had feared because the grounds included a library where I spent all of my free time." The bad news was that he now had some idea of where he and his company were almost certainly going next: the Pacific theater.

"I telephoned Whitehill, who was now in Washington. He was not encouraging. The commission had been denied because of my weak eyesight. Whitehill reported he was not giving up, nor was the division chief, commander Percy T. Wright, a retired submariner who knew little history but saw the wisdom of gaining someone with my expertise."

Dick assumed his chances for a commission were gone and urged his mother to resign herself to that reality when he wrote on December 7, 1942, that his "application for a Navy Commission had been finally and definitively rejected." His "eyes were too weak to justify even a waiver on vision for a commission. So that is that."

But the next day, Whitehill sent a telegram instructing Dick not to accept any furlough before contacting him. Dick responded immediately: "Telegram received. Furlough cancelled. Will await letter and developments. Many thanks for your efforts."

On December 10, German and Russian soldiers were locked in mortal battle at Stalingrad. Dick was working KP duty when a messenger came to the kitchen: "Is there a Private Leopold here?"

"Yes," came Dick's tentative reply.

"You are to report to the discharge office at once," the messenger responded.

"Even sixty years later," he told me, "you can still practically hear the china falling to the floor."

Whitehill's telegram awaited him: "Commission issued today—advise remaining at present post to await developments—letter follows. Whitehill."

A longer letter followed on December 15 when Whitehill explained, "This whole business has been fantastic. A week ago, I thought that nothing except [a] problematical Act of Congress . . . would get your eyes through, but Commander Wright has again done the impossible without waiting for the Act of Congress."

Thereafter, Dick spent all of his time at Jefferson Barracks in the library while the other men in his unit went through basic training on their way to the Pacific. He was "the old man" in the group and had no real friends among them. Occasionally after a day of grueling training, the commanding sergeant would wander into the library to find Private Leopold sitting among the books. Before recognizing him as the beneficiary of a pending discharge from the Army, the noncommissioned officer would approach and say, "Soldier, what are you doing in here. . . ."

And then the sergeant would stop himself in mid-sentence and with disappointment, saying, "Oh, it's you."

In mid-December, he received word that his official papers were ready: "When I reported to the CO's office, I was more relaxed than I should have been. I was afraid I had blown the whole discharge when the CO remarked, 'You're supposed to say, "Private Leopold reporting, sir," but you did not do that, soldier.' I apologized and the paperwork was completed." He later learned that when the orders came to ship the rest of his Jefferson Barracks unit overseas, the name "Richard W. Leopold" still appeared on the list of departing soldiers. He had come that close to active duty in Burma.

"On the New York Central train bound for New York, I hoped for a private room," he told me as he described the trip to his next assignment, "but got only the upper berth of a Pullman, which meant I'd had no privacy since October 5. At Albany, I changed to the local for Boston and moved to the coach section. I was lounging with my jacket unbuttoned when roving military police quickly spotted me. 'Soldier, button your blouse,' one of them barked at me. 'Let me see your travel orders.' I told them I didn't have any and, of course, my incomplete response only tantalized them. Their eyes lit up as they moved in for the kill. Then I calmly reached into my pocket and said 'But I do have these. . . . ' and handed up my discharge orders. The MPs said they wished they had theirs and moved on. I do not know why I behaved as I did when they first started questioning me, especially because I was not particularly confident at that time in my life." He eventually arrived in Boston on a Friday. There the Harvard Coop hurriedly outfitted him in a Navy uniform for his trip to the nation's capital.

* * *

Pop's path into World War II was more straightforward, but what Dick would call fortuity played mightily in shaping his military career and his life, too. "When we were ready to finish school in 1937," he later wrote, "we were offered commissions—just sign up. So I did." On a visit from Chicago to Cleveland over the Labor Day weekend in 1940, Pop's mother handed him a letter he would keep forever. "If physically qualified," it said, "you will report for one year of active duty in the Continental United States. Report 7 October 1940 to Ft. Thomas Ky. By Order of the President. Signed: Franklin D. Roosevelt."

Pop's status removed the kind of uncertainty torturing Dick from September through December 1942: "We started out as First Lieutenants, one rank ahead of everyone else newly commissioned as a recognition of the years in getting the M.D. degree. When the war really started, many physicians began as Majors. . . . When the draft began, I spent a month setting up draft board examinations in Huntington and Clarksburg, W. Va." That experience made even Fort Thomas look good to him.

"One's decisions are frequently formed and modified by uncontrolled events," Pop continued. "This happened." His father had a heart attack in 1941; a few days later, he died. It was a devastating blow, but the timing of the tragedy became fortuitously beneficial. A few months earlier, the Army had invited medical personnel to volunteer for foreign service at the base of their choice. In sharp contrast to Dick's reluctance to experience the unknown, Pop enthusiastically embraced the offer.

"What better time to see distant parts of the world at no cost? We spoke with officers who had had service abroad, asking their advice. Panama was O.K., but nothing special. Rather boring. Hawaii was great; good living, pleasant Army posts, but quite expensive. We did not have much to spend, so that had to be considered. Best place, they said, was the Philippines. Nice climate. Plenty of servants to do work at home, good company, all at low cost. Why not? When later might we be able to do this? Let's go. We applied."

The answer to "why not?" came with his father's passing only a few months after submitting his application. As the only child in the family, he felt responsible for the well-being of his mother and maternal grandmother, who lived together. "We couldn't just run out of the country, so we canceled the Philippines trip. . . . It is now clear that had we gone to the Philippines in 1941, my chances of surviving the Japanese attack would have been slim."

By July 1941, he was a captain; he and Sue were living at Camp Atterbury, Indiana. June 1943 was particularly eventful: Their first daughter was born and Pop was promoted to major. Shortly thereafter, he was shipped overseas where he helped to run an Army hospital in Naples, Italy.

NINE

INTERLUDE

"We have to treat the war years somewhat differently," Dick continued. "Although I regard it as, perhaps, the most exciting period of my life, there is not much of a written record. Once I entered the Army in 1942, I stopped maintaining my personal diary." He was clearly disappointed that an otherwise complete documentary trail spanning almost a century lacked any significant writings for the period defining his generation. It was the ultimate irony for a historian reflecting on his own life.

"Why is that?" I asked. "It's interesting to me because very little of Pop's correspondence during that period survived, either."

"When I entered the Army, they told us that we could not maintain any personal diaries. I could have resumed my daily aide in Washington because I was basically doing civilian work in Navy garb, but I did not. It is one of the biggest regrets of my life. Because there is very little we can rely upon in the way of my writings during this period, we will have to go with my memory." Fortunately, his recollections provided an ample source from which to reconstruct a critical time of his life—including a personal relationship putting him on a path leading to marriage, but the end of the war effectively terminated that prospect.

* * *

After the Harvard Coop completed work over the weekend on his naval uniform, he left for two days in New York City because, as he said, "Mother would have disowned me if I had not visited her on my way to Washington."

He then recounted his wartime experience: "As for my time in D.C., we should start with the people with whom I deepened relations, or formed new ones. First among them would have been Myron Gilmore. He was married to Sheila Dehn—does that name mean anything to you?"

"No," I admitted.

"Well, I'm not surprised, but her grandfather—although not by blood relation—was the famous philosopher, Alfred North Whitehead. He had risen to prominence in his native Britain and maintained his stature at Harvard. Interestingly, Sheila was Jewish, but not practicing. In any event, Myron and I had become very close friends as members of the Harvard fist-ball group and as tennis rivals. A week before Christmas 1942, I arrived at their home at 2708 First Street NW and stayed for four months. At the time, they had two baby girls, Janet and Diana. With a third child on the way and expected in July, my stay there became temporary. Fortunately for me, Sheila had made it her personal mission to locate suitable replacement accommodations. She used all of her Cambridge connections in finding me a place to live. Through a friend, she eventually secured a room for me on the third floor of the Frank Hammond home, which was certainly better than my mother's proposal: she wanted to move to Washington and take an apartment where we both would live!"

Eventually, I reviewed the letter in which he carefully explained to Ethel why her suggested change of residence from New York was impractical, if not impossible. Although he had not kept copies of his correspondence during the war, this particular letter survived because Ethel had retained Dick's original letter to her. It was clear that his mother remained an emotionally challenging presence throughout Dick's life, especially after her husband died.

"I moved into my room with the Hammonds in April 1943," he resumed, "but I continued to take all of my dinners at the Gilmores. Sheila was a good cook, and she was grateful to have my red and blue ration stamps to supplement theirs. It was a beneficial arrangement for all of us.

"Myron's military assignment was cryptanalyst. He later joined Elting Morison, who worked on the administrative history of the Navy during the Second World War. They eventually added John Blum to the team, so you can see it was a very distinguished unit of my closest friends."

His next Washington family members, the Hammonds, lived at 3221 Macomb: "I had not known them in Cambridge, but Franklin T. Hammond Jr. had graduated from Harvard College in 1922 and the law school three years later. When I moved in, he was a major working for the assistant secretary of the Army. He and his wife, Caffie, who was the most beautiful woman I had ever known, had three sons—John was nine, Henry was six, and Frankie was three. Caffie was pregnant with their daughter Kate when Frank was shipped overseas. At that time, I slipped into the familiar role of big brother and father figure for the three sons left at home with their mother."

Two other Cambridge friends, Elting and Anne Morison, also entered his wartime picture: "At first, they were living in New York City where Elting was stationed while compiling the history of the eastern sea frontier. I visited them when I went to see my mother, which was about four times yearly. After his transfer to

Washington, they moved to Falls Church, Virginia. I became close to them and their children. One daughter reported that I had the softest lap in Washington."

* * *

In addition to the Gilmores, Morisons, and Hammonds, Dick developed close relationships with the men working with him. The first was Captain Walter Muir Whitehill, who had recruited Dick to the Office of Naval Records and Library: "Walter's wife was the daughter of Julian Coolidge, who had been master of Lowell House at Harvard. Walter drove a Ford to work and picked me up every morning at the downtown restaurant where I always ate breakfast. He also gave me a ride home every night. Sometimes we would sit in his old Ford for hours in front of the Hammond house as I educated him on the history of the profession to which he was a relative newcomer."

Dick then listed his other fellow workers in the ONR&L: "I already mentioned commander Percy T. Wright, a retired submariner. Before I joined the office, Knox had recruited lieutenant Marion Brewington, a banker from Philadelphia whose interest was sailing ships during the Revolutionary War; lieutenant John H. Kemble, a historian who had written his doctoral dissertation on the interoceanic canal and had taught at Pomona College; lieutenant Nelson Blake, who had been in charge of naval records in the National Archives; and lieutenant George Porter, a former *Washington Star* reporter who was the publicity guy. Kenneth Grant, who rose from yeoman second class to chief, is also deserving of note. So is the fact that, although I was only an ensign, I took the lead and became principally responsible for the Pacific side of our work while Whitehill handled Europe.

"Jack Kemble and I became good friends. Knox had persuaded Kemble to apply for his commission in the late 1930s, so he was a full lieutenant when I arrived. Kemble left for Pearl Harbor in the spring of 1943, but we corresponded regularly. If someone were interested in what was happening in the Office of Naval Records and Library during the war, I think that correspondence would present a complete picture."

* * *

Dick's duties were to read and organize operational records as they came into the office. Much of the material, especially relating to German submarine warfare, was heavily edited. Only years later did he learn why. A distinguished group of allied scientists had gathered in England where they worked with an Enigma cryptography machine seized from a German submarine in May 1941. The submarine had used the machine to decode secret orders from the German High Command, but an enterprising British captain had seized it from an abandoned submarine during a naval battle. If disclosed, the redacted portions of documents coming into Dick's office would have revealed what only a handful of people knew: The Allies were now using Enigma to translate the secret communications from Berlin to the German fleet. The Allies had also broken the Japanese code used to direct naval operations in the Pacific. The resulting top secret information contributed to America's decisive victory at the Battle of Midway. It also made possible the assassination of Japan's top naval officer, Admiral Isoroku Yamamoto, who had planned the attack on Pearl Harbor. With intercepted knowledge of Yamamoto's precise itinerary, American fighters flew from Guadalcanal to complete a stunning midair ambush on April 18, 1943, in the northern Solomon Islands. To maintain secrecy about the Allies' knowledge of Japan's code, Yamamoto's death would not be revealed as an assassination until the war was over.

"By May 1943," Dick continued, "I was receiving the flow of correspondence and reports involving the Battle of Coral Sea a year earlier; by June, I was working on the Battle of Midway. I organized the materials and developed finding aids. I devised an innovative index card system for essential information on each document: name, ship, operation, and so forth. During my first year, I read all incoming documents for the Pacific Theater myself. But as the volume eventually became overwhelming, I trained a WAVE officer and two enlisted men in my system of three cards: one each for ship, command, and area. The method I devised for organizing the materials was a major departure from the approach used during World War I and remained in use for decades. My personal review of the materials coming into the office gave me an intimate familiarity with virtually every battle in the Pacific from 1942 to 1944."

Commenting on his wartime work sixty years later, Dick concluded, "In retrospect, we did a good job. The records are still kept in the same form; the finding aids are still in use for those who want to find records. The system is in the National Archives, along with the records to which they refer."

Returning to the topic of his wartime acquaintances, he continued, "While I was in Washington, I saw a number of familiar faces: fellow Princeton alumnus and former Harvard graduate student George Elsey was working in the White House map room; Rod Paul, who had been the next ranking tutor in American history at Harvard below me, drove us around Civil War battlefields after gas rationing was lifted; Harvard's Sam Morison made his headquarters in the ONR&L office because he spent much time overseas and needed a stateside base. He had risen from lieutenant commander to captain, and Roosevelt had made him the official historian of naval operations during the war. I also saw my old friend, Ernie Gillespie, at least twice during the war. Ernie had completed his Ph.D at Princeton, taught at Exeter, and married Janet Wicks—the daughter of Princeton's chaplain, Bobby Wicks ('who knew the soul's most inward tricks . . .'). After securing a naval commission, Ernie was stationed in Greenland. On two occasions, he returned to Washington during a leave and we had dinner together. I could not help but notice that his stutter had improved dramatically since our Exeter days."

* * *

"What events do you recall as most prominent during your war years?" I asked.

"Among the many I remember, I would say that, after Pearl Harbor, five stand out above the rest. First was D-Day. I was in New York City as it dawned in the United States. On the train back to Washington, full news of the landing began to circulate. I will never forget Roosevelt's eloquent prayer for the soldiers and sailors involved."

"What did you think about the event itself?" I asked.

"That's an interesting question. I knew the reports coming in were inconclusive, but I never doubted the ultimate success of the invasion. I'm not sure why."

"What's the next one?" I continued.

"Roosevelt's death—April 12, 1945. It was late afternoon and I was heading to the Gilmores for dinner. I took the crosstown bus to Tenley Circle and heard people talking about it. I had known about the reports of his poor health. Two months earlier, he had surprised everyone when, after his return from the Yalta Peace Conference, he addressed Congress from a seated position. It was the only time he had ever done so, and that was taken as some indication of his physical difficulties. Still, his death came as a complete shock.

"Third was Ike's return to America. I recall standing at a window in the National Archives when his motorcade drove down Pennsylvania Avenue after V-E Day—the end of the war in Europe. It was a great procession. The captivating smile on his face lighted up the whole affair. It was as if he was smiling at the entire world. It was quite something.

"The fourth and fifth events occurred a week apart. One will surprise you: October 31, 1945. That's when I attended congressional hearings with Elting and Anne Morison on the unification of the armed forces. The former secretary of the Navy during World War I, Josephus Daniels, was testifying. His name had been anathema in the Morison household because he had publicly questioned the intelligence of his wartime commander, Admiral Sims. Anne Morison was Sims' daughter. We had gone to the hearings expecting to hiss; we wound up applauding instead. He was a remarkably charming old man and he completely won over the room.

"The last was Navy Day—October 25, 1945. I went to New York and walked along the Hudson River where I saw the *U.S.S. Enterprise*—the sole carrier to go through the entire war—and the *U.S.S. Missouri*—on which the Japanese had just surrendered to General MacArthur. I stood near the very spot where, twenty-seven years earlier, I had been a six-year-old boy watching the Navy return from World War I—a very different fleet to be sure. The circularity of history was never so evident to me as it was at that moment."

* * *

Having learned the lessons of history in the failure to grant President Wilson's request that America join a new international peacekeeping organization after World War I, the Senate this time overwhelmingly approved the United Nations Charter in December 1945. In August 1946, it accepted the optional clause to join the International Court of Justice as well. The war in the Pacific had ended in August 1945 after atomic bombs landed on Hiroshima and Nagasaki.

Dick was honorably discharged in March 1946. From his initial commission as an ensign, he had been promoted twice and left the service as full lieutenant. In later correspondence, he often mentioned his regret in failing to have kept any diaries or daily records during the period from his 1942 draft to his 1946 discharge. He spoke less often about another regret, one relating to a Navy WAVE with whom he had developed a close personal relationship.

"Ruth Delano was several years younger than I, had light brown hair, blue eyes, and was good-looking, but not what you would call beautiful. She joined our staff at the Office of Naval Records and Library in 1944. Most female naval personnel were not commissioned. Ruth was one of two female officers in the department and among the most effective in performing the tasks I assigned to her. We lunched regularly together and I often took her to dinner at our favorite restaurant on Connecticut Avenue, just above DuPont Circle. When my mother visited, I introduced her to Ruth. But I did nothing to suggest the seriousness of the relationship, probably because I myself had little sense of it."

In February 1946, he wrote to Ruth while she was away from her duties and attending to a dying relative. He expressed his "sincerest sympathy" upon her "great loss" and urged her to "just take good care of yourself, don't overwork, and hurry back just as soon as you can. It will be good to see you again." He also reported that "in private life, I have lost both my 'bed' and my 'board.'" The Gilmores had left for Cambridge on December 28 and the Hammonds followed on January 1. With Elting Morison and many other friends already departed, Washington hardly seemed like the same place. From the Hammond house, he moved into a room at 3301 Highland Place.

By March, Ruth had returned and joined Dick and the Whitehills in visiting an ailing Dudley Knox in the Naval Hospital at Bethesda. Afterward, they dined together before delivering Dick to the Union Station platform for the train that would eventually return him to Harvard: "As best I can recall, I said, 'Goodbye' and urged her to carry on the work of the department. We said we would keep in touch." She tried.

*   *   *

Similar to the hole in Dick's correspondence files, very few of Pop's letters during the war survived; however, I found three. The first was dated April 20, 1944, in which he wrote about a "distinguished patient" whom he had recently treated in Italy: Marlene Dietrich. "Looks better than she does in pictures and considerably younger than she must be," he reported crisply. He also described that "censorship has been lifted on the Vesuvius business. Saw the whole affair. If it weren't for a little war going on, it would probably have been the biggest news of the time." He set forth in detail his close observations of the volcano's eruption after climbing up the mountain one evening: "The big rocks would keep rolling down and send showers of sparks. Then the molten lava rolled down in a fluid state. A bit would touch a tree and the tree would immediately blaze up in a flame and disappear. . . . A little added attraction to the main show—but much worth seeing."

Pop's second surviving letter is dated June 3, 1944. By the time it finally arrived in the United States, D-Day had come and gone and the battle to liberate Europe was under way. On his daughter's first birthday, he wrote, "You are old enough to enjoy everything that happens, because everything is new to you. And you are too young to bother with all the troubles that are around everyone else. In fact, you are the only person of all those I love who isn't upset by this war. That is as it should be. . . . At this time, the war will not leave any scars on you. The rest of us who are fighting it, at home with you and over here with me, will never be quite the same. We can't be. But you will gather all the benefits of our work and troubles. . . ."

A year later, he wrote from Italy of his hope to be home soon: "Your mother writes that you are very good with puzzles. I don't suppose you have tried to puzzle out such things as credit points or the redeployment programs yet. But if you have, you will know that you are a most important factor in getting me headed back home to see you and mother. . . . As it is now, I hope it will come to pass before many months are past."

In certain respects especially ironic for a historian, Dick possessed only limited contemporaneous knowledge of events defining and shaping postwar perceptions of Jews. In 1991, he wrote, "Most of us had become hardened to Hitler's treatment of the Jews beginning in 1933; and although I was in Washington during the war— reading the *New York Times,* the *Washington Post,* and the *Washington Star*—my ignorance of the death camps was colossal."

I think Pop knew more than he would have preferred on the subject of the Nazi treatment of Jews. Concluding his 1945 V-Mail to his daughter on her second birthday, he wrote, "Until I return, be a good girl. You are very lucky, because you have a much nicer home and a much better place to grow up than many of the little girls I have seen during the past two years."

TEN

Casualties of War

As the war raged, three of Dick's favorite undergraduates did not return: "The first was Warren Winslow. I had tutored him during my first year of teaching. He was the captain of the Harvard hockey team during his senior year, 1939–1940. Being a final club member, Winslow did not live in Adams House. A graduate of the NROTC at Harvard, he was called to active duty in 1942 after his first year of law school. He died in a needless accident off Staten Island where his destroyer exploded while loading or off-loading ammunition."

"The second was Carroll Binder Jr., known as 'Ted.' He came from the same Chicago suburb of Highland Park where my cousin Alice lived by that time. His father was the foreign news editor of the *Chicago Daily News* until it was bought out by the Knight organization. Ted's plane was shot down over Europe before D-Day. Despite his father's contacts and the use of private planes to search for him, Ted's body was never found."

"The third hit hardest," Dick said in making a point he reiterated in his correspondence half a century later. By his own reckoning, Dana Reed had been one of his favorites.

When he headed "off to war" in October 1942, Dick ceased his scrupulous retention of daily aides, appointment calendars, and correspondence. For the rest of his life, he regretted what became this stark omission in an otherwise complete documentary record of his life. But thirteen letters Dana wrote to him between November 1942 and October 1944 survived. They comprise only half of the dialogue between the two young men because, with the exception of a single letter, Dick's missives are gone; however, they still reveal a remarkable friendship and tell a poignant tale about fate and fortuity. Never before in our discussions had I seen a tear in his eye. I probed very delicately as he told a story that continued to haunt him.

* * *

Dana had been one of his closest friends among the Adams House undergraduates. He was a member of the distinguished class of 1943 and had helped Dick pack before reporting for duty in September 1942. As he had with so many young Harvard men trying to sort out their military service options, Dick counseled Dana to consider the Air Corps because, as he told me, "I thought it needed strengthening."

Dana followed Dick's advice. Two months after his mentor boarded a train for Fort Devens, Dana wrote from Cambridge that he had handed in his "papers to get in the Air Force Enlisted Reserve." He was to be examined on the day after Thanksgiving, at about the same time Dick would be told his own commission would almost certainly never be approved. Dana's letter continued: "I guess you realize that it was your advice that started me on the trail towards getting in the Air Corps. If you ever read about me bombing Tokyo, you can give yourself a private pat on the back."

By January 1943, Dick had received his commission and Dana wrote he was "greatly impressed with [Dick's] switch from Army to Navy, and can imagine how much more you are enjoying yourself in your present job than in the old one. I presume that this is the position for which you were filling out reams of applications back in September, and therefore I presume that what you termed a 1000 to 1 chance worked out the right way." He went on to report that he "was accepted in the Air Corps. I just squeaked under the wire—I was sworn in on December 3 and the President clamped down on the 5th. I call that figuring it pretty fine. But even though I asked to be put on the active list, I don't think I will be called until April, May, or June. As usual, I will probably be taking your advice again—this time about what to do in the meanwhile." Dana said he "still wanted to be a pilot," but was "trying not to get my heart set on it so that if they tell me I would not do well in it or if I wash out I won't be too disappointed." He wrote that Dick had managed "to mold my military career as though I were putty in your hands. . . ."

In February, Dana was "drilling" at Brigantine Field near Atlantic City and awaiting his promotion to aviation cadet. In April, Dana wrote from Meadville, Pennsylvania, that he thought the Army was keeping him and other prospective aviation cadets there as it "stalled for time" while new training facilities were being built. He was happy to report that the base was "co-ed," which meant he had already been on a number of "dates." By May, he was in Nashville waiting to be classified—pilot, bombardier, or navigator—after four days of tests: "I put down pilot as my first choice, but I think they are going to make me a navigator. That's o.k. by me, because I want to do whatever they think I'm best fitted for. But I hope I won't get stuck in some hole waiting for navigator schools to thin out." He also hoped to be "at pre-flight school" when he next wrote to Dick.

Two weeks later, he was at Maxwell Field where he told Dick with delight, "I'm a full-fledged aviation cadet. Although I believe I'm better qualified as a navigator than as a pilot, apparently they don't need navigators, so I've been made a pilot. As I may have written to you, that's o.k. by me—I'll get the pilot experience and if I wash out I can still be a navigator. The reverse is not true." He said life at Maxwell was his most difficult to date, "but it is doing me a lot of good." The hazing by the upperclassmen did not bother him as much as "1) the heat, and 2) the lack of free time." His days began at four-thirty in the morning and included "drilling and parading in the heat . . . as well as a two-mile grueling cross-country run called the Burma Road." He expected to be in Florida for primary flight school by August 1.

At Dorr Field in Arcadia, Florida, Dana was thrilled: "At last I've got somewhere in the Army—I might even become useful in the not too distant future. I'm here at what is virtually a country club, deep in the heart of Florida." He said he had left Maxwell ahead of schedule: He was promoted to "an accelerated super-squadron . . . because I had the luck to be a college graduate." With the resulting extra time at the end of the training, he was furloughed for fifteen days that he divided among home, Harvard, Martha's Vineyard, and a Washington, D.C., visit to his sister. He called Dick while he was in the nation's capital, but his mentor "had gone to the National Archives Building on some ultra-vital mission," so he gave up. He was happy to report that only twenty-five percent of pilots "washed out" from his present station, but said if he did, "I can still be a navigator."

In September, Dana responded to what must have been Dick's previously expressed pleasure at having encouraged Dana into the Air Corps where he was clearly thriving: "You're off your nut if you think that *someday* I *may* admit your advice was sound about joining the Air Corps. . . . Heck, I'll never cease to be endlessly grateful to you for convincing me to join this outfit. I sometimes get irked at seeing classmates of mine sail off overseas with gold bars on their collars, but I wouldn't trade this job for any other in the Army. God bless RWL for making DR a pilot!"

In October, Dana was at Gunter Field in Montgomery, Alabama. He described at length his joy in flying for the first time a BT-13 (Basic Trainer) that was far more powerful and sophisticated than the biplanes he had flown at primary training school. "At the moment," he was "for FDR in '44. Wilkie is the only good GOP man, and I wouldn't trust his assistants in a Republican administration." In early December, Dana was at twin-engine advanced school in Columbus, Mississippi. He hoped he was "coming down the home stretch" as a cadet—and ready to receive his wings and see action. He continued to worry about a Republican administration that might take over after the 1944 election.

On February 8, 1944, Dana graduated from Columbus Army Flying School. He sent Dick a short note expressing his hope to see him in Washington soon. A month later, Dana wrote from Smyrna Army Air Field in Tennessee that he was "getting quite fond of the Liberator—it's an enormous plane, and, as they tell us, it's not a boy's airplane." Having soloed the B-24 for the first time a few days earlier, he concluded, "You never thought I'd actually be flying a Liberator some day, did you? Well, neither did I. And I shall always be grateful to you for persuading me to go into the Air Forces—I can't think of another job I'd rather be doing."

In April, he completed his flying instruction and awaited orders to be shipped overseas. He hoped for the European theater. On the subject of American politics, he expressed disappointment that Wilkie's chances for the 1944 Republican nomination had faded "because it indicates to me that the reactionary movement in America is more widespread than I feared. I think I would have voted for FDR even if Wilkie had run against him, but I'm sure that I shall not vote for the G.O.P. candidate now." He closed by asking Dick's views, noting that earlier letters had suggested a belief that "it was time for a change in administration. What think you now?" He also congratulated his mentor on a recent promotion: "Remind me to salute you when next we meet."

From there, Dana went to Westover Field in Massachusetts for a two-week assignment to a crew. He "got home for two weekends, met some nice girls at Smith, and enjoyed life in the North again." Then it was back to the South—Chatham, Georgia—where he wrote, "My crew is a young and 'eager' bunch. I never thought I'd feel like an old man for a long time, but I do when I see my 18-year-old sperry ball turret gunner, tail gunner, and assistant engineer, all of whom came into the Army this January. But they're all good boys, and I'm really enjoying this experiment in leadership."

He said he had flown a "formation gunnery mission over the Atlantic, with my gunners peppering a target towed by a B-26. We've also dropped bombs, had instrument checks, etc. . . . We should leave here around July 1, get our own ship at Mitchell Field, and get sent to England or Italy." He was interested in Dick's "views on FDR vs. Dewey. I'm still sure I won't vote for Dewey, however." He thought Americans "will be less reactionary when the casualty lists start coming in. When this country has suffered as Britain and Russia have, the voters will troop back to FDR in a big way. I can't see why Dewey isn't just another Hoover or Coolidge. I don't fear him—it's his administration and the men around him."

On D-Day, June 6, 1944, "the greatest amphibious force ever assembled stormed ashore in Normandy," as Dick would write in his 1962 book. On October 31, Dana sent him a notice of change of address card permitting only a short note: "Having a great time. Have seven missions in now. What's new in the states? DR."

Dick immediately shot off a "prompt reply to the postal giving me your current address, a promptness which is in sharp contrast to the long period of silence that followed the receipt of your last letter some time in May or perhaps June. For that long silence I can offer only apologies in the humble manner with which you are familiar." In his one and only letter to Dana that still remains, he reported Harvard college enrollment as still declining and prior expert predictions of an end to the

European war by autumn as obviously wrong. He also identified a trend he saw developing and predicted its continuation after the war: emphasis on scholarship and graduate work and de-emphasis on undergraduate instruction. But he hastened to add: "I did not say I approved the trend; I merely recognized it. Maybe I am wrong."

Dick also reviewed American presidential politics: "When last I wrote to you, I think I expressed—long before Dewey—the thought that it was time for a change. I did not care for Dewey's nomination and definitely did not like the substitution of Truman for Wallace [as Roosevelt's vice-presidential candidate]. I remained on the fence until early August when I began to realize that I had no choice but to vote for FDR. As the campaign wore on, as I saw how Dewey hoped to gain votes, all hesitation disappeared. By election eve I was as rabid a Rooseveltian as you were likely to find." As for the war, he said he "was never very optimistic and some time back predicted 1945 for the end in Europe and at least 1946 in the East." His postscript stated: "Congratulations on your promotion. I expect to be addressing you as 'Sir' when next we meet."

On November 28, Dick's letter in its six-cent postage envelope was returned to him unopened. It bore the stamp: "Missing."

* * *

Twenty years later, Dick learned from William Witkin, Dana's classmate at Harvard and his best friend among fellow pilots in Italy, what had happened. On November 11, Dana's squadron (which included Witkin and his crew aboard another B-24) took off in bad weather. Flying in formation, the planes encountered even worse conditions over the Adriatic Sea. Witkin disregarded the standard instruction to fly a tighter formation in such circumstances, left the group, and flew on his own for a time. That decision may have saved his crew, his plane, and himself. Unfortunately, Dana instead adhered to the stated protocol. When the weather cleared, Witkin rejoined the squadron's formation. He did that several times on this particular mission before eventually losing sight of the other planes and breaking out of the clouds alone at 26,000 feet, which is a high altitude for a B-24. Eventually the mission was aborted; Witkin returned to the base.

Dana's was one of two planes in the original squadron that did not return. For the next two days, search missions failed to find any trace of them. Witkin was convinced that Dana's plane collided with the plane either directly ahead of or behind him in the formation. The mission never should have occurred in light of the weather conditions, but that was small consolation to Dick, who had first encouraged Dana to join the Air Corps two years earlier.

A picture of Dana in his dress uniform appeared in the December 8, 1945, issue of *Harvard Military Intelligence,* along with the following: "Dana Reed, '43, 1st Lt., Air Force, AUS, was killed in action in the Mediterranean theater, November 11, 1944. He was a Liberator bomber pilot." Classmates later established a prize for "excellence in undergraduate writing" in his honor. In 1982, Dick sent copies of Dana's thirteen letters to the Harvard Archivist. His accompanying note was straightforward: "They reveal a great deal about an extraordinary young man whose life was cut short by the tragedy of his era."

In a 1995 letter expressing gratitude to Witkin for the additional information he had supplied concerning Dana's final flight, Dick wrote, "Many of my Harvard students gave their lives in the war. I mourn especially three: Dana, Warren Winslow '40 whose ship blew up in New York harbor, and Carroll Binder, Jr., '43 who was shot down over the Dutch coast. Of these, I feel the loss of Dana most deeply, and the fact that two strangers are corresponding about him fifty-one years later indicates his enduring appeal."

It was still true ten years after that. "When I read your treatment of Dana," he told me after reviewing the first draft of this chapter, "it brought a tear to my eye." I am sure Pop lost people close to him during the war, too. I wish I had asked him about them.

ELEVEN

"THE UNITED NATIONS
AND THE PEACE"

Even while I was an undergraduate at Northwestern during the early 1970s, much lore surrounded the question: How did Harvard let Dick Leopold get away decades earlier? It was common knowledge he had obtained his doctorate there, but no one could explain why that institution would have permitted the departure of such a talented teacher and scholar. Mystery and mythology shrouded the entire topic as a matter of Northwestern student gossip. Now I would finally learn the truth.

* * *

"When I was separated from the Navy in March 1946," Dick continued, "I hoped to pick up the life that had been broken off in October 1942. In many ways, this was relatively easy to do. I had three years remaining on my five-year appointment as an assistant professor. As was done with all returning veterans, I was placed immediately on the Harvard payroll; however, I did not have to resume teaching immediately."

"Why not?" I inquired.

"I had help from Paul Buck on that one. You'll recall he had been the first person to tell me, as I swam in the Adams House pool in the spring of 1938, that the history department was likely to offer me a five-year teaching appointment, provided that I change my field from intellectual to diplomatic history. Well, during the war, Buck had advanced dramatically. In fact, his entire career is a remarkable story of fortuity.

"As I already told you, his connection to author Benny DeVoto had been crucial to the Pulitzer Prize that Buck won for his dissertation. That, in turn, got him tenure at Harvard. Then he and a more senior faculty member—mathematics professor William Caspar Graustein—were appointed assistant deans. As far as I was concerned, Graustein's most important act had been his creation of the 'Graustein

95

table'; it had mapped out all future openings in various departments after Conant had decreed there would no longer be open-ended appointments to nontenure track positions. The history department did not fare well in that exercise and neither did I personally. In any event, because Graustein was very much Buck's senior, he had also been identified as the person who would become Harvard College's next dean of the faculty of arts and sciences. But in 1941, Graustein was killed in an automobile accident. As a result, Buck became dean in early 1942."

"So, there's the fortuity," I interjected.

"There is more: By October 1945, President Conant was spending much time in Washington, grappling with the problems of the new atomic age as chairman of the National Defense Research Committee. He needed someone tending to administrative matters in Cambridge, so he created the new position of provost and gave it to Buck. When I returned to Harvard, Buck said I was not required to teach until the beginning of the new semester in September. I suspect all of that is a longer answer than you expected."

"What were your living arrangements when you returned?" I asked.

"Dave Little had reserved a suite suitable for a resident tutor and had made clear he wished me to become the senior tutor in the fall, all of which would enable me to return to the life I had left four years earlier. Even the Sunday noon dinners at the Demoses were resumed. So certain aspects of my life returned to familiar routines.

"On the other hand, Adams House in March 1946 differed in many ways from that of October 1942. The student population was entirely new, so I had to start over in getting to know the undergraduates. Three meals a day were still available, but the earlier table service with menus had yielded to a cafeteria-type line with fewer choices. And I made clear almost immediately that I would not become senior tutor because I knew that it was imperative to press ahead with my research and writing. Because Harvard had constructed graduate housing and dining facilities on the site of the old Sargent Gymnasium, my fist-ball games did not survive the Second World War, either."

Neither did single-sex education. In 1943, Radcliffe women began to attend classes alongside Harvard men to offset the wartime drop in Harvard enrollment. No longer would Harvard instructors give their lectures twice in the same day— once to the men and then across the Cambridge Common to the women—as Dick had done before the war.

"The history department to which I returned had also changed," he continued. "In the fall of 1945, Arthur Schlesinger Jr. had been made a full professor with tenure following the acclaim that had greeted his *Age of Jackson,* for which he had won the Pulitzer Prize. His appointment contradicted the earlier statements to me—based upon the 'Graustein table'—that there would be no tenured position in American history during the remaining term of my Harvard assignment. Even before there was any public announcement, I learned about Schlesinger's appointment from Myron Gilmore, with whom I had been dining almost every evening while in Washington. But I decided to discover the facts for myself. Shortly after Myron had informed me of what the department had done, I went to Cambridge on a short leave. I spoke briefly with history department chairman Fred Merk, who, according to graduate student lore, had been seen crying when Arthur Jr.'s appointment confirmed beyond any doubt that I had no long-term future at Harvard. But the main goal of my visit was to speak with the senior Schlesinger.

"When I asked him what Arthur Jr.'s appointment meant to my future, his response was direct yet oblique: 'I did not go to the meeting at which my son was appointed, and so I cannot tell you what it means.' I certainly understood that a father would recuse himself from the vote affecting his son, but I doubted that any important appointment in the department could be made without Schlesinger's knowledge. He was a powerful figure at Harvard." In a 2001 letter to Arthur Jr., Dick would write: "It was the only time your father failed to be completely frank with me."

The final result remained unchanged, as Dick reported to Ethel: "I have heard further from Cambridge; and everything, including what I learned when I was there, leads me to believe that I shall not stay at Harvard permanently. That, of course, is not a new situation; but until the recent turn of events, there was always a possibility. Now I do not think that there is even a possibility."

He adjusted to the reality he had always expected, although the precise manner of his exclusion from a position on the Harvard faculty was surprising. After all, Schlesinger Jr. had not received and never would receive a Ph.D. Even so, the Schlesingers were and would remain among his best friends and staunchest supporters. He never charged anyone in the department with bad faith. Quite the contrary, as he wrote to Merk in 1945: "It is now more than twelve years since I arrived in Cambridge to begin my graduate studies. In that period I have experienced nothing but the highest consideration and utmost kindness from the history department. It has been a rare opportunity, first to study under and then work with men whose greatness was manifest not only in their scholarship and teaching but in their character and democratic manner. I venture to say that there is no department in any university in which a junior feels more at ease and more that he is genuinely contributing to the work of the group than the one over which you have the honor to preside. For being granted that opportunity, however brief, I shall be eternally grateful and always consider myself to have been highly privileged."

He remained forever loyal to those in Cambridge who had mentored, befriended, and promoted him, as he reconfirmed his earlier sentiments while speaking to the Massachusetts Historical Society in 1983: "Almost four decades later, after a rewarding career at another major university and knowing much more about the historical profession than I did in 1945, I would not wish to change a single word in that tribute to my former mentors, colleagues, and friends."

During the late summer of 1946, Dick received a telegram from Scripps College, part of the Claremont College system in Southern California, asking him to consider an immediate appointment to teach in the fall. Because he was already committed to teach at Harvard in September, he declined while leaving open the door to any later interest the school might have in him. In December, Scripps renewed its offer when Dick met with its president Frederick Hard in Washington, D.C.

"I refused primarily because of the long distance between California and all of the people with whom I had become close. I would have known Jack Kemble and John Gleason in the Claremont College system, both of whom were friends from the war, but no others." With my new knowledge of Dick's life and tendencies, I can now see clearly that a move to California would have meant an impossible transition for him.

* * *

Outside academia, life in the broader Leopold family moved forward. In 1946, Harry and his wife, Lucy, had their one and only child—a son, John. Dick's personal life fared less well. After Ruth Delano bade him farewell at Union Station in March of that year, she followed up with an April 6 letter poking fun at him for taking his Washington office keys with him: "I know it must have hurt that perfectionist soul of yours to have forgotten them and marred an otherwise perfect 'leave taking.' It is said, 'to err is human.' 'Tis nice to know that you are." A month later, she wrote that she was "at a complete stalemate as to what I want to do come September" when she would be out of the service. In early June, she visited Dick in Cambridge where she stayed with the Whitehills in their North Andover home.

"We saw a Red Sox game and went to dinner at the Demoses. Jean Demos was eager to play matchmaker for the man she regarded as one of the Harvard faculty's most eligible bachelors—me," Dick told me with a wide-eyed grin. On June 10, Ruth sent him a typed letter of thanks "for the wonderful time" he had shown her, signing it "As always." She followed with a similar note a week later.

On July 15, she wrote that she would "become a civilian on July 17" and that the "ONR&L is no more." By August 15, she was back in her native Minnesota, reporting on the ongoing polio epidemic and telling him she was returning to the East Coast because "the final instructions for arriving and registering at Yale arrived yesterday." She also described how one of her German cousins had lost everything in the war and had spent most of his time working as an interpreter for the British during his time as an Allied prisoner. She once again thanked Dick "for the very pleasant day in Cambridge and Boston. It was nice to see you again."

Ruth had done everything a woman of her time could do to make clear her interest in Dick. She was even on her way to New Haven for a year of medical training, probably as a nurse. There she would be only a short train ride away from him. But he did not respond to her overtures.

* * *

Meanwhile, Paul Buck had found a place in another department for Dick's history colleague, Oscar Handlin, a Jew. In 1946, Handlin was moved to the social relations department where, unlike in Dick's situation, a decision on his future as a historian could be deferred. Although Handlin thought he had no prospect of tenure, somehow he received it a few years later, shortly before he was about to accept an offer to teach at the University of Iowa. In 1952, he won the Pulitzer Prize for *The Uprooted: The Epic Story of the Great Migrations That Made the American People,* a study of immigrant adjustment to America.

* * *

Forty years after the events, Dick wrote to a former Northwestern graduate student, assessing the situation that had produced tenure for Arthur Schlesinger Jr. and Oscar Handlin while Dick was told to look elsewhere: "I suppose one could conclude that Buck and the Department by 1945 and 1948 thought more highly of Arthur and Oscar than they did of me, or perhaps they thought more highly of the fields that Arthur and Oscar represented. Certainly, they chose two of the ablest historians of our day." But even in the gracious acceptance of his fate, Dick did not let his old institution off the hook altogether: "Certainly, too, they fumbled for six years over the field of diplomatic history. Not until 1954 was Ernest May, a rank beginner (as I had been in 1938), appointed an Instructor. Not until 1959 was he given tenure; not until 1963 was he promoted to Professor."

Insofar as Arthur Schlesinger Sr. had any role in Harvard's decisions about the future careers of Dick Leopold, Oscar Handlin, and other Harvard Jewish graduate students in history, his words and actions suggest he must have been a very complex person. In promoting Bert Loewenberg, a Jewish graduate student who received his Ph.D from Harvard in 1934 and later taught at Sarah Lawrence College from 1942 to 1971, Schlesinger described him in 1930 as equivalent "to the whitest Gentile I know." He similarly recommended Oscar Handlin with the assurance that Handlin had "none of the offensive traits which some people associate with his race."

One element of Schlesinger's complexity emerges from the fact that he himself descended from Prussian Jews. His Jewish father had emigrated to America in 1860 and made his way west after the Civil War. Arriving in Xenia, Ohio, in 1872, he married a Roman Catholic woman the following year. Their grandson, Arthur Jr., would later write, "[T]he young people resolved whatever religious dilemma there may have been by turning Protestant and joining the German Reformed Church." Raised without any religious or cultural connections to Judaism, perhaps Schlesinger Sr. completed his internal separation from all things Jewish by reference to its traditions: He was not the child of a Jewish woman; that ended the line of Semitic succession under Jewish law. It remained severed when a Congregationalist minister married Schlesinger Sr. and Elizabeth Harriet Bancroft of Columbus, Ohio.

Or, perhaps, he was actually trying to promote the advancement of certain Jews through his assurances to others about their characteristics. Even nonpracticing Jews had little chance for an academic career in history, unless those who made the hiring decisions could overcome their anti-Semitic concerns and suspicions. Ironically, when I told Dick about Schlesinger Sr.'s description of Handlin, he laughed and said, "Oscar spoke and acted in almost every way that one would regard as 'typical' for a Jewish person at that time."

Time apparently made a difference to Schlesinger Sr.'s approach. In the 1950s, a newspaper reported that the national convention of his Ohio State undergraduate fraternity, Phi Delta Theta, had reaffirmed a constitutional exclusion of Jews and African Americans, at which point he sent a letter of protest to the alumni president and resigned. When the alumni president responded that resignations were not recognized and that expulsion was the only path out of the fraternity, Schlesinger Sr. took that route.

* * *

Meanwhile, Pop wanted to establish his postwar medical practice in Alaska—a place he regarded as America's last frontier. But just as his impulse to embrace the Army's offer of a year in the Philippines yielded to his sense of familial duty to his mother and grandmother, so, too, he scuttled his mission to the great North. He returned to Cleveland, began his own medical practice, and became chief of ENT (ear, nose, and throat) at Euclid General Hospital. He and Sue added twin daughters to their family in 1946 and bought a small home in a modest area of Shaker Heights. At the time, it was one of Cleveland's most affluent suburbs and its streets were lined with mansions; however, most assimilating Germanic Jewish families lived elsewhere. "Their" suburb was still Cleveland Heights, where both Pop and Sue had grown up.

Pop's family expanded while he himself yearned for adventure, new experiences, and wide open spaces; Dick suffered a tragedy in his extended Cambridge "family." The loss removed one of the ties binding him to the comfortable environs of his Harvard community. Ruth Delano remained on the sidelines at New Haven—close, but not quite close enough.

TWELVE

A Loss in the Family

Dick's Harvard family had grown continuously from his first days on the campus in 1933. But three couples and eventually their families stood above the rest: the Gilmores, Demoses, and Littles.

"As you know, I had met Myron Gilmore, another Harvard Ph.D in history who was a year ahead of me, in May 1937. His field was Renaissance history and he had received his five-year teaching appointment a year before I received mine. I spent much time with him and Sheila. Indeed, when I arrived in Washington in December 1942, I lived with the Gilmores until they moved in May 1943 to a smaller house in a more fashionable neighborhood on Alton Place. Even then, I continued to take most of my evening meals at the Gilmore home, which by the end of the war included three children—Janet, Diana, and Tom. After the war, they had their second son, John."

Dick had likewise reviewed with me the origins of his relationship with the Demoses: "You already know how fortuity played its hand during my 'Annus Mirabilis' that really began with a chance invitation to join the fist-ball group and my introduction to Raphael Demos that resulted. His wife, Jean, was absolutely delightful. She attended Radcliffe as a graduate student and was ten years younger than Raphael, whom she married in 1935 or 1936. Their first son, John, was born while they were living in their Adams House suite. Their daughter, Penny, was born in early 1938. After Raphael's year as acting master, the family moved into a small home on Scott Street, where they lived for about two years before moving to a house on Francis Avenue during the summer of 1940. They did not have a car and I still remember a very hot moving day when I carried lamps from their old home to their new one.

"I dined with the Demoses every Sunday from mid-1940 until I left for military service. Of the children, I became closest to their son, John, both because he was older and because I identified more readily with a boy. I took him to Red Sox games, track meets at Harvard Stadium, and the movie house in Harvard Square. Raphael, Jean, and I also made occasional trips to the Boston Symphony together. I especially enjoyed Beethoven's third symphony (*Eroica*), along with the sixth (*Pastoral*), the ninth (*Choral*), and Mozart's *Gran Partita*. I also spent several late summer vacations with the Demoses in 1939, 1940, and 1941.

"As for the final couple, when Dave Little replaced Raphael Demos as Adams House master in the spring of 1938, he brought his wife, Henge, with him. The Littles had four children. The oldest was Priscilla, who was grown and married when I first met her. Next was David Jr., who was in the Princeton class of '41, I think. We played tennis together and he eventually went to medical school. The third child was Adam, who struggled. Their youngest was Katherine, who was born in the mid-1920s."

I wondered if, with all of his closest Cambridge friends married and having children, Dick had not wished that Jean Demos had been more successful in her matchmaking efforts involving Ruth Delano. The Gilmores, Demoses, and Littles became the heart of Dick's new extended family. He certainly would have remained in close proximity to them, if that option had been available. But the door to a tenured position in the Harvard history department had been nailed shut, so, as he put it, "I had three years to find an acceptable position elsewhere."

* * *

Meanwhile, another former Schlesinger graduate student, Ray A. Billington, had left his Smith College teaching position in American history to join Northwestern University in 1944. Dick had first become acquainted with Billington at the weekly Schlesinger Sunday teas they attended while Dick was a graduate student, and Billington would come from "wherever he was teaching at the time—which was either Clark University or Smith College." Dick's only other interaction with Billington had occurred in 1942, when they served together on a committee of former students raising funds to commission the portrait of Schlesinger Sr. to honor his election to the presidency of the American Historical Association.

Dick described to me how recruiting Billington to Northwestern was the first step in an effort to rebuild a department that in 1935 had numbered five, but had subsequently fallen apart: "It all started when James Alton James retired in 1935. Isaac Joslin Cox became James' successor as the William Smith Mason Professor of American History, and the department got two for one—Tracy E. Strevey, a Ph.D from Chicago, and Franklin D. Scott, who got his degree from Harvard—to compensate for the loss of James. But then Cox, the department's most productive scholar, retired in 1941. Clyde L. Grose then held the William Smith Mason chair briefly until he died in 1942. Arthur Guy Terry, who had been appointed in 1906, retired in 1943. Raymond Carey—the fourth member of the department—was commissioned in the Navy during the War, but his return to teaching remained uncertain in 1944. Finally, a complex extramarital affair had eliminated a fifth member when his mistress discovered him cheating on *her* as well. Billington joined the department in 1944."

* * *

On March 12, 1947, the president announced what would become known as the Truman Doctrine: "I believe that it must be the policy of the United States to support free peoples who are resisting attempted subjugation by armed minorities or by outside pressures. I believe that we must assist free peoples to work out their own destinies in their own way." Five months later, former United States counselor in Moscow George F. Kennan anonymously published an article in which he advocated "a long-term, patient but firm and vigilant containment of Russia's expansive tendencies." Kennan suggested the West's superior economic and military strength permitted it to apply counterforce "at a series of consistently shifting geographical and political points, corresponding to the shifts and maneuvers of Soviet policy." Communism, Kennan argued, contained the seeds of its own demise, but they would require time to bloom. Dick would eventually have an opportunity to discuss Kennan's famous containment doctrine personally with him in 1951 and again in 1961.

* * *

In late 1947 and as an example of what Dick later called the "good ol' boy network" featuring Arthur Schlesinger Sr. at its center, Northwestern University invited him to teach during the 1948 summer session. The course would be a mutual test for the school and the prospective faculty member. Unbeknownst to Dick, Northwestern had recently tried to recruit a more prominent diplomatic historian, Stanford's Thomas A. Bailey.

"Many years later, I learned that in January 1946, Bailey visited the campus," Dick recounted. "He was offered the chairmanship and the highest salary in the department, but declined. If he had accepted, he would have pre-empted any possible position for me. But he chose to remain on the West Coast where he was born and had lived all of his life. When the opportunity came to me, I concluded that, for the first time in my professional career, all signs pointed in favor of a permanent departure from Cambridge.

"First, I already knew four current Northwestern faculty members, which gave me an immediate core of friends to offset the isolation I expected to feel from the absence of my dearest Cambridge colleagues. In addition to Billington, Richard C. Overton and Howard F. Bennett had been acquaintances at Harvard. Bennett had been in my first-year graduate seminar in 1938. Medievalist historian Gray Boyce had been an assistant professor at Princeton while I was doing my undergraduate work there and had been recruited to Northwestern in 1946—the same year Leften Stavrianos joined the faculty.

"Second, I had family in the area. My first and second cousins from the

Churchill and Ballenger families still lived on Chicago's North Shore. My cousin Alice had married into a family in the leather business. I had always felt especially close to her. The frequent train trips with Mother during my childhood had also given Chicago itself a comfortable familiarity.

"Finally, Northwestern's campus was accessible by inexpensive public transportation to Chicago and beyond. Evanston itself had a sufficient population to support all I would need within an easy walk from almost anywhere I lived." Dick accepted, but even before observing his trial run performance during the 1948 summer session, Northwestern enhanced its invitation.

"I arrived at the Orrington Hotel after a long train ride in January 1948," he continued. "There I met Howard Bennett, who took me to Dick Overton's house and then to the Billingtons, where I met history department chairman Tracy Strevey and his wife. I was very favorably impressed and it certainly helped that during my first visit to Evanston I encountered so many familiar faces. Later that first evening, I spoke with Gray Boyce and asked him what I should request in the way of an annual salary when I saw college dean Simeon E. Leland the next day. I was receiving $4,500 from Harvard, plus room and board at Adams House. Boyce and I concluded that the most I could reasonably seek was $5,500."

Leland himself was relatively new to Evanston. An Indiana native, he had received his Ph.D from the University of Chicago in 1926, joined its faculty in 1928, and eventually chaired its economics department from 1940 until he accepted an appointment as professor of economics and dean of Northwestern's college of liberal arts in 1946.

"When I met with Leland, he offered me a five-year appointment as an associate professor with an annual salary of $6,500! That tells you something about the seriousness of the university's efforts to strengthen the department, as does the failed attempt two years earlier to hire Bailey at an even greater salary. Leland then escorted me into the office of assistant dean J. Lyndon Shanley, who had been a year ahead of me at Exeter and Princeton." The two men had never met as students, when Shanley had dealt with the sometimes unpleasant treatment the two predominantly Anglo-Saxon Protestant institutions doled out to Catholics as Dick withstood the even more difficult challenges confronting a Jew. They would become close friends in the coming years.

On January 31, the day after a Hindu extremist killed pacifist Mahatma Ghandi, Dick wrote to Ethel, "I can think of only two mottoes for this letter, one from Shakespeare and the other from American history. 'There is a tide in the affairs of men' and 'Westward the course of empire takes its way.'"

He then described how his initial appointment included a "reasonable expectation" of promotion to full professorship and tenure. Although he regretted the loss of free room and board Harvard had provided him, he also reminded his mother (and himself) that such a situation would not last forever and obviously "could not survive a marriage," suggesting perhaps that Ruth Delano remained somewhere in his consciousness. But in the final analysis, the pecuniary arrangements were the least significant factors to him because, he wrote, "Most important of all the university is moving forward. It is well endowed and there is a spirit of progress and optimism for the future. Evanston is a nice place to live; and in a sense it's like going, if not home, at least to a place with which I am familiar."

He concluded with the suggestion that his mother "tuck" his letter away for the future, but then observed, "It is bad for a historian to write letters because he is always thinking how they will sound ten years from now." His letter did not mention Henge Little's recent hospitalization because he did not know the seriousness of her illness. When she passed away shortly thereafter, he wrote to Ethel that her death had made his decision to leave Cambridge easier. He reaffirmed that view in his discussions with me:

"I had been especially close to both Dave and Henge Little—maybe too close. I was sometimes the confidant of each in private discussions about the other, which at times could make things somewhat awkward for me. But when Henge died in February 1948, it was a tremendous blow to me personally and to all of us. Words cannot describe her importance to the life of the Adams House community. Somehow, things were never quite the same after her passing. Only after her death did I learn that she had cancer. While she was in the hospital, I certainly did not know she was dying. People did not talk about cancer in those days. We were all told she had phlebitis."

* * *

By the end of February 1948, the Communist Party had seized control of Czechoslovakia. In June, the Soviet Union blockaded Berlin in an attempt to isolate it from the West and force its will on the city that had been divided into four sectors after World War II, one for each of the Allies to control: American, French, British, and Soviet. Five days after the state of Israel was born in May 1948, Harvard professors Myron Gilmore and Dave Little joined Massachusetts Institute of Technology professor Elting E. Morison in hosting a farewell dinner honoring Dick. There is no doubt about the attendees because he noted them in his daily aide entry for May 19. They comprised a "who's who" of the century's leading and soon-to-be leading historians: Samuel Eliot Morison, the Schlesingers Sr. and Jr., Fred Merk, David Owen (modern English history), Donald Cope McKay (French history), Charles Holt Taylor (medievalist—and fellow fist-ball player), Crane Brinton (European and revolutionary history), and Elliot Perkins. Also present was Harvard's future dean of admissions Wilbur J. Bender.

On May 21, Dick was honored at an Adams House dinner where, as Dick put it, "Dave Little lavished the customary praise on a member of his staff." Then senior tutor Frederick L. Gwynn observed that Dick "probably knows more about the curious working of the Harvard undergraduate mind than most deans and certainly more than the majority of professors. . . . Dick has always made the mental health and—I do not hesitate to use the word—the moral health of Adams House undergraduates his primary concern, even to the point of running an informal symposium three hours a day at meal-time. I have watched him operate at breakfast, lunch, and dinner, and in the pleasant Sunday evenings at home he had as senior tutor before the war, and have been constantly amazed at the originality and germaneness of his conversational pace. We can safely pay him that highest of compliments to a teacher—that he has the true Socratic stimulus."

Dick then took the floor for one of the most difficult speeches he would ever give. "Henge's death and my special relationship with each of the Littles," he told me, "made it almost impossible for me to get through it." He reminded his audience that "we sometimes forget and certainly take for granted what the house system means to a young instructor. When I was first permitted to join the staff of Adams House, thanks to good friend Raphael Demos, I was probably pretty much like most young instructors of that day. I knew a few senior members of my own department, not all by any means, and practically no one outside of it. Membership in the house allowed me to broaden my acquaintanceship, to cut across departmental lines, to come to know and benefit from such people as Joe Walsh, Bright Wilson, Raphael, and others." He concluded with an oblique reference to Henge: "Finally, in closing, I would like to pay tribute to my good friend, Dave Little, for the inspiring leadership that he has always given to us as master. And I know that I speak the sentiments of all of us when I add to that tribute another to the one whose passing we have so recently mourned and whose memory we shall always cherish."

Soon thereafter, as he made his way from Adams House to Harvard Square to catch the subway to South Station for the train taking him westward, he encountered Payson Wild. Dick had first met Wild during his Annus Mirabilis at a February 1938 World Peace Foundation luncheon, but had never been to his home at any time thereafter. Nevertheless, Wild had become a friend in Harvard's political science department and, more recently, had been promoted to dean of Harvard's graduate school. One of his former students, John F. Kennedy, was running for re-election to the United States House of Representatives. Wild had also taught John's older brother, Joe, who had died in the war. Neither Dick nor Wild knew they would soon find themselves together in Evanston, Illinois, for a very long time.

* * *

One loose end still remained in Dick's life: Ruth Delano. In the fall of 1946, she began study at Yale, where she received some type of medical training and wrote in October, "It seemed like old times this morning to have breakfast with Walter, see Jane, and ride in the old Ford. Only you were missing." She was still there in March 1947 when she wrote, "It was nice to hear your voice again"—an obvious reference to a recent telephone call between them that Dick could not recall when we spoke about her sixty years later. Her note congratulated him on the "offers of jobs" that kept "flowing in" and expressed disappointment in his decision to decline Yale's offer to teach for a single year in place of Samuel Bemis: "There is nothing I would like better than to have you here, if only for a year. However, I know about Yale's one year offers with no promise of anything."

"One year at Yale would have been a dead end, professionally," Dick explained to me. "I never really considered it seriously."

In December 1947, Ruth was working in Washington and wrote that one of his letters had "made me lonesome for the sight of you and the sound of your voice. It was all I could do to keep from getting on a train bound for Boston." She then became even bolder in her effort to move him and their relationship along, writing that "the Fates—all three of them—are against me. I was counting on seeing you this summer since I am scheduled to work at Butler Hospital in Providence during July and August—so—o—o—o—you go to Northwestern in Chicago when I go home on vacation the 1st of September. Why don't you come to Washington for a weekend on your way to and from Cleveland? PLEASE ?!"

She must have scared him off. The next letter in Dick's "Ruth Delano" correspondence file is dated six months later, and it is from him: "This letter is long overdue, and I am afraid that you have probably learned indirectly what I should have told you myself. The Northwestern job that began to percolate just after I left Washington in March 1946 materialized last Friday, and I go out to Evanston permanently in September." He signed it, "Best ever, Dick."

She answered him a month later. "Your long overdue letter was very welcome as you well know," she wrote politely, but with a new and obvious distance. After that brief and superficial note, his correspondence file for her goes dark for more than two years. Their next and final communication is dated December 27, 1950. It responds to a card or letter from her that is not among his papers: "Quite a feat to acquire a husband and a three-year-old son all in one fell swoop," he told her. "My belated wishes for a lifetime of joy and happiness." The letter was addressed to Mrs. Kirwin Butler of Oklahoma City.

* * *

Reflecting on the relationship more than half a century later, Dick used phrases uniquely his: "If the war had continued for another six to twelve months, I believe I would have asked Ruth Delano to marry me and I believe she would have said yes. And I believe the marriage would have been a successful one. Never again was I as close to getting married as I was then." Especially in later years, Dick identified himself in his writings as "an unfortunate example of bachelorhood" and regretted "he had no wife for support." The latter became a regular excuse for his refusal to attend class reunions at Princeton, but it seems to me that wedded or not, he would have missed those events because they were unpleasant reminders of a somewhat unhappy college experience.

"So, you see," he summarized for me, "timing is everything. War interrupted a possible marriage; my return to the familiar environs of Cambridge further moved me along the bachelor track; Henge Little's death actually made it easier for me to accept Northwestern's offer and leave Harvard. But that last event sealed my fate as a single man." I found his last point particularly striking, since he was only thirty-five years old when he took the job planting him in the Midwest for the rest of his life.

* * *

Pop's life seemed less complicated. In addition to his private practice and positions at two Cleveland-area hospitals, he published several articles in professional journals. He continued to develop his medical practice while maintaining his reserve commission in the Army. He and Sue retained their lofty positions in Cleveland's east suburban social structure.

With respect to family matters, Sue's perspective on her Jewish pedigree diverged from Pop's. She had grown up among wealthy Jewish families on Arlington Road in Cleveland Heights, in sharp contrast to the one-half of a rented double house where Pop spent his childhood among the non-Jews in that suburb. Although she remained firmly embedded in Cleveland's Jewish "high society" as an adult, she and Pop did not involve themselves exclusively in that social scene. I think Pop would have shunned it altogether if the decision had been solely his. The impetus to assimilation remained his dominant theme as he tried to move his family steadily away from all traces of ethnic, religious, and cultural Judaism.

In that crucial respect, World War II and the Holocaust did not change the way he viewed himself. If anything, Pop's wartime experience reinforced his belief that separate and identifiable categories for human beings led to mischief and worse. Pop had been raised in an entirely nonreligious way; his existence had been secular from the beginning. He was a Jew only because that is how others classified him, not because he regarded himself as one. If he had been asked what it was about him or his background that made him Jewish in the eyes of others, he would have been hard pressed to identify it. He probably would have said it was the residue of religious belief and ethnicity persisting from prior generations, but it was a distant past bearing no relationship to his life or belief system.

"In the end, the labels should not really matter. People is people," he often remarked. "Everything should all just come down to people." The problem, of course, is it rarely does.

PART THREE

"Whether I could have done these things at Harvard,
we shall never know."

THIRTEEN

Northwestern

In June 1948, Dick arrived in Evanston. During his negotiations with the university, he had sought a residence close to the campus. He also wanted at least one bedroom and a separate living room. The result was a two-bedroom apartment at 1725 Orrington Avenue, recently constructed university housing for faculty and graduate students. When I was an undergraduate twenty-five years later, I thought it odd that any faculty member would live among students. But I now realize that Dick's days at Adams House had actually made him more comfortable living near young adults than anywhere else.

* * *

"Location was everything to me," he continued. "The Northwestern Apartments were next to the public library, two blocks from the bank, one block from the airline ticket office, and across the street from a hotel that ran a regular shuttle bus to the airport. Within a few blocks were clothing stores, Marshall Fields, the A&P, a dry cleaner, tailor, and various haberdasheries. The history department offices in Harris Hall were two blocks away.

"I had barely finished unpacking my belongings when the department's grand old man, James Alton James, knocked on my door. James had been a faculty member from 1896 to 1935. He had studied with the most famous historian of the American West, Frederick Jackson Turner—a fact he was eager to share with anyone who would listen. The only problem with turning on James' 'Turner switch' was that you could not turn it off.

"I didn't know it when we first met, but James was also an outspoken anti-alcohol crusader who helped the Women's Christian Temperance Union keep the location of its national headquarters—Evanston, Illinois—'dry' even after the passage of the constitutional amendment repealing Prohibition. As James continued to speak well beyond my ability to bear it, I tried desperately to develop some graceful way to bring our discussion to a close. Not yet aware of James' aversion to alcohol, I inadvertently hit upon the solution to my dilemma when I offered him a glass of sherry. James politely refused and beat a hasty retreat."

The only drawback to Dick's second-floor apartment on the south side of the building was its location directly above the laundry room, which began operating loudly and in earnest at six in the morning, even on Sundays. Eventually, he spoke with the building manager, who confessed he did not know how he could limit access to the area and remedy Dick's noise complaints.

"How about a lock on the door to remain locked until a designated *later* time when you would unlock it?" Dick suggested.

"Oh, a lock . . ." came the bewildered reply, as the light dawned from within.

His living situation would improve dramatically in 1952, when he moved to a sixth-floor apartment on the north side of the building.

* * *

Shortly after his arrival, Dick learned that his friend Payson Wild would join him. Even before Dick had moved to Evanston, his views of Wild as a candidate for the Northwestern University presidency had been solicited. He had known Wild since 1938 and endorsed him enthusiastically, but heard nothing more about the matter before the announcement that the dean of Northwestern's medical school, J. Roscoe "Rocky" Miller, had won the position. However, Miller appointed Wild to be his number two person, a position eventually renamed provost. With that outcome, Dick now had an important friend from Cambridge in a very high place at the university.

Dick added others as he built a new family in Evanston. He and Shanley became close friends. In fact, Dick became such a regular dinner guest for special occasions at the Shanley home that Lyndon's son, F. Sheppard, eventually came to regard him as a fixture there after the family of four (including Shep's sister, Molly) moved to a larger house in June 1951. "Nearly every summer afternoon beginning in 1951," Shep told me, "My mother drove our Plymouth to the Northwestern Apartments, picked up Dick, and headed for the beach behind Sargent Hall. We all had a great time there." Dick met home economics professor Ruth Bonde, who never married, at a Shanley dinner party in 1951. Dick and "Ruthie" would serve together for many years on Northwestern's Council on Undergraduate Life and remain close friends to the end.

Dick became a Northwestern fund-raiser in 1949. President Miller requested his presence on a visit to Charles G. Dawes, who had been running for vice president when Dick wandered into the Coolidge/Dawes New York campaign headquarters in 1924 and picked up some buttons for his friends. Dick had met with Dawes the previous summer to ask about an unpublished diary the latter had kept during the Spanish-American War.

"Unfortunately, it was of little historical value," Dick said. "As for my trip with Miller, Dawes had already promised to bequeath to the university his mansion in Evanston, and we were seeking more from him. I don't recall that we succeeded, and even the house he had previously donated had a leaky roof. For awhile, we were told the mansion would become the history department's offices where each professor would receive palatial rooms. That was a pipe dream. After repairing the roof, the university leased it to the Evanston Historical Society for one dollar a year.

"Although Miller and I were seeking additional financial support for the university, all we got for our efforts were Dawes' endless stories about his World War I service under General John J. Pershing—the same ones I'd already heard when I'd gone to ask about his diaries."

* * *

Dick described how his new geographic location in Evanston influenced the development of his career. "I had joined the American Historical Association in 1933 or 1934," he said. "While in Cambridge, I had attended most of its annual meetings since 1935 because they were in the East. Although I had joined the Mississippi Valley Historical Association in 1937, I had attended only one of its annual meetings prior to my move to Illinois. Thereafter, I went to those Midwestern conferences regularly. I still attended AHA meetings in Washington and New York because I linked them to visits with my mother, which I would have made anyway."

Meanwhile, Pop continued his otolaryngology practice in Cleveland and published articles in professional journals. He also spent one Wednesday every month and two weeks every summer at Army reserves training camp. The summer sessions were held at Fort Knox for the first few years. Then the site moved to his former World War II outpost and the location of his oldest daughter's birth in 1943— Camp Atterbury, Indiana. Sometimes life's journey seems circular.

FOURTEEN

BUILDING THE

HISTORY DEPARTMENT

"The department I agreed to join in 1948 consisted of four full professors (Ray A. Billington, Tracy E. Strevey, Franklin D. Scott, and Gray Cowan Boyce), two associate professors (Leften S. Stavrianos and Richard M. Brace), two assistant professors (Leland H. Carlson and Philip W. Powell), and one instructor (George T. Romani). In May 1948, Strevey resigned to accept a top administrative post at the University of Southern California.

"When I accepted the appointment at Northwestern, it was understood that my teaching load would include one quarter of the yearlong sophomore survey course, a three-quarter sequence on American diplomatic history, and a two-quarter graduate seminar. Strevey's departure created an immediate need for someone to teach the third quarter of the survey course. As the junior member of the department, the responsibility fell to me."

Dick's presence helped the department's American history section become one of the nation's best for its size. Billington and Leopold formed the nucleus around which the remaining constellation of academic stars would gather. The third member of what Dick would call Northwestern's "American quartet" was added when Arthur S. Link joined the faculty in 1949. The fourth, Clarence L. Ver Steeg, would arrive in 1950. The addition of Link to his life also gave Dick the best friend he would ever have in the profession. That led to our next topic.

* * *

The historic professional collaboration of Leopold and Link had persisted as a matter of undergraduate legend to the time I was a student in the 1970s. I now discovered they were an unlikely pair. In most ways, they could not have been more dissimilar. Link was born in 1920 and raised in a rural area of North Carolina; Dick came from affluence in New York City. Link's devoutly religious upbringing in a strict Protestant home remained a central part of his identity throughout his life; Dick was raised as "nothing" when it came to religion and eschewed every aspect of his Jewish heritage. Link went to the University of North Carolina at Chapel Hill because it was the best school he could afford; Dick received an Ivy League education at Princeton after preparatory school at Exeter. Link did not serve during World War II because childhood polio had left one leg two inches shorter than the other and a shoulder slightly slumped; Dick was in the Navy for four years, despite his poor vision. Link married in 1946; Dick remained single throughout his life. Yet somehow in the ways that mattered most, the two men connected to form an immutable bond of friendship.

Although Link remained devoted to his family, both men shared a dedication to their profession. For Link, history was akin to a religious calling; Dick may have shared that view without ever adopting that language. Whatever the basis for their interpersonal chemistry, their mutual respect and admiration fostered genuine affection. But it did not begin that way.

*   *   *

"I had first heard of Link when Princeton University Press published his 570-page book, *Wilson: The Road to the White House,* in April 1947," Dick told me. "Three months later, I wrote to one of my former Harvard students on the Princeton faculty, Thomas Pressly '40, expressing my surprise that Link was only an instructor. In May 1948, Dean Leland informed me of Strevey's resignation and solicited my thoughts on a successor. I immediately wrote to Billington because I did not want to give Leland any specific names without knowing more about the departmental situation generally. Billington responded with a request for my response to a list of potential candidates. He alluded only briefly to Link as someone who, he believed, did not have the personality or reputation for the open position. I commented on Billington's list, telling him what Pressly had previously told me: Link was not regarded as an outstanding teacher or colleague, but was a bearcat for work and very ambitious. I also suggested that Billington consider another person whom he had not included, David Potter. I told him Potter might be interested because Yale had publicly stated its unwillingness to make any promotions in the near future and Potter might have been caught in that squeeze.

"After I arrived in the fall of 1948, Northwestern first approached Potter, then Sam Brockunier at Wesleyan and, finally, Bell Wiley at Louisiana State University. Potter turned us down because Yale offered him an unexpected promotion. Brockunier and Wiley visited Northwestern and the department recommended that offers be extended, but Leland and the outgoing president, Franklin Bliss Snyder, rejected both men on the stated grounds that the department could do better. At that point, acting on a suggestion from a former colleague, Leland told us to take a closer look at Link."

Dick first met Link at the American Historical Association's annual meeting in December 1948, where Link accepted the department's invitation to visit Evanston for interviews, which went well. Dick later learned that Link's conversation with Northwestern's dean went as follows:

"Leland: Professor Link, we very much want you at Northwestern.

Link: Thank you, sir.

Leland: We are prepared to go well beyond your Princeton salary.

Link: That is very generous of you.

Leland: As to rank, it might be best, since you have just been promoted to assistant professor, to come in at that rank but at a very high salary; but if you insist, we are ready to make you an associate professor.

Link: Thank you. Again you are generous. I shall be happy to consider an appointment as an associate professor."

By March 1949, Dick's earlier diffidence about Link had transformed into euphoria over the prospect that the budding Wilson scholar would join him on the faculty. He reported to Arthur Schlesinger Sr. his surprise at Link's acceptance of Northwestern's offer: "I say surprise because I felt Princeton would not let him go—that it would feel compelled to jump over the heads of his less distinguished seniors. That action, apparently, they refused to take. . . . So Link comes to us to help me with the survey course, to teach his seminar, and to offer lecture courses on Southern and recent history. I think you will agree that we have strengthened our department, at least on the side of scholarship."

* * *

As the department was recruiting Link, research seminars brought the total teaching load for Dick's first year to a staggering eight units. "You'd never get any newcomer to teach that many courses today," he told me with a proud smile. "But Ray and I agreed that the survey course had not gone well during the 1948–1949 academic year. Billington had taught the first quarter; I had taught the second and, with Strevey's abrupt departure, the third. We had been disappointed with the students' performance throughout the year. The entire class of about 300–350 heard lectures thrice weekly—from Billington in the fall and from me in the winter and spring. In addition, graduate students taught the course's small-group sections that met weekly and contained twenty-five to thirty participants. Departing from tradition, I decided to conduct a different section each week until I had covered all of the students for each teaching assistant. That approach broke down the distance separating the lecturer from the student. It also enabled me to learn the names and faces of a very large class."

After teaching the 1949 summer session in Evanston, Link assumed Billington's responsibility for the first quarter of the survey course in the fall. Dick followed with his uniquely personalized approach to the individual sections in the second and third quarters. Link then left during the 1950–1951 academic year to enjoy a previously deferred Guggenheim Fellowship he had received shortly before accepting his Northwestern appointment. The two growing giants in American history resumed their team teaching in the fall of 1951. That was also when they met George F. Kennan, author of the famous 1947 article outlining a policy of "containment" in dealing with an ambitious Soviet Union's desires to expand its sphere of geographical and political influence. The university had invited Kennan as a distinguished lecturer in connection with its centennial celebration.

"The university distinguished itself greatly at that event," he told me, "because the noted theologian-philosopher Reinhold Niebuhr spoke, too."

Eventually, Dick and Link concluded that Billington's textbook, which had been the course standard for the last few years, did not measure up to their standards and requirements. "Together," he told me, "we did what neither of us could have easily accomplished alone. We gave Billington the unhappy news that his royalty payments would decline by the number of Northwestern students who took our American history survey course. The truth was that we were more concerned about the reaction of his wife, Mabel, than that of our departmental colleague."

Meanwhile, the last member of Northwestern's American quartet was added when Clarence L. Ver Steeg joined the department in 1950 as an instructor with the understanding that he would be promoted to assistant professor when he completed his dissertation at Columbia. His work focused on the colonial period; Dick correctly recognized Ver Steeg as a rising star in his field.

"Ver Steeg was born in Iowa and had graduated from Morningside College in '43," Dick said. "During the war, he served in the Army Air Corps and was stationed in the southwest Pacific. After the war, he attended graduate school on the GI Bill of Rights. He had been a graduate student for only two or three years when he sent Gray Boyce an unsolicited letter about a possible position at Northwestern. Boyce was extremely taken with the letter. But with the department's recent hiring of Billington, Link, and me, our request for another American historian was greeted with skepticism. Leland agreed to hire Ver Steeg, provided that Northwestern's Technological Institute paid half of his salary. As a result, Ver Steeg taught a survey course for the engineers. He lived with his wife and son, John, in the Northwestern Apartments for a few years before the family moved to a house in Evanston."

The combination of Billington, Leopold, Link, and Ver Steeg gave Northwestern a collection of American historians arguably second to none. For Leopold and Link, it was only the beginning of a remarkable decade-long collaboration that would become historic in its own right.

* * *

In Cleveland, Pop was collaborating with Sue to raise a family and build an independent medical practice. He also maintained his Army Medical Corps Reserves status and lieutenant colonel rank. When the Soviet Union blocked all rail and road access to West Berlin to create the first Cold War crisis in 1948 and continued that blockade into 1949, Pop's unit "was alerted for probable active duty. No question," he wrote. "I saw the orders. But the Allies set up a 24-hour air supply to Berlin . . . known as the Berlin Air Lift. No active duty for my unit."

FIFTEEN

The Leopold-Link Decade

at Northwestern

A major crisis erupted on June 25, 1950, when communist North Korea invaded its democratic neighbor, South Korea. The United Nations authorized action, and President Truman assigned America's most distinguished soldier, General Douglas MacArthur, to lead the troops in defense. As the war bogged down during the winter and into the spring, MacArthur became frustrated at Truman's unwillingness to permit pursuit and combat engagement of hostile forces deep in North Korean territory. He became openly critical of Truman's policies and, eventually, the president relieved MacArthur of his command on April 11, 1951.

* * *

In the same month that Truman brought MacArthur home, a representative of Prentice-Hall approached Dick and Link about a new project. He wanted them to edit a book that would be suitable for use in American history survey courses at colleges and more demanding secondary schools. They agreed to the enterprise and *Problems in American History*—edited by Leopold and Link—became the first of their many collaborative efforts outside the classroom. They asked Dick's fellow Harvard alumnus, John Hope Franklin, to contribute a chapter on the Reconstruction. Sometimes, as with this volume, the work of Leopold and Link together revealed itself in the presence of both names on the final product. More often, they served as each other's toughest and most respected critics in reviewing drafts of books and articles they published individually.

In addition to the publication of *Problems* that year, 1953 became important to Dick for additional reasons. First, the manuscript for his next book circulated for comment among an impressive group of advance readers: Billington, Link, Elting Morison, John Morton Blum, and McGeorge Bundy. It was a short interpretive biography of Elihu Root, who had served as secretary of war and secretary of state during the McKinley and Theodore Roosevelt administrations and had won the

Nobel Peace Prize the year Dick was born. Dick's book had a much different purpose from Philip C. Jessup's lengthy and definitive two-volume work that had drawn, in part, on the author's interviews of his subject. It also considered historical documents that Jessup had not seen.

Second, Dick's success in the classroom, together with the anticipated publication of his book on Root, resulted in his promotion to full professor with tenure at the age of forty-one. Northwestern would now remain his home for as long as he wanted. Given his aversion to change and transitions, that would be a long time. He also acquired the Royal standard typewriter on which he composed letters and most other written communications for the next half century.

"It was at this time," he continued, "that Al Knopf, the president of his own publishing company, was discussing with me the writing of a treatise on American foreign policy. You will find that I took full advantage of the dangerously long period he gave me to complete it."

Finally, he was offered the prestigious Harmsworth Professorship and its opportunity to teach for a year at Oxford University, but he refused it. "You're probably wondering why I turned down the Harmsworth," he told me. "Just as Cambridge had become comfortable for me in ways causing me to settle back into Massachusetts after World War II and ending any chance for a continuing relationship with Ruth Delano, a similar fear of the unknown prompted me to remain in Evanston, rather than accept the Harmsworth. When in doubt, I didn't." It was another theme of his life. Passing up that particular opportunity also cost him uninterrupted time away from teaching obligations; such a respite from classroom responsibilities might have allowed him to produce another book.

He ended the summer of 1953 in an automobile, traveling with Arthur and Margaret Link through Iowa, South Dakota, Yellowstone, the Grand Tetons, and Colorado Springs during September. Originally, the Links had planned to take their children on the trip, but, as Dick later told Ethel, he persuaded them otherwise: "I thought it was a mistake to take three small children. They would not appreciate what they saw, and Margaret would get no rest." The Northwestern Archives has the collection of postcards he sent Ethel on that trip—one for every day he was away from Evanston.

* * *

As newly elected President Eisenhower tried to bring the Korean conflict to an end, Dick's appointment to full professor carried with it an unexpected challenge: He also became acting chairman of the department. His remarkable promotion came about in strange fashion. Chairman Gray Boyce was taking a two-quarter leave—the first and last time he had ever done so. Franklin Scott was the department's next-reigning elder, and he initially agreed to serve as acting chairman in Boyce's absence.

"Notwithstanding his other strengths, Scott could sometimes be indecisive," Dick told me. "He accepted the acting chairmanship and the board of trustees approved it; however, he then changed his mind. With Billington already on leave, I was the next ranking member of the department." In addition to teaching his full load, among his major accomplishments was to recommend increases in the salaries of two American history scholars whose retention he viewed as essential to the department's growing strength and reputation, Billington and Ver Steeg. "Leland typically asked, 'Who is your best man?'" he told me. "I succeeded in expanding his focus in my effort to create one of the best *departments* in the country."

* * *

After the Soviet Union's first detonation of an atomic bomb in 1949 and Nationalist China's fall to communism later that year, a modern-day political witch hunt followed as Americans searched for someone to blame for these apparently devastating blows to the nation's security. Wisconsin's junior Senator Joseph McCarthy gave them a simple, seductive, and incorrect answer: communist infiltration of the American government. By the summer of 1954, it seemed that no one would stop him as all eyes turned to the Army-McCarthy hearings broadcast live on national television over thirty-six days.

Along with millions of other viewers, Dick watched the beginning of McCarthy's end unfold during a riveting session on June 9, 1954. The Army's attorney, Joseph Welch, was cross-examining a vicious attorney on McCarthy's staff, Roy Cohn. McCarthy interrupted and sought to divert Welch and the national television audience to a wholly unrelated matter. McCarthy said that Fred Fisher, a young associate in Welch's Boston law firm who had no connection to the Army case, had belonged to what McCarthy characterized as a communist-sympathizing organization while attending Harvard Law School. When McCarthy demanded that Welch acknowledge the young man's former associations, Welch calmly took the senator apart and then concluded, "It is, I regret to say, equally true that I fear he shall always bear a scar, needlessly inflicted by you. If it were in my power to forgive you for your reckless cruelty, I would do so. I like to think I'm a gentle man, but your forgiveness will have to come from someone other than me . . . Let us not assassinate this lad further, Senator. You've done enough. Have you no sense of decency, sir? At long last, have you left no sense of decency?" Dick would long remember Welch's final sentences and, in a much different setting, later use them himself.

* * *

Dick did not confine his commitments to scholarship and teaching alone. In 1954, he began a five-year term on Northwestern's Council on Undergraduate Life. The success of the Harvard house system was not lost on him, and he sought to utilize lessons he had learned there to enhance the quality of student life in Evanston. In many ways, he became every undergraduate's best friend, although not all of them realized it.

At the same time, his collaboration with Link continued to thrive. Dick produced his second book in 1954: *Elihu Root and the Conservative Tradition.* "But," as Dick described to me, "none could match Link's prolific written output while he was at Northwestern. Arthur published four major books: *Woodrow Wilson and the Progressive Era: 1910–1917* in January 1954; *American Epoch: A History of the United States Since the 1890s* in April 1955; *Wilson: The New Freedom* in December 1956; and *Wilson the Diplomatist: A Look at His Major Policies* in November 1957. But that was not all. He co-edited and contributed to two editions of a textbook designed for classroom use, wrote five articles, and wrote eleven book reviews. Along with his wife, Margaret, I became his most trusted advance reader."

In September 1954, Link began a year-long sabbatical at the Institute for Advanced Study at Princeton, where he planned to complete his second major volume on Wilson. Two weeks into his stay, Princeton associate professor of history Jeter A. Isley suffered a fatal heart attack, and the Tigers' press to keep Link in New Jersey permanently began. By February 1955, Link had decided to remain at Princeton and placed a telephone call to his closest confidant to explain his decision. Dick persuaded him on the basis of friendship to make no final decision until returning to discuss the matter in Evanston.

As soon as he hung up, he wrote Link a letter revealing the depth of their friendship: "I realized that you might have been struck by my ostensibly unemotional and matter-of-fact attitude. I want to assure you that such was not my true feeling, that it took the greatest will power to discuss your problem objectively and without intrusion of personal feelings and appeals. I have always acted upon the assumption that between such close friends as you and I, certain things do not have to be said. On the other hand, that policy can be carried too far. And thus I want to say once and for all that your leaving Northwestern University will be for me a personal and professional loss, the extent of which I shudder to contemplate." He went on to describe the professional and personal dimension of their relationship, which had included their automobile trip west, a close relationship with the family that made him a regular guest in their Evanston home, and even Margaret's service as a proofreader for the Root manuscript.

"It has been my fondest hope," he concluded, "that we could keep the American quartet together. I knew it would be difficult, and you constituted the greatest difficulty . . . I fought for Ray Billington last year. I did everything I could to keep Clarence Ver Steeg. And yet neither mattered as much to me as you. These things you and Margaret must have sensed; I hope you will forgive me for saying so now. For I say them for the record and for the record only. Your decision must be reached on other grounds. You must do what is best for your family and your career. Loyalty and affection for friends and other institutions must be a secondary consideration. I deplore these facts, but I recognize them. So there will be no appeal to you on the grounds of friendship and emotion."

When Link returned to Evanston that "one last time," Dick had enlisted Payson Wild's support in gaining for the Wilson scholar a huge salary increase. Link pondered his dilemma as Wild told him, "Wilson belongs to the nation, not just to Princeton." After all, even though Wilson had started his career as Princeton's president before becoming governor of New Jersey, he eventually led the entire country. The decision became easier when Link returned to Princeton and found its president, Harold Dodds, somewhat aloof and indifferent. Margaret Link had made clear all along her preference for Evanston, but the decision would always remain his. He chose Northwestern, at least for now.

On March 25, 1956, Link's second volume of the Wilson biography was published. He dedicated it to "colleague and collaborator, Professor Richard W. Leopold." In early September, Dick accompanied the Links on another joyous and festive motor trip to the South. Aside from Dick's cousin Alice and her children, the Links were as close as Dick came to having an immediate family in the Chicago area, although the Shanleys and the Wilds were not far behind.

* * *

Meanwhile, Dick's advanced course on American diplomatic history was renamed "The History of American Foreign Policy" and listed as History C-13 in the course catalog for 1955–1956. Oxford University once again invited him to be its Harmsworth Professor and, once again, his aversion to change prevailed. He refused the offer, but suggested an eager Arthur Link as a candidate to serve in his stead. When Link got the nod, he immediately accepted as the two men were completing their first set of revisions to *Problems in American History.* Their earlier volume had gained sufficient prominence to remove an albatross Dick had borne since 1924.

"By the time of the second edition of *Problems* in 1957, the coupling of the names Leopold and Loeb had finally changed to Leopold and Link . . . except for the occasional idiot who would see us together at some conference of historians and say, 'There go Leopold and Loeb.'"

Link's acceptance of Oxford's Harmsworth Professorship allowed him to spend the entire 1958–1959 academic year on the next installment of his Wilson biography. "He wrote the whole thing in longhand and in pencil," Dick recounted. "It was so long that they decided to break it into two volumes." Link said later that his only regret about accepting Oxford's offer was it caused him to miss the football season in which Northwestern defeated both Michigan and Ohio State in Evanston. He typically attended all such Saturday afternoon home games with Dick.

* * *

Dick's aversion to risk did not interfere when an unambiguous professional opportunity for advancement presented itself, and he did not have to change residences to accept it. Such was the case in 1955 when he was invited to become a member of the Navy's Advisory Committee on Naval History. Appointment to the committee was for an indefinite duration. Its charter was particularly significant to Dick: Every eighteen months it reported on where the Navy should spend its time, energy, and financial resources relating to historical document preservation activities. Two long-time friends and colleagues—James Phinney Baxter and Walter Muir Whitehill—comprised part of its exclusive membership and, undoubtedly, enthusiastically recommended the addition of Dick to their ranks.

"You see the circularity of life and the role of fortuity?" he told me. "Almost by chance, Baxter and Whitehill had been central to the direction of my life in 1937 and 1942, respectively. Now I was serving on a committee as their equal, but I was the youngster in the group." He properly regarded the invitation as a significant honor for such a young historian. It was his first postwar opportunity to influence the process by which government materials would become available for future generations of historians. It would not be his last.

* * *

Dick also continued his efforts to strengthen the Northwestern history department. When Philip Powell left in 1949, Dick recommended Howard F. Cline of Yale, his former tutee from the Harvard class of 1939, to fill the Latin American history position. Cline accepted Northwestern's offer. "When Cline left in 1952 to head the Hispanic Foundation in the Library of Congress, Dean Leland said that because the political science department already had a Latin American scholar, we should find a person for East Asian studies, which we did, Roger F. Hackett," Dick explained. "In the spring of 1953, Hackett became the first history department appointment in that area. In the spring of 1954, Leland Carlson resigned to become president of Rockford College and, a year later, Lacey Baldwin Smith was appointed to teach courses on England. One of Lacey's faculty colleagues at MIT, my former undergraduate student John Morton Blum, had strongly recommended him to me. Adding to the circularity of all this, Blum had been recruited to MIT after the war by my old friend, Elting Morison, for whom Blum had worked in the service. But returning to the subject at hand, Northwestern, even with the changes I've described, the department was relatively stable throughout the decade. It had numbered seven in 1940, eleven in 1950, and twelve in 1960. But that stability would soon come to an abrupt end."

Dick published his biography of Root in the same year—1954—the Supreme Court declared in *Brown v. Board of Education* that "separate is not equal" and that the nation's public schools should be desegregated "with all deliberate speed." A year later, a young African American boy from Chicago named Emmett Till was brutally killed, and race relations moved to a higher level in the national consciousness. These increasingly tumultuous times eventually touched the Northwestern campus. Dean of students James McLeod was a former Marine who had risen from the position of university chaplain to occupy his post. Unfortunately, he held racial views that combined with an inflexibility to exacerbate growing tensions on the campus. In one particularly unpleasant episode at a large gathering in the university chapel, the dean aimed inflammatory comments in the direction of an African American student. When reporters for *The Daily Northwestern* asked Dick to comment on the incident, he categorically condemned the dean's remarks and conduct. In such matters, especially as they affected students, Dick was relentless and unflagging.

"I believe that many other faculty members would have similarly spoken up if asked about such issues," Dick told me. But according to a former student from the class of 1958 who sat with us on a Sunday morning in 2005, the reporters for *The Daily* were less certain. They regularly turned to Dick for public comment on and reaction to controversial university administration policies and statements because they knew he would speak his mind.

* * *

For Dick, the Link years had been magical in almost every way. The Links completed his Evanston family and were central to a period he would always remember as one of the best in his life. In 1982, he wrote to a former Harvard undergraduate (and Adams House protégé): "The years from 1948 to 1960 were ones of pure joy and some fulfillment. From being one of the lowest men on the totem pole at Harvard, and a shaky perch at best, I went to one of the top positions at Northwestern and, because of personal quirks, became probably the second most influential in a department of ten or eleven. Arthur Link arrived in 1949 and, because our scholarly interests overlapped, became my closest friend."

He then described the steady progression of his career: "Since in those years I was primarily responsible for the large survey course (450–500 students), I became well known on the campus and filled several important University, College, and Departmental committees. I also began an ascent in the profession, especially in the Mississippi Valley Historical Association: Board of Editors, 1952–1955; Program Chairman, 1956; Executive Committee, 1958–1961. For the American Historical Association, I was on the Beer Prize Committee, 1951–1952, and on the Committee on the Historian and the Federal Government, 1956–1965. I was one of the first three representatives on an advisory committee for the Department of State in 1957 and stayed on for eight years." He completed his reminiscences of that period with the nagging question that would always linger for him, namely: "Whether I could have done these things at Harvard, we shall never know."

He had also navigated through another potentially serious problem: Two of his most beloved friends, Merk and Billington, had locked in mortal combat. At Harvard, Billington had studied under Merk who, in turn, had patterned his lectures after Frederick Jackson Turner's. When Billington published his lectures in 1949, Merk complained that his own unpublished work had somehow been usurped. He even threatened to file suit, although any theory of legal liability was elusive at best. It was easy for Dick to come down on the right side of the issue and in favor of Billington because, as he told me, "Ray had done nothing wrong." Unfortunately, even after Billington revised the preface of his book to heap Merk with praise and to credit him for inspiration, Merk was not moved and held a grudge against Billington for the rest of his life. Dick managed to preserve his relationships with both men.

* * *

Meanwhile, Pop saw the orders that would have activated his reserve unit for the Korean War, but reported that, as with the Berlin Crisis of 1948–1949, "We missed out again and stayed home." He continued in the reserves throughout the 1950s, as a 1956 photograph taken at Camp Atterbury conclusively proves. He is shown with future Israeli leaders, including Moshe Dayan. Standing less than five and a half feet tall, Pop was the shortest in the group by several inches, but his compact stature was no obstacle to his becoming a full colonel in 1957. The irony of the picture is that Pop was vehemently anti-Zionist because it ran counter to his assimilation principles.

"In 1959," Pop explained, "someone in Washington decided on one weekend a month instead of Wednesday nights" for reserve training. "For me, it was not possible. Couldn't be away from the medical work all day Saturday and Sunday. At the same time, having completed more than twenty years of service, was eligible for retirement. That I did."

Professionally, he was a pioneer in his field. "Because my bronchoscopic work was done by only three people in Cleveland in the early 1950s," he later wrote, "I went to several east side hospitals as a consultant." Among his consultancies was an experimental alternative health care system, Kaiser's Health Maintenance Organization—one of the nation's first HMOs. "[T]hey built a new hospital," he wrote. He set up the ENT department—meaning "all of the instruments required for the operating room, for out-patient clinic, and for in-patient care."

He also established and supervised Cleveland's first ambulatory surgery unit at Mt. Sinai Hospital. It arose from overcrowding and a hospital bed shortage. "At Mt. Sinai, the hospital was outgrowing its space," he reported. "Surgery was only five rooms—not nearly enough. About 1952, we set up an ambulatory surgery unit, which I set up and ran." After starting with tonsils and adenoids work, "we developed the ability to do eye surgery, simple general surgery, some orthopedics, and more. Ambulatory surgery has come a long way since then, but we started it."

Pop's medical career thrived as he became director of otolaryngology at both Mt. Sinai and Case Western Reserve University Hospital. The latter had been off limits to Jewish interns in 1937, as had St. Luke's, where he had now become an attending physician. He even obtained a patent for one of his diagnostic and surgical inventions. The event in his life most important to me occurred in 1955 when the last of his four daughters, Kit, was born. She eventually became my wife. Her favorite family time by far was Christmas; Santa Claus always put very nice presents under their tree.

Unfortunately for both men, the "times of pure joy and some fulfillment"—the phrase Dick used to describe the decade plus two years that began in 1948—would soon be "a-changing" . . . and not for the better.

SIXTEEN

ARTHUR LINK LEAVES EVANSTON

Dick's 1962 treatise concluded with the inauguration of John F. Kennedy. He wrote his final pages as the Soviet Union had once again blockaded Berlin and the world stood on the edge of disaster. He titled the last section "The Continuing Test: Neither Peace Nor War, 1953–61—in which the American people remain suspended between peace and war, undertake unprecedented commitments, and dwell in dread of a nuclear apocalypse."

He concluded the book with a prescient paragraph: "The struggle for men's minds will be won by those who articulate a dynamic, relevant, and compelling system of values for a world that can either lapse into barbarism or advance to heights yet unscaled. In that contest, the American people can succeed if they mobilize their material and spiritual resources; if they sacrifice some of their debilitating luxuries; if they exhibit courage, tolerance, and compassion; if they do not attempt to remake mankind in their own image. But for that victory to be meaningful, the same creative intelligence must find a way to live with the fire of the gods and spare humanity from a nuclear apocalypse." He had no inkling of the national, international, and personal upheavals that would characterize the decade he himself had just entered when he penned those words.

* * *

As the McCarthyism of the 1950s gave way to relative quiet before the storm of the 1960s, Dick's career progressed. In 1958, the Department of State asked the American Historical Association, American Political Science Association, and American Society of International Law to nominate from their respective ranks a total of eight candidates to sit on its advisory committee and supervise the publication of its documentary series, *Foreign Relations*. In addition to Dick, the AHA chose fellow Harvard alumnus Dexter Perkins, who was teaching at the University of Rochester, and Stanford's Thomas A. Bailey. "The prestige of the nomination led me to believe that perhaps my earlier change of fields from social and intellectual history to diplomacy had not been in vain," he told me. "Bailey served only for one year, but you can see the circularity of history in the way he kept returning to my life." Although Dick's formal term ran only from 1958 to 1964, he actively participated in the committee's work for almost two decades thereafter.

But Dick suffered a serious personal setback in 1960 when Arthur Link accepted Princeton's offer to rejoin its faculty. To keep Link in Evanston after Princeton had tried to lure him in 1955, Dick had swung the full force of Northwestern's administrative apparatus into high gear. Less than a year later, he himself unwittingly contributed to a process eventually taking his dear friend to Princeton forever.

"At a meeting of the American Historical Association in 1957, the secretary of the congressionally created Woodrow Wilson Centennial Commission asked Link and me about the feasibility of a project whereby a scholarly collection of Wilson's papers could be prepared. We responded that the task would be enormous—at least thirty volumes when published—but that it could be done. From there, the Woodrow Wilson Foundation took the baton from the expiring Centennial Commission. The chairman of its board of directors, Princeton alumnus Raymond B. Fosdick, solicited my thoughts on who should head the project. Emerging as the nation's pre-eminent Wilson scholar, Link was the obvious front-runner for the job. I told Fosdick that the only logical candidates for the project were Link and one of my former Harvard students, John Morton Blum. Link knew Wilson better than any other living historian; Blum had more editorial experience."

In early 1958, the committee unanimously chose Link as editor of "The Papers of Woodrow Wilson." Dick joined Link's wife, Margaret, in expressing their concern that Link's ongoing work to complete Wilson's massive and comprehensive biography would be interrupted—perhaps permanently—if he embarked on the Woodrow Wilson Papers project. They urged that with five volumes completed just for the period to April 1917, it would be tragic if the enterprise ended there.

"Surprisingly," Dick continued, "Princeton then entered the picture when Link learned it wanted to house the Wilson project headquarters on its campus. The battle for Link was on once again. I worked valiantly with Northwestern to persuade him that the undertaking could be manned from Evanston and that Link would have all of the flexibility and support necessary to fulfill his tasks. With Billington and Ver Steeg, the four of us comprised one of the strongest collections—for its size—of American history scholars in any college or university. I wanted to keep it that way. With Link's April 1959 election to the executive committee of the Mississippi Valley Historical Association, Northwestern held two— Link and me—of its eleven prestigious seats for the second consecutive year."

Dick then explained how things began to slip away: "In the end, proximity to Washington, D.C.'s historical resources and Princeton's superior Firestone Library tipped the scales of Link's decision in favor of New Jersey." In October 1959, the members of Northwestern's history department officially learned that Arthur Link was headed for Princeton.

Dick was angry and bitter. When he related the saga in a letter to Blum, Princeton agents and alumni bore the brunt of his ire. He described Link's belief that God was "calling" him to the Wilson Papers project: "Arthur's impending departure is a cruel blow to the university, to the department, and to me personally. And it came about in an ironical way that few outsiders can appreciate. You will recall how it all began soon after the New York meeting in 1957. The task was then to persuade Fosdick and Company that they should choose Arthur. And that task had to be faced only when Margaret and I, fortified by your advice, were unable to persuade Arthur that God was not calling him to the task."

Outlining his personal effort to keep Link at Northwestern, he expressed frustration at Princeton's entry into the contest: "Making a virtue of necessity, we then strove to bring the Wilson project to Northwestern in order to anchor Arthur in Evanston. Then at the last minute the Princeton boys got in the game. Why shouldn't they? It would cost the department there not a cent, and they would draw upon Arthur's prestige. I was pretty certain in June 1958, when Arthur left for Oxford, that we were beaten."

He went on to reveal the emotional roller coaster he had ridden while the battle for Link raged. He persuaded Northwestern's leadership to pull out all the stops to keep the Wilson scholar, only to lose in the end: "Then a breath of hope appeared as he was genuinely flattered by the efforts made by Payson Wild and others to make it possible for him to stay here," he continued in his letter to Blum. "He was still undecided when the Wilson people jumped the gun with a statement that he was moving. In mid-September he went to Princeton where [university president] Goheen played it just as skillfully as Dodds had bungled a comparable situation in 1955."

In the end and just as Dick had counseled five years earlier, "grounds of friendship and emotion" were secondary to what Link concluded was best for his career. Even Link's family would have preferred to remain at Northwestern, as Dick observed in his letter to Blum: "At that point we lost to the facts of geography and distance. You know, and Arthur will tell anyone who talks with him, that he prefers to stay with this department and to live in Evanston; but he believes, and he is probably right, that the job can be done more efficiently along the Atlantic seaboard."

After the Northwestern board of trustees accepted Link's resignation on November 30, 1959, he issued a lengthy statement that the campus newspaper printed in full: "I have . . . not only admiration but also deep affection for this university—its students, faculty, and administrative leaders. . . . One does not break easily such ties. . . . We will move next summer, but when we go we will leave much of ourselves behind, and we rejoice in the thought that we will never be strangers in this place."

The Links finally departed from Evanston permanently in the spring of 1960 and returned to the institution that had let Arthur Link slip away a decade earlier. The difference was that in his intervening years with Dick at Northwestern he had become the nation's premier Wilson scholar. "When he left Northwestern," Dick told me, "it was one of the saddest days of my life."

Dick's fearful predictions came true. At Princeton, Link's immersion into Wilson's papers came at a high price: The final volumes of what would have become Link's definitive biography of Woodrow Wilson were never written. For the remainder of his career, Link never produced the quantity and quality of original scholarly work he had generated at Northwestern during the Leopold-Link decade. There was a personal cost as well. Link would say years later that he was never as happy as he had been during his eleven years as Dick's colleague at Northwestern. The feeling was mutual.

* * *

The blow of Link's departure was initially softened when Dick uncharacteristically accepted an invitation to leave his Evanston home and spend a sabbatical year at the Institute for Advanced Study at Princeton, starting in the fall of 1960. There he planned to complete the final steps in transforming his twenty years of classroom lectures into a textbook, a project that had already taken him far too long. In November 1959, more than five years had passed since Dick had initially agreed to write the volume when his publisher Al Knopf wrote to him, "How is our book coming along?"

Shortly after his arrival at the Institute, Dick's earlier acquaintance from the Northwestern centennial celebration, George Kennan, took him to dinner with Institute director J. Robert Oppenheimer. "Oppenheimer was just performing his duties," Dick said in describing to me his encounter with the man who had overseen the creation of the first atomic bomb. "He was friendly and interested, but I never saw him again before I left."

It was unfortunate that Dick and Oppenheimer did not spend a little time discussing their common early experiences. As Dick and I read the most recent Oppenheimer biography, we marveled at the parallel paths of their early lives, even though the similarities were first revealed to him more than forty-five years after the men had met in 1960. Eight years Dick's senior, Oppenheimer was born on the upper west side of New York City, about three blocks from Dick's birthplace. He had a younger brother Frank, who was Dick's age. Like the Leopold boys, Robert and Frank Oppenheimer grew up in affluence—with live-in domestic help, nursemaids, and chauffeurs. Like the Leopolds, the Oppenheimers were nonpracticing Jews who eschewed all aspects of any Jewish heritage.

Robert Oppenheimer did not attend the Franklin School. Rather, he and his brother were enrolled in the Ethical Culture School on Central Park West. It had begun as an outgrowth of the Reform Judaism movement in Germany. The school had evolved into a secular institution instilling in its students the belief they were a vanguard for positive change in the world. The story of Oppenheimer's early education caused Dick to wonder aloud why the Leopold boys had not been sent to that school, too: "It certainly would have been more consistent with my parents' assimilation efforts, I think." Oppenheimer attended the almost entirely Jewish Camp Koenig for a single year during the summer of 1920; that was Dick's first summer there and Harry's third. However, the reported story of Robert's vicious hazing experience at the camp came as a complete surprise to Dick.

Oppenheimer also attended Harvard University during its distinctly anti-Semitic period under President A. Lawrence Lowell, but as an undergraduate. He studied under physics professor Percy Bridgman, who would be among Dick's fist-ball team members a decade later and an eventual Nobel Prize winner. Bridgman's letter of recommendation described Oppenheimer as "a Jew, but entirely without the usual qualifications of his race. He is a tall, well set-up young man, with a rather engaging diffidence of manner, and I think you need have no hesitation whatever for any reason of this sort in considering his application." Bridgman's language about Oppenheimer lacking "the usual qualifications of his race" struck both Dick and me as remarkably similar to Arthur Schlesinger Sr.'s description of Oscar Handlin. Of course, one interesting difference between Schlesinger Sr. and Bridgman was that Schlesinger Sr.'s father was Jewish. Another was that Bridgman's description of Oppenheimer's assimilated demeanor was truthful.

Dick's appointment to the Institute placed him in close proximity to the Links for another year. A younger member of his Evanston "family," Princeton freshman Shep Shanley, was also nearby. Dick invited him to dinner monthly. "Dick also let me study in his office when he wasn't using it and I wanted to get away from campus," Shep told me. "And he reassured me over Christmas vacation, when I was fretting over my first set of college final exams."

Dick's time at the Institute also permitted him to spend almost every Sunday with Harry's family, who now lived in Yardley, Pennsylvania, just across the Delaware River from Trenton. With Dick's mother still living at the Wyndham Hotel in New York where she had resided since 1937, he spent six months beginning in September 1960 living near those he loved most. It certainly eased temporarily the withdrawal of Link's physical presence from his life.

* * *

With the uninterrupted time that his sabbatical year in New Jersey had provided, Dick completed his landmark survey, *The Growth of American Foreign Policy.* Dedicating the treatise to his history teachers at Exeter (Whitman), Princeton (Sontag), and Harvard (Merk), he wrote in the preface: "My greatest debt is to my loyal friend and former colleague, Professor Arthur S. Link of Princeton University, who struggled with the first overly long version and showed me how to shorten and improve the work. His frequent encouragement, his generous sharing of an unmatched knowledge of the Wilson era, and his constant readiness to assist helped enormously at every stage of my labors."

The text received favorable reviews and, as Dick explained in 1981, "It sold surprisingly well, was widely reviewed even in professional journals, and became a History Book Club selection. It was the only volume of its type to be included, with a descriptive paragraph, in *The Foreign Affairs 50-Year Bibliography, 1920–1970* (1972)." In our discussions, he expanded on his 1981 remarks: "Publisher Al Knopf was a good friend and was actually disappointed that the book did not sell even better. I think it was too good, if I can say that. What I mean is that I had colleagues, Tom Bailey in particular, tell me they could not use it because the vocabulary was too sophisticated. Nevertheless, I am proud to say that until it became outdated as all such texts eventually do if they are not revised and updated, it was a standard text for advanced courses at Harvard, Yale, Stanford, Princeton ... need I go on?"

In fact, he accomplished the most important mission he had intended for his book. With the ability to convey substantive factual material through assigned readings in his new volume rather than oral presentations, he converted what had been his demanding three-quarter lecture series into a discussion format. Starting with the fall of 1962, C-13 assumed the form that would eventually make it legendary. With the Cuban missile crisis in October of that year, he could not have orchestrated a more dramatic backdrop for the first classroom use of his new book. As he watched that drama unfold, he was grateful that his long-time friend, Arthur Schlesinger Jr., was among the inner circle of President Kennedy's closest advisers. Dick knew the younger Schlesinger would provide reasoned analysis, historical context, and sound judgment to the nation's young leader. He could only hope the advice would be heeded.

* * *

In 1962, Dick returned to Exeter for a short stay as a visitor to appraise its history department. There he spent time with Ernie Gillespie, who was assistant principal after many years of service as a classics teacher—the same job Ernie's father had held when Dick first met his friend as a "lower-middler" in 1926: "I did not know it at the time, but I would not see Ernie again," he told me sadly. I knew we would have to come back to that topic.

"After a year's leave, the Northwestern history department to which I returned in the fall of 1961 had begun to change," Dick continued. "The full-time history faculty numbered twelve during the academic year 1959–1960 after a decade of unusual stability. Ten years later, there would be twenty-two of us. With Link's departure we had gained two men, Robert H. Wiebe and Grady McWhiney. They handled the survey course, which meant I was free of it. More changes were on the horizon as we added James E. Sheridan and John R. McLane in 1961. E. William Monter came in 1963."

In 1963, Dick went to Johns Hopkins and gave the prestigious Albert Shaw Lectures on Diplomatic History, which dated from 1899 and typically produced a book from the lectures that its invited speaker gave over several days in Baltimore. Tom Bailey had given the lectures in 1941. Dick's topic was the battle between the executive and the legislative branches for control over foreign policy.

"The publisher of the Johns Hopkins Press was very disappointed that I did not think my one hundred pages of lecture materials warranted a book," he told me. "But in the end, I was a victim of my own standards because the material was clearly publishable with minimal additional effort by me. I spent the next several years fleshing it out, but I became so busy with other things that time ran out." During the same period, he was also the Taft Lecturer at the University of Cincinnati. His presentation dealt with the conflict between the president and the Senate over treaty making.

Northwestern's American quartet, which had become a trio after Link's departure, shrank to a duo in the spring of 1963 when Ray Billington, who had recruited Dick to Evanston fifteen years earlier, left for California. "Ray had taken several trips to examine the Frederick Jackson Turner papers at the Huntington Library in San Marino," Dick said. "While spending time there on a leave of absence from the university, he decided to embark upon a full-scale biography of the most famous historian of the American West. Because he had the independent financial means to do so, Billington accepted a much lower-paying staff position at the Huntington when he left Northwestern."

In the alumni magazine, Billington explained his unique opportunity and lamented his loss: "I leave Northwestern with great regret. . . . No other university could have attracted me, for I know that none promises so much for the future as Northwestern." Dick assumed Billington's chair as the William Smith Mason Professor of American History in the fall of 1963.

* * *

A few months later, President John F. Kennedy was assassinated. Like Pearl Harbor, it was an event anyone old enough to understand could never forget. Dick was working at home in the early afternoon of November 22, 1963, when his friend Lyndon Shanley called to ask him if he had heard the president had been shot.

"How is Rocky doing?" Dick responded, assuming Shanley was referring to Northwestern's chief executive, J. Roscoe Miller.

"No," said Shanley, "the president of the United States."

Along with most of the world, Dick spent the next several days in front of his television set, mourning the loss of America's young leader who had energized him and an entire generation. He was stunned and disheartened for himself, his country, and his students. "I remember in particular the large gathering of students, most with tears streaming down their cheeks, attending a memorial service at the newly constructed Alice Millar Chapel," Dick remembered with a sadness still lingering forty years later.

* * *

Almost a year after Lyndon Johnson's 1964 landslide election victory, Dick learned that the health of his closest childhood friend, Ernie Gillespie, was failing. The condition seemed to respond to periodic blood transfusions; Dick hoped Ernie's optimistic notes reflected the reality of his situation and, for a while, they did. Meanwhile, Dick served on Northwestern's General Faculty Committee and University Discipline Committee. He also collaborated with Link in producing the third edition of *Problems in American History*.

Although Ethel's health remained relatively good, a series of falls resulting from what she called "blackouts" caused concern, so she moved to Trenton in 1963—to be near Harry's family. By 1966, she was on her way to an Evanston nursing home. "With the inevitable guilt accompanying such a move," Dick wrote long afterward, he found a place for her in Pembridge House, within easy walking distance of his apartment. He prepared a lengthy script for use by those accompanying Ethel on her trip to Chicago. In it, he described with great detail what should and should not be discussed as she made the difficult transition to a new living situation in September 1966. "Above all," he later told me, "no one was to mention that Mother was on her way to a nursing home."

Meanwhile, Dick continued to add government service to his professional resumé. In addition to serving on advisory committees for the Navy and Department of State, he accepted a similar position with the Army. He also became chair of the Northwestern history department in the fall of 1966 as its unprecedented expansion continued.

"By 1966, Gray Boyce, Leften Stavrianos, Richard Brace, and George Romani were the only history faculty who had taught at Northwestern longer than I had," Dick said. "Al Rieber had been hired in 1957 as a one-year replacement for Stavrianos to teach Russian history, but then invited back in 1959 when Stavrianos started concentrating on world history. Rieber was a superb instructor, but left in 1964 for Pennsylvania. James J. Sheehan and George H. Daniels came in 1964. David Joravsky and John A. Rowe joined the department in 1965. In August 1966, Gray Boyce stepped down after eighteen years of service as chairman—a tenure in that position never to be repeated—and I became his successor."

In sharp contrast to Dick's earlier tour of duty as the department's leader, this time there was a contested election, a vote, and a winner. Some faculty members resisted his candidacy and persuaded his esteemed colleague and friend, Clarence Ver Steeg, to run against him. Although the voices of dissent did not prevail, they set the stage for divisiveness that would haunt his tenure as chairman and the entire department itself for years thereafter.

"In my first year as chairman," he continued, "five new members joined the department, the largest number in any single year: Christopher Lasch, Ivor G. H. Wilks, George M. Frederickson, Frank R. Safford, and Conrad D. Totman."

* * *

Unfortunately, Ernie Gillespie's health took a dramatic turn for the worse in the spring of 1967. On June 11, Ernie summoned the strength to deliver a commencement address to Exeter's graduating class. It became an instant classic that remains part of Exeter's proudest traditions. As the struggles over racial inequality and Vietnam swept the country, the man who had been known for his childhood stutter spoke eloquent words that still endure at the Academy.

"I am not advocating docility," he said, "but it is equally useless to disown all allegiances to the government however blind and perverse its policies may seem on some issues. One can best work to change policy as a member." His final remarks provided a glimpse into why Ernie Gillespie had remained one of Dick's best friends for forty years: "You have a lot to do. This is no time to concern ourselves with nostalgia. As a matter of fact, I don't believe anybody has ever claimed that Exeter is a warm nest. But I hope, and I expect, that when you find yourselves involved in skirmishes on the frontiers of barbarism, which are not very far away, you'll strike some shrewd blow in favor of civilization. Some day you'll come to show us your trophies and your scars, and we'll be glad to see you." Among those in the audience was Exeter history instructor F. Sheppard Shanley, the son of Dick's close friend and Northwestern colleague J. Lyndon Shanley.

On October 30, 1967, Ernie wrote his last letter. Thanking Dick for a note praising Ernie's commencement address, he explained the background of his speech: "We had a fairly steady succession in late winter and spring of visiting speakers advocating everything from civil disobedience to treason and I'd have been even more unhappy if I hadn't believed this was a minority view. All the speakers were invited by extreme liberal groups of students. The response of the seniors was heartening. . . ."

After describing yet another decline in his health, Ernie concluded with the topic that had bound the two friends since adolescence: "How did you like the Red Sox? Incredible. With one pitcher and one hitter, a bunch of journeymen jerks and a daring manager, they stumble their way to the series and carry the Cards to seven games. Joe Vosmik and Earl Averill never played in the series, but

George Thomas, batting in the low 100s and not good enough to play for Simmy Murch, actually got into one of the games." Vosmik and Averill had played in the 1920s and 1930s for Ernie's favorite team, the Cleveland Indians; Murch was Exeter's baseball coach; and Thomas was a former student at the school.

Ernie Gillespie died on November 5, 1967. In anticipation of his sixtieth class reunion in 1989, Dick wrote, "The class of 1967 never had the opportunity to show him its trophies and scars. But it had heard and the alumni had read a message of challenge and hope from one of Exeter's most illustrious sons."

* * *

Pop's career continued its climb throughout the 1950s, too. Although remaining in Shaker Heights, the family moved from its modest home on Rolliston Road to one of the small mansions on South Park Boulevard. Pop was elected to numerous professional medical societies and traveled with Sue to conferences around the world. His talents alone produced his success; the earlier obstacles to a Jew's advancement prior to the war seemed less formidable.

As a direct and opposing reaction to the Zionist movement, Pop and Sue left Rabbi Abba Hillel Silver's congregation and founded an even more "Reform" temple than the one she had attended as a child. Later, their daughters went to "Sunday school" there and were "confirmed" after eighth grade, but none of them went through a bat mitzvah process or ceremony. Apart from the requirements for confirmation, they rarely went to temple.

There was a continuity to Pop's social life for which Dick had no parallel experience. During adolescence, Pop had attended parties and dances held at the Excelsior Club. "This was THE social club of the community," he wrote, "the members being exclusively the 1840 German Jewish families again. . . . The Oakwood was the golf/country club, with almost the same membership." During the Depression, the Excelsior merged with the Oakwood Club, in which Pop and Sue retained their respective families' multigenerational memberships as adults, even though neither Pop nor Sue played golf or tennis. "[Oakwood] provided summer activities for the younger kids, until they grew up and went to seasonal camps," he reported. "Dined there with friends. Attended parties there. Not being golfers we were limited to the social life of the club. Membership was then mostly the old families who came from Germany in the 1840s, several generations ago."

Notwithstanding the Jewish exclusivity of the Oakwood Club, the process of his daughters' assimilation continued in important and systematic respects. All of the girls attended an exclusively ("by invitation only") Jewish dancing school where they met boys of similar background and upbringing. Depending on bloodlines, there was an "A" group and a "B" group. As "sixth-generation Clevelanders," Sue Goldsmith Loeb's daughters were always in the "A" group. But the overriding purpose of Flossie's Dancing School was not to serve as matchmaker for Jewish adolescents. In fact, the experience ended when high school began. Rather, it was a finishing school in the truest sense of the concept. Its aim was to train its young charges in proper social etiquette and to facilitate the process whereby the next generation entered mainstream secular society. Perhaps Exeter had played that role in Dick's life; however, it is a shame he never became sufficiently confident as a young man to ask a girl to dance with him.

SEVENTEEN

1968

It was a momentous year in modern American history. Ironically, subsequent polling demonstrated that many of those who had voted for Senator Eugene McCarthy of Minnesota in the March 1968 New Hampshire presidential primary thought the McCarthy on the Democratic ballot was Joe, the notorious anticommunist crusader who had embarrassed the nation fifteen years earlier. In fact, they were voting against their intent and in favor of the liberal antiwar candidate whose stance on the single issue of Vietnam would help drive Lyndon Johnson from the presidential race two weeks later, even though Johnson actually won that early primary by a narrow margin.

Only three days after Johnson announced he would not seek or accept his party's nomination to serve another term, Martin Luther King Jr. prophetically told his audience that, like Moses, he had "been to the mountaintop. It really doesn't matter what happens now. . . . Like anybody, I would like to live a long life. Longevity has its place, but I'm not concerned about that now. . . . I've seen the Promised Land. I may not get there with you. But I want you to know, tonight, that we, as people, will get to the Promised Land. . . . Mine eyes have seen the glory of the coming of the Lord. . . ." Less than twenty-four hours later, an assassin's bullet ended King's life as he stood on his Memphis motel room balcony.

* * *

A few weeks after King's murder, Dick was making his way down the stairs from his apartment when he encountered a suspicious group of African American students. It was the day student activists took over the Northwestern administration building.

"I followed my usual route to Harris Hall. I went out the back entrance of my sixth-floor apartment and walked down the stairs," he told me. "As I passed the laundry area, I was surprised to see a large number of African Americans gathered.

143

Aware of the rioting in the immediate aftermath of King's assassination and concerned about what might be afoot in Evanston, I walked briskly to my office and phoned Payson Wild. The line was busy."

Before the morning was over, that assembly of students had moved from its position in the apartments and into the administration building across the street at 619 Clark, which housed the offices of Northwestern's president and senior leadership, including Payson Wild. The group had no trouble taking over the defenseless structure, from which it declared its demands: There should be more African American faculty members; there should be more African American students; and there should be more financial aid for them. The insurgents made racial strife at Northwestern a national news story, and Dick had walked past them only a few moments before it had all begun.

"If only Payson had answered the phone," he continued. "Although what, if anything, he could have done is an entirely different and unknown matter. But Payson would have done something. That's for sure."

* * *

Throughout the spring, senators Eugene McCarthy and Robert F. Kennedy competed for leadership of the antiwar and racial activist constituencies of the Democratic Party as another Minnesotan, Vice President Hubert Humphrey, carried forward the incumbent administration's banner. Humphrey had an easy ride to the nomination after an assassin took Kennedy's life on the night of the California primary in June. Humphrey's losing fate in the November general election was sealed during the violent convention in Chicago that nominated him two months later. Northwestern's Evanston campus was only a few miles to the north.

When classes began at Northwestern in the fall of 1968, the Students for a Democratic Society (SDS) were trying to ride the coattails of protests around the country, but with relatively little impact on the campus. Richard Nixon won a close presidential contest in November, but the more important event for Dick personally came a few days later on November 7, when assistant professor of philosophy and education Hugh G. Petrie placed before a meeting of the college faculty a seemingly innocuous motion with potentially dramatic consequences. He wanted Dean Robert Strotz to appoint a committee "to investigate the purposes, functions, and relations of the Department of Naval Science to the College of Arts and Sciences of Northwestern University. Such an investigation should indicate the history of the relationships as well as present conditions. It should be aimed at determining what form future relations should assume."

Dick smelled trouble and the obvious assault on the Naval Reserve Officers' Training Corps (NROTC) that lay behind the motion. He immediately wrote to Strotz, expressing his concerns: "During the debate this afternoon on the Petrie resolution, I was struck by the fact that on this issue, as on so many under current discussion, the advocates of change are persons who are relatively new on the campus and who cannot, therefore, have full knowledge of the historical antecedents of the problems under consideration. . . ."

Dick offered Strotz the perspective he thought his chosen profession provided: "As a historian, who is aware of how much easier it is to tear down than to build up and of how quickly one can destroy by one act an edifice that has been constructed over the years, I strongly urge that you appoint to the committee to investigate the role of the Department of Naval Science one of the members of the faculty who have been on the scene for some time." Strotz honored Dick's request, but the battle to save the NROTC at Northwestern had only just begun.

* * *

Northwestern had been one of the original six NROTC programs created in 1923, along with Harvard, Yale, Georgia Tech, the University of California at Berkeley, and the University of Washington. When first established, the program provided no financial support to its student participants—just uniforms and related military paraphernalia. As America moved closer to entering World War II, Congress created many more NROTC outposts throughout the nation's campuses. When the war ended, Congress gave the Navy a tremendous recruiting advantage over its Army and Air Force ROTC competitors with the establishment of financial scholarships for student participants in the program.

The NROTC program at Northwestern had faced earlier challenges before the Petrie resolution. During the 1966–1967 academic year, the managing editor of the student newspaper launched a one-woman crusade to get the program removed from the campus, but the effort failed. Nevertheless, student radicalism pervaded colleges and universities, and the NROTC remained a target throughout the period.

But directing criticism at the NROTC was only one aspect of the radicals' tactics. By 1968, widespread interference with daily lectures grew. Student dissidents targeted particular classes for "liberation," which meant that once the radicals entered the room, everyone could either sit around and talk about the war or go home. Eventually, the history department had to consider its approach to such conduct. The entire issue damaged Dick's close friendship with a younger colleague; it took more than a decade to complete repairs.

"The department had continued to grow," Dick explained, "and I think that made it more difficult to maintain the spirit of collegiality that had developed among a smaller group who had come to know each other well over a long period of time. Robert H. Lerner joined in 1967; Edward E. Malefakis, Robert J. Bezucha, and T. William Heyck in 1968; T. H. Breen first appeared on the 1970–1971 faculty roster. Robert H. Wiebe was initially hired in 1960 and had gained tenure in 1966. He had exploded onto the scene with his 1967 book, *The Search for Order*,

1877–1920, which offered unique and imaginative interpretations of the Progressive Era in American history. Wiebe and I had been quite close until an incident shattered our friendship for a long time."

In November 1968, Wiebe received a letter from Dick, then the department chairman, that was, to say the least, stern. The facts surrounding the episode remained unclear to Dick when we spoke about it almost forty years later; however, his harsh words communicated dismay over a recent history department meeting at which he felt that Wiebe's suggestions for dealing with the classroom "liberation" problem had ambushed him. Dick did not like surprises.

Wiebe responded with an equally blistering missive, suggesting that Dick should be grateful for Wiebe's efforts to maintain departmental harmony and noting particularly Wiebe's success in dissuading a group of student radicals from disrupting Dick's foreign policy discussion class. Dick had the last word; he said Wiebe overestimated his own influence because the reason Dick's course had escaped liberation was the class's early meeting time: "I wish you had not dissuaded 'a group of undergraduates from creating a scene' in C-13. I might have discovered what I had done or not done to cause them anguish, and a protest at eight in the morning would have had some novelty."

"Radicals," Dick later told me, "will not get up at eight in the morning, however noble the cause."

* * *

"To maintain my balance I did more teaching than any chairman, before or since," he wrote twenty-three years later. He also added to his public service when he assumed the post he would come to regard as among his most important professional contributions outside the classroom: member of the National Archives and Records Service Advisory Council. Eventually, he became its chairman. The council had an enduring impact on the rules governing access to the country's most significant records. He continued to pry open the secret pockets of government so future historians could shine the light of day on them. Such access afforded the necessary factual foundation vital to a true understanding of history and to the functioning of a democratic government.

Dick's unprecedented teaching load as department chairman combined with outside commitments to leave him with less time for the scholarly research and writing he loved. It was a subject to which he often returned in our discussions: "In that regard, I had already lived through a setback of sorts when I accepted Harvard's offer of a five-year appointment. It had required that I change fields from social and intellectual history to diplomacy. After I had started over in a new area unrelated to my dissertation, World War II next had provided an unwelcome interruption. When I finally landed what looked to be a permanent position at Northwestern in 1948, I spent several summers in the early 1950s reading materials in the manuscripts division of the Library of Congress in the hope that I could complete a scholarly work on the history of Anglophobia, but that topic was too broad. Moving instead to the narrower question of American foreign policy since 1890, I felt the frustration of all scholars who maintain high standards. In other words, I simply did not have the time required to do all that I wanted to do at the level I wanted to do it."

* * *

Although Pop's career flourished, he found the 1960s to be a tough time, too. As the decade began, his mother suffered a fatal heart attack while taking the European vacation that had been her lifelong dream. As social and political unrest intensified, he became increasingly conservative politically. Some of his views arose from very personal experiences: Teenage gang problems in the park across the street required him to leave the South Park Boulevard home in Shaker Heights that he loved. The family's new house was located in the predominantly Jewish suburb of Beachwood; the move seemed to take his assimilation efforts a major step backward.

He defended his conservatism on international politics as the fundamental lesson learned from Hitler and the war in which he had fought to destroy the Nazis. He fervently believed that America's dominance in the world required it to resist tyrants and dictators in Southeast Asia and anywhere else they appeared. Hitler— Stalin—Khrushchev—Castro—Ho Chi Minh—the names were unimportant to him; all embodied a dangerous megalomania that civilization could not tolerate. Most other members on Sue's side of the family had become progressively more liberal. Just as the Vietnam War had divided America, political discussions at Thanksgiving dinners and holiday gatherings at Pop's house developed into verbal combat and intense emotional exchanges leaving open wounds for years.

Dick's politics moved him in the opposite direction from Pop's, but his actions sometimes rendered him enigmatic to those who did not know him well. For example, most people assumed that a political liberal in the late 1960s would have fought, as many did, to banish ROTC programs from the nation's universities. Yet, as Dick would write more than twenty-five years later, "Immodest as it may seem, I did more than anyone—administrator, faculty member, uniformed officer, or student—to save the NROTC program here and to prevent Northwestern (one of the six original units) from surrendering, as did Harvard and Yale (two of the other six), Princeton, Stanford, and Dartmouth. But that belongs to a chapter in my autobiography, not yours." Indeed it does, and it comes next.

EIGHTEEN

The Assault on the NROTC

It was the worst of times for Dick—and getting worse. January 1969 began with the inauguration of Richard Nixon as president. The Northwestern history department he had chaired since the fall of 1966 and helped build to greatness over the prior seventeen years became increasingly and publicly divided; private disagreements among colleagues became fodder for *The Daily Northwestern*. With the earlier departures of his closest colleagues Link and Billington, he felt alone professionally, but there was more bad news to come. When Dick's mother died "rather painlessly" of a cerebral hemorrhage in March 1969, he suffered his most serious personal loss since Ernie Gillespie's death and Arthur Link's departure to Princeton earlier in the decade. After cremation, a private interment at Rosehill Cemetery joined Ethel with the previously transported ashes of Harry Sr. Meanwhile, the NROTC program was still in danger at Northwestern.

* * *

"By April 1969, those attacking the NROTC had sought to expand Petrie's initial request of November 1968," Dick told me. "The move was on to use the investigating committee as a vehicle for a full-blown challenge to the program's continued existence. The student newspaper became the critics' strongest ally. In May 1969, a new group of student editors assumed command of *The Daily Northwestern*. They had been freshman compatriots of the managing editor who had failed in her 1966–1967 mission to banish the NROTC program from the campus. Her successors had now taken up the cause and made it theirs. The student newspaper reflected their goal. The fact that Harvard, Yale, Dartmouth, Stanford, and other institutions with which Northwestern liked to compare itself had banned ROTC programs on their campuses virtually guaranteed faculty and administration attention to the controversy. The additional publicity that *The Daily* was giving the issue, coupled with the increasing agitation provided by the SDS, meant it was only a matter of time until some event precipitated a campus explosion and a public university-wide debate on Northwestern's relationship to the federal government and the Vietnam War."

That time and that event came on May 15, 1969, during an NROTC drill session in the middle of the campus on bucolic Deering Meadow. The SDS interrupted the proceedings, hurling insults at the midshipmen and putting on a guerrilla theater that mimicked and ridiculed their fellow students. They even tried to move onto the field and break ranks. Even so, Dick was convinced that the whole episode was mild and any furor over it might well have disappeared if the dean of students had handled it differently.

"Rather than allow the largely ineffective demonstration to spend itself with little impact, the dean brought some of the protesting students before the University Discipline Committee. Now the SDS had achieved exactly what it had sought: escalation of and continued attention to the matter. Five students were charged with misconduct. One was acquitted; three were placed on disciplinary probation; one was suspended until September 1970. Although the proceedings had been conducted fairly, *The Daily* now had what it needed to exploit the matter as a free speech issue, divide the campus, and sway moderates to their cause. In all of this, the NROTC was an innocent bystander, but a logical whipping boy."

Dick thought that *The Daily*'s "blatant misrepresentations" had allowed the SDS to enlist sufficient support to disrupt entirely the NROTC drill scheduled for that afternoon. When the weather intervened to force the drilling inside at Swift Armory, the protesters followed. By the end of May, Dick became convinced that there was a majority sentiment among the faculty to detach NROTC from the college of arts and sciences, but not yet enough votes to banish it from the campus altogether. The issue of credit toward graduation for naval science courses remained open.

"Faculty members who opposed the program wanted to force its withdrawal from the campus as a demonstration of unified academic outrage at a hostile government and the Vietnam War," he later told me. "The first step in that effort was the attempt to cease granting any credit toward graduation for course work taught by naval officers who simply could not measure up to faculty standards. If the university disallowed such credit, midshipmen would confront increasing course loads that would effectively force their abandonment of the program. The Department of Defense threatened to up the stakes when it decreed that any university failing to give academic credit for ROTC course work would be denied government grants."

The issue came to a head during the academic year's final faculty meeting in early June 1969. Dick's position was straightforward—"fair play," as he explained in his address: "I beg the indulgence of the faculty to make a speech, not a few remarks, on the subject under discussion. I have been waiting ever since last fall for an appropriate moment to speak; although I am not certain that this is the best opportunity, it may be the last at which my thoughts have any influence. In retrospect, I am sorry that I did not have my say earlier . . ."

After acknowledging the work and good faith of those who had labored to produce recommendations with which he disagreed, he went to the heart of his concerns: "What, Mr. Dean, is the issue we should deliberate upon? The subject under discussion is not the Vietnam War. It is not the Military-Industrial Complex. It is not the Selective Service Act. It is not the University Discipline Committee. It is not the action of the faculties at Harvard, Yale, or Dartmouth. It is not even the role of the ROTC in our universities. The issue is the NROTC program on this campus—what it means to Northwestern University, what it means to our students." He then outlined the three reasons why the NROTC had a place on the campus.

"First, it is good for the nation. The armed forces need officers who have been trained in the best universities. We do not want an officer corps trained solely at West Point, Annapolis, or Colorado Springs. The nation needs a reserve component. Anyone whose memory goes back to 1940 will recall that there could be no rapid expansion of the fleet after the fall of France if there had been no NROTC graduates. The need for experienced reservists was demonstrated again in June 1950 after the invasion of South Korea.

"Second, the NROTC is good for the university. I will not belabor the scholarship assistance that the regular program provides, except to say that the suggestion of the critics—that the university assume the payment of scholarships—is both impractical financially and wide of the mark. The best midshipmen come to Northwestern because they want both a Northwestern education and a naval commission. Certainly, the program has attracted, while I have been on the faculty since 1948, a large number of able yet diverse students. It is somewhat ironical, in view of *The Daily Northwestern's* current crusade, that two *Daily* editors since 1948 were members of the NROTC—Herbert Hart in 1949 and Jon Dressel in 1956, while another midshipman, Paul Stanford, was managing editor in 1964. The diversity of this group was well illustrated in 1961, when one midshipman was president of the Young Republicans and another president of the Young Democrats. The achievements of this group are evidenced this year when one midshipman was elected to Phi Beta Kappa and named the outstanding senior in political science, while another was chosen by both students and faculty for the annual Eshbach award, which goes to the outstanding senior in the Technological Institute. . . ."

By now the room was completely silent, except for his strong and unwavering baritone. He proceeded to the point nearest and dearest to his heart, but listed last for this audience: "Third, the NROTC is good for those who wish to participate. I find it completely unhistorical and illogical to argue that our universities should not provide training for those who want to make the military a profession, just as it provides training for future ministers, lawyers, doctors, and professors. Not all midshipmen, of course, will end up as professional officers. Indeed, the majority will not. But during their days of active duty and during their years of reserve status, they will be better for having combined their military preparation with a liberal arts or other academic preparation. As to the emotion-packed argument that 'teaching killing has no place in a university,' I might remind the faculty that we do not ban the teaching of nuclear physics because someone might make a bomb; that we do not avoid the study of Marxism because the student might become a Communist; and that we do not discourage investigation of social deviants because the student might become one himself. In short, let us play fair with these young men who feel they want to serve their country, whose judgment on the morality of any given war may differ from those of other students."

His audience remained quiet as he concluded, "Finally, as to the current agitation among the undergraduates. I do not myself believe that the vast majority of students demand an end to the NROTC. There has been no continuing demand in the past; indeed, there was little demand this year until the classic pattern of provocation, response, and indignation—on matters for which the NROTC was not responsible—took place. But even if I am mistaken in my reading of true campus sentiment, I would like to make the well-worn point that Northwestern University is not the property of a single generation of students; it is the product of many years of efforts and dedication by those who have gone before. As has been well-said elsewhere, 'It is the right of every student generation to seek orderly change and renewal in the university; it is the duty of students, faculty, administration and alumni alike to make sure that change does not destroy the very values of free inquiry and individual rights.' It is easy, gentlemen, to destroy in one year what has been built up painfully over a long period of time. By its very nature, the NROTC has little with which to defend itself. The staff is transient in character; the midshipmen constitute a small fraction of the undergraduate body. It is in the sense of fair play that I appeal to the faculty to deliberate fully, to take into account what the NROTC on this campus—and I speak only about this campus—has accomplished, and to consider how this viable and worthwhile enterprise can be made still more valuable and creditable in the future."

When he sat down, the room erupted in sustained applause—an extraordinary occurrence for such staid meetings. Telephone calls, messages, and letters of praise came from all quarters and from those on both sides of the issue. Although Dick's views did not prevail on the specific vote taken at that time—whether the NROTC should separate from the college within a few years—he had made his point and turned the tide of the debate. The next issue would be whether to confer any grad-uation credit for naval science courses, but Dick's address provided NROTC sup-porters with a critical boost in the only battle that mattered: whether the NROTC should be terminated altogether.

Shortly thereafter, he addressed the new naval officers in the class of 1969 at their commissioning ceremony and told each to hold up his end of their implicit bargain with him: "You are about to enter the naval service. . . . Some will become part of the naval profession. You do so at a moment when criticism of the armed forces is again rampant. Each of you, it seems to me, has an obligation, an oppor-tunity, to prove how unfounded and unjust most of this criticism is. As midship-men, each of you had the opportunity, by your words and deeds, to counter the at-tacks this spring. Some of you responded intelligently and courageously; all of you must do so in the future. If those of us who believe in the NROTC program, be-cause we have seen its value for over thirty years, are to be effective on the nation's campuses, we need your support, your help, but most of all your example—your example of pride in service and excellence in leadership. Do not fail us. And so goodbye. Come back soon. Come back often. We will not forget you." He crossed out from his prepared remarks what would have been his penultimate line: "Do not forget us."

On October 2, 1969, the "Report of the General Faculty Committee on the NROTC" was formally presented. It confirmed that Dick's efforts aimed at pre-serving the NROTC program at Northwestern had hit their mark: "While there are many points to be made, one is predominant in our thinking," the report con-cluded. "This is the need to have as many of the career officers in our armed forces as possible educated in civilian universities. The combination of the liberal arts courses available at these schools and the constant contact with students who are not military cadets and who may have quite different views of current events can-not help but give a broad base for their future careers. The two major sources of officers are the military academies and officer candidate schools (OCS). While academies serve a function, the education they give is definitely limited. And ex-cept in time of full mobilization, most OCS candidates come from the enlisted ranks, again giving narrow background. Therefore, in order to help provide offi-cers with a broad educational background, we recommend that Northwestern University continue to participate in the NROTC program. . . . In our discussions with students and faculty, we have found two major concerns expressed in con-junction with the NROTC program. One arises from the opposition to and frus-trations with the war in Vietnam. The other is the fear of the influence of the industrial-military complex on our nation. We do not mean to dismiss or minimize these concerns, but for the reasons stated above, we feel that they can best be met by training officers for the military in universities such as Northwestern."

When Dick spoke to the University Senate on October 9, 1969, he opposed only the report's conclusion that naval science courses should not count toward satisfaction of degree requirements. He asked that this issue be reserved for a later time, after the revised NROTC curriculum could be assessed. He urged special caution in light of the Navy's threats to act against institutions failing to grant any credit for such courses. But on the most important issue, he supported the report. In the key purpose of his original mission, he was well on his way to success.

The Curriculum Committee issued a report resulting in another faculty meeting on January 29, 1970. Although on sabbatical, Dick returned to speak one last time on the recommendation favoring degree credit for only a few naval science courses: "I hope that the recommendations of the majority will pass. They seem to me to be a reasonable compromise. They make life more difficult for future midshipmen, but without working so many obstacles as to discourage enrollment. They leave us with a viable program. If to some, the majority report seems to err on the side of generosity, I would remind you that the faculty has tended, of late, to be generous in curriculum matters and that such an attitude in this case will enable us to maintain a program that, over the years, has proved beneficial to the nation, advantageous to the university, and—above all—rewarding to students who have freely chosen to participate."

On the all-important vote on an amendment to the report that would end all degree credit for all naval science courses, those who sought to drive the NROTC off campus lost by three votes—sixty-nine to sixty-six. Dick had assured that the NROTC program would remain at Northwestern. He had persuaded a sufficient number of his colleagues that sentiments about the Vietnam War should not cloud a clear-headed decision about a program that had benefited the country, the university, and the students who chose to participate. He became the program's most articulate defender and, without his support, it would have been terminated.

Dick was also correct in his assessing the difference between the ease of destroying something built over many years and the more daunting task thereafter of bringing it back to life. On all of the campuses that eliminated the NROTC programs in the 1960s, including Harvard, Yale, Stanford, and those "other institutions with which Northwestern likes to compare itself," the program has never returned. Nevertheless, by 2006 the program's declining enrollment at Northwestern once again placed it in harm's way. So it is certainly possible that Dick's efforts postponed the inevitable, but the many Northwestern midshipmen who graduated and became officers during the thirty-five years after it survived the 1969 assault remained forever grateful to him.

* * *

Regardless of political ideology, Dick always insisted that discourse remain civilized. During the Vietnam War protest days in the late 1960s, he was hosting a guest speaker in Northwestern's Tech Auditorium, the largest gathering place on the campus and the site of his survey course lectures to more than five hundred students at a time. Student demonstrators appeared and began to disrupt the event. Dick walked to the podium and projected his distinctive baritone that boomed throughout the cavernous room: "You will desist! You will desist!" A remarkable testament to his stature among all factions, Dick needed to say nothing else. The demonstrators left the auditorium, and the guest speaker resumed without further interruption.

That all of Dick's efforts were first and foremost about the individual students there can be no doubt; his experience with student John W. Duffield '68 proves it. In October 1969, Duffield found himself in the Army and sent Dick an urgent message, asking that he vouch for the sincerity of a belated petition for conscientious objector status in connection with the Vietnam War. Dick and a colleague, economics professor Karl deSchweinitz (a Quaker who had opposed Dick's position on the NROTC program), supported the request. Two months later, Duffield's petition was granted, even though it had come far too late in the process for anyone to think it stood any realistic chance for success.

*　*　*

Pop had to accept an additional appointment at a Cleveland area hospital to pay his twin daughters' college tuition bills during the 1960s. Sue wanted him to raise his standard fee for an office visit, but he refused because he feared it would price low-income families out of decent medical care. When the twins graduated from college, the financial pressures eased. He took Sue and Kit to several European medical conventions.

The family also continued a tradition it had established earlier with the help of a program called Cleveland International. Through it, a college-age student from a foreign country lived with the Loeb family for the entire summer. They came from around the world—Sweden, Chile, India—and most were not Jewish. In retrospect, this appears to have been another component of Pop's personal assimilation program—specifically, to advance assimilation to the next generation. He wanted his daughters to understand that "people is people"—and hoped his guests would take that message home to their respective countries. The foreign student who remained closest to the family for decades after her first visit in 1964 was an Iranian Jew whose aristocratic family traced its roots back twenty-five hundred years. In 1967, she returned to Cleveland for graduate study; the rest of her family left Iran during the Islamic revolution of 1979.

NINETEEN

THE ROOSEVELT LIBRARY
INVESTIGATION

As the academic year 1968–1969 was ending, Dick was ready for a rest and the long-awaited sabbatical he had planned for the following year. Even so, in August 1969, he wrote to a colleague that he would continue to assist the effort to save the NROTC program, which he did: "I shall be on leave next year, but I probably will not wander very far from Evanston. Hence, I should be available to give support and aid and, if necessary, I will even come to an occasional faculty meeting." With a Northwestern presidential fellowship to pursue research and writing, he anticipated a happy return to the intellectual pursuits that had always nourished and revitalized him. Unfortunately, life would not be as easy in the coming year as he had hoped.

* * *

"I had returned from a conference in Japan in August 1969 and was just settling back into Evanston when, on Wednesday, September 3, 1969, I received a telephone call from Paul L. Ward, executive secretary of the American Historical Association," he told me. "While I was at Harvard, Ward had been a resident tutor at Adams House. In 1934, he received a master's degree and in 1940 his Ph.D. He was calling me because he had a mess on his hands."

The mess was that a day earlier, the *Washington Post* had run a major story covering Rice University professor Francis L. Loewenheim's accusations of civil and potentially criminal wrongdoing directed against the federal employees who ran the Franklin D. Roosevelt Presidential Library in Hyde Park, New York. He said the AHA, the Organization of American Historians (OAH), and the National Archives and Records Service of the General Services Administration (NARS) were refusing to investigate his charges. His claims of initial wrongdoing had now exploded into allegations of an organizational cover-up. The most prestigious organizations of American history scholars in the world were under siege.

Ward wanted Dick to chair a joint ad hoc AHA-OAH committee to investigate Loewenheim's assertions fully, fairly, and completely, letting the chips fall where they may. What had begun as a researcher's simple complaint that he had been deprived of access to a handful of historical materials had mushroomed into a national news story. The situation would continue to command public attention in a way that put the entire profession on trial, along with NARS and the staffs that were running presidential libraries throughout the country. The publicity now swirling around the controversy required a distinguished man to head the investigation; Dick's reputation and integrity in the profession were widely known and above reproach. The inquiry had to be thorough and its conclusions trusted. Ward told Dick that he could think of no others who commanded the stature Richard W. Leopold could bring to the task.

"Ward said that the entire job could be completed in two weeks," Dick told me. "Heh, heh, heh . . ."

Dick reluctantly accepted the assignment. Four days later, on September 7, 1969, he viewed with amazement the *New York Times Book Review*'s reprint of a letter signed by nineteen of the nation's leading historians. The letter summarized Loewenheim's charges and demanded a "complete investigation" of them. Most of the signatories were well known to Dick, including his old friend and former Northwestern colleague Ray Billington.

As set forth in the *Times* letter, Loewenheim's assertions were serious and shook the very core of the profession. He claimed that while he was conducting research at the Roosevelt Library, the staff had deliberately and systematically withheld materials it knew would have been useful to him. Library archivist Edgar Nixon had subsequently included the documents in question among fourteen hundred items in a three-volume book, *Franklin D. Roosevelt and Foreign Affairs, 1933–1937*. As Dick was leaving Princeton to begin graduate study at Harvard in 1933, United States ambassador to Nazi Germany, William E. Dodd, was corresponding with President Roosevelt. Although not specifically mentioned in the *Times* letter thirty-five years later, the supposedly withheld materials actually boiled down to six letters exchanged between the men.

The *Times* letter also claimed that the Harvard University Press's private publication of the three-volume work in 1969 was illegal and improper. According to Loewenheim, the Government Printing Office should have published the presidential papers. Harvard's two unsuccessful attempts to copyright the volumes likewise raised troubling issues of private rights to public materials. Moreover, the letter stated, other scholars "had various documents at Hyde Park denied or withheld from them, seriously affecting their work."

Loewenheim urged that these concerns were sufficiently serious to warrant a complete investigation into the recently published three volumes of material from the Roosevelt Library, as well as the operation of all presidential libraries. As he read the *Times,* which also reprinted the reply of the nation's archivist James B. Rhoads, Dick began to fear that what was supposed to be a two-week job appeared to be developing into much more. The assignment filled Dick's life for a year and took an immeasurable personal toll.

* * *

"In our first conversation about the ad hoc committee on September 3, Ward had told me that two others had already agreed to serve as members," Dick summarized. "One was Alfred D. Chandler Jr., who taught at Johns Hopkins and had graduated from the Harvard class of '40. Al had sat in on one of my classes while he was an undergraduate; Paul Buck had been his tutor. The other was Dewey W. Grantham Jr. of Vanderbilt, a noted historian of the South. But before I could even get the work of the committee off the ground, I learned that Loewenheim's lawyer, William D. Zabel from New York City and a member of the Princeton class of '58, was already on the attack. The day after the publication of the *Times* letter, Zabel wrote a letter to Ward questioning the jurisdiction of my committee and asserting mysteriously that one or more of its three members had a 'conflict of interest.'"

Zabel's subsequent telegram remained conspicuous in its omission of any evidence to support his conflict-of-interest allegations, and it recast the September 7 *New York Times* letter as suggesting that the demand of twenty historians (the nineteen other signatories plus Loewenheim) was "for a congressional investigation." In fact, the *Times* letter had made no such demand and at least one signatory, Ray Billington, later told Dick that he was surprised to see the letter reprinted in the *Times* because he had never given any permission for such a use of his name. "The problem," Dick said as he recalled his old friend, "was that Ray would sign almost anything that someone put in front of him. He was too trusting."

Nevertheless, the prospect that Congress might involve itself in the fray, as Loewenheim and his lawyer persistently urged, gave Dick's committee an even more profound sense of urgency and seriousness. Yet for more than two months, Ward and Loewenheim jousted with Dick over the role of the Leopold committee in the planned investigation.

"We were stymied as we limited our work during that period to reviewing the documentary record framing the controversy," Dick told me. "I gained an uncomfortable insight into what lay before me when I read Loewenheim's December 25, 1968, letter to Ward."

In that letter, Loewenheim described a telephone call with Max Hall, an editor at the Harvard University Press, in which he described Hall as one who "throughout the conversation—maintained a studied air of who in effect was I (connected with no more prestigious school than Rice) to question the almighty decisions of the Harvard University Press." Dick quickly realized that Loewenheim had a gigantic chip on his shoulder and a lawyer who seemed determined to help him keep it.

* * *

At the end of October 1969, the AHA reaffirmed the charter of Dick's committee and urged the completion of initial findings by December 20, 1969. Loewenheim countered with a letter to Congressman George H. W. Bush of Texas; it reiterated an earlier request to representative Bob Eckhardt for a congressional investigation into his charges. Bush placed the letter in the *Congressional Record.* On November 17, Dick's committee sent initial letters of inquiry to the signatories of the *Times* letter. On December 2, the administrator of the General Services Administration sent Bush a lengthy rebuttal to Loewenheim's earlier letter; Bush placed it, too, in the *Congressional Record.*

Loewenheim responded to the Leopold committee's initial inquiry through his attorney, who claimed that he wanted Dick himself to explain what he regarded as an attack on his client's honesty by Ward's assistant. Characteristically, Dick responded immediately and directly. He said that he regretted Zabel's view of the committee "as part of a conspiracy" and chastised the attorney's letter as "the shoddiest treatment of an important problem of ethics among scholars that I have known since I began teaching in 1937." Expressing the hope that "you and I could correspond as men of good will and mutual trust in an attempt to resolve equitably an extremely serious and complex matter," he continued, "I regret to say that I have found no evidence to date that you desire to proceed in that spirit."

For Dick, who had volunteered his time, skill, integrity, and reputation in the service of his profession, the experience went downhill from there. Undeterred by the failure of cooperation from the instigator of the complaints, he still proceeded as the outstanding historian he was. He would marshal the facts, try to learn the truth, and report fully and candidly all conclusions. As the AHA had requested, Dick's committee published its interim report on December 20; it consisted principally of a few key items of correspondence describing the subject and framing the issues for further investigation. Among the materials was a statement from Herman Kahn, former director of the Roosevelt Library and assistant archivist in charge of presidential libraries. Dick had known him as a Harvard graduate student in 1933, but Kahn left after a year without obtaining a Harvard degree. Kahn's statement had been developed from two letters he had sent to Dick in October and November 1969. The statement would eventually lead Zabel to make unfounded personal attacks on Dick. If Loewenheim and his lawyer truly sought a fair process aimed at understanding the truth, they could have had no better ally than Richard W. Leopold. But they appeared to have a much different agenda, as Dick would continue to learn.

* * *

It was always best to start with basic facts and then work outward from there. Both sides agreed that Loewenheim had visited the Roosevelt Library on twenty-one occasions between September 1966 and February 1967. They agreed on little else. Loewenheim maintained that the staff should have informed him about six letters exchanged between Ambassador Dodd and FDR in 1933. The staff responded with research records indicating that a thorough examination of what was made available to Loewenheim proved his access to a file containing the very letters he now claimed to have been withheld from him; as a sloppy researcher, he simply had not requested that file. Likewise, those records proved that other scholars who had visited the library had used and referenced the file.

Loewenheim also asserted that the supposedly withheld letters, along with three printed volumes of other FDR correspondence, were the subject of an improper publishing arrangement. In particular, Loewenheim claimed, Harvard University Press undertook the publication of FDR's letters (including the six specific Dodd letters from 1933 that Loewenheim's accusations had put at issue) in violation of the law. Although the underlying legal question had not been resolved, Loewenheim argued that a private press could not lay claim to publication rights associated with the papers a president had given to the country. Two facts supposedly added fuel to Loewenheim's "conspiracy" fire: First, the Roosevelt Library's archivist Edgar Nixon had enhanced his stature with his editorship of the Harvard-published collection; and, second, the United States Copyright Office had twice denied Harvard's requested application to copyright the three volumes of FDR correspondence.

Once the Leopold committee finally got moving in November 1969, Loewenheim and his lawyer transformed the controversy in a way that sought to make Dick's investigation itself the story, rather than the underlying claims creating the fracas in the first place. They complained that the AHA and the NARS had "dragged their feet" in investigating and responding to Loewenheim's accusations. In response to Dick's earlier letter criticizing Zabel's approach to the investigative process, Zabel countered that Dick was failing to proceed in good faith. When Dick replied, Loewenheim himself returned fire with a request for all of the materials in the possession of Dick's committee.

The exchanges between Loewenheim and his lawyer on one side and Dick on the other continued for months. The complainants seemed not to be searching for the truth. Rather they appeared determined to scandalize the process by which Dick's committee was now seeking to find it. And then they turnd to attacks on Dick himself. Loewenheim and his lawyer complained that Herman Kahn's written statement published in the Leopold committee's December 20, 1969, interim report had not been provided to them previously. They accused Dick of deliberately withholding the statement as part of an effort to "defame" Loewenheim. In a letter to Dick dated February 28, 1970, but postmarked a week later, Loewenheim's attorney took the entire proceeding to a new low.

"How long and how well have you known Mr. Kahn?" Zabel asked. "Are you on a first name basis with Mr. Kahn? Have you ever entertained each other socially? Did you see Mr. Kahn at the American Historical Association meeting in Washington and discuss with him, in any way, the scandal at Hyde Park or the investigation or work of your committee? How, when and why did you decide—and was it in consultation with or perhaps at the suggestion of Mr. Kahn?—to print parts of these two letters to you, but carefully omitting an entire paragraph relating to the financial benefits that Harvard University Press might derive from this project, a key paragraph which makes the whole Harvard contract appear even more senseless? How many letters, altogether, have now passed between you and Mr. Kahn as regards this whole scandal, and what are their dates? Similarly, have you had any phone conversations, or indirect contact, with Mr. Kahn, perhaps through mutual friends at Yale or elsewhere?"

Dick drew a line in the sand. For months Loewenheim had refused to participate meaningfully in the committee's factual investigation. The Leopold committee declared that all interviews aimed at gathering the facts of the underlying controversy would be completed by a date certain. If Loewenheim wanted his version of the events to be told, he would have to comply with the deadline. Prolonged negotiations with Loewenheim's attorney over the nature of his client's appearance before the committee followed. The parties finally agreed that Loewenheim would answer in person a set of nine questions the committee would provide to him in advance.

The extraordinary session convened at the AHA offices in Washington on Saturday, May 2, at ten-thirty in the morning. It continued until four o'clock that afternoon with only a short break to eat sandwiches delivered to the room. One of Dick's former students, John C. Roberts ('61), an associate at the law firm of Covington and Burling, also attended.

"It was a waste of time," Dick told me. "Loewenheim provided nothing new, but when we adjourned because most of us were rushing to catch our planes home, he was still complaining that we had hurried things too much. Loewenheim did not fly and had taken the train, so he was not particularly worried about our flight schedules." In a remarkable testament to Dick's interpersonal skills under adverse conditions, Zabel wrote afterward, thanking him for his "very substantial part in making the meeting . . . a success. . . . I want you to know that I have told my client that I sincerely believe that you and Professors Chandler and Grantham are making a conscientious effort to reach a just result in this matter."

Dick announced that the record of the investigation would be closed on June 30, 1970. Loewenheim had earlier complained that the AHA and the Leopold committee were moving too slowly to investigate and report on the original accusations. Now that Dick declared the process to be approaching its end, Loewenheim sought to slow it. After June 30, the committee planned to focus all attention on drafting and issuing its final report. Although Loewenheim was given additional opportunities after his May 2 appearance to make corrections "on the factual recitation" in the report, none came. Rather, he renewed conflict-of-interest allegations, finally disclosing the basis for his charge: Ad hoc committee member Alfred B. Chandler had accepted an offer to serve for one year as the Ford Distinguished Visiting Professor at the Harvard Business School, commencing in September 1970. Loewenheim also repeated the shot previously taken at Dick personally based on some allegedly inappropriate (but never explained) relationship with Herman Kahn.

"Loewenheim was relentless," Dick continued. "He even wrote to Northwestern Professor Lacey Baldwin Smith, who had done his graduate work at Princeton while Loewenheim was there. He also wrote to one of my history department colleagues, Bill Heyck, who had taught at Rice. In essence, he asked both men to go directly to the university's new president, Robert Strotz, and complain about me. But, of course, Smith and Heyck ignored him."

* * *

The Leopold committee rendered its findings on August 24, 1970. It concluded that there had been no conspiracy against Loewenheim. Dick was the principal draftsman of the 448-page final report, itself a historical document he would always identify as his "fourth book." Meticulously researched with every available source consulted and referenced, it stated unequivocally that there "has been no scandal at the Roosevelt Library." In fact, the report found that Loewenheim should have been able to find "on his own . . . either at the Roosevelt Library or at the Library of Congress the few Dodd-Roosevelt letters that he lacked."

"Dewey Grantham personally went to the Library of Congress and got his hands on the letters immediately," Dick later explained to me. "That told me everything I needed to know about Loewenheim's shoddy research methods."

The report also concluded that Harvard University Press committed "amazing ineptitude" in pursuit of its twice-denied application for a copyright of its publication including those and, literally, hundreds of other Roosevelt letters. But the copyright application was denied in any event. The report found no proof of Loewenheim's claim that other scholars had been denied access to the Roosevelt Library materials under consideration. In fact, the committee found "impressive" the Roosevelt Library's handling of the complex problems confronting it.

The report described miscommunications, unintentional lapses by the library staff, and unfortunate delays—all of which related to the handling of Loewenheim's initial complaint, but not to his actual access to the documents in question. The report criticized NARS and the AHA for failing to respond more quickly to Loewenheim over the several months preceding Dick's appearance on the scene.

But none of these were deliberately malicious acts aimed at Loewenheim. Rather, the situation resulted from inadvertent human failings and the absence of a systematic process for handling the trauma that Loewenheim and his lawyer had wrought on an organization of scholars unaccustomed to such behavior among fellow professionals.

Despite the personal attacks Dick sustained at the hands of Loewenheim and his lawyer as the investigation proceeded, the Leopold committee produced a balanced report offering constructive suggestions for presidential libraries, the AHA, OAH, and NARS. The clamor for a follow-up congressional investigation died after Dick's committee declared such government involvement unnecessary and counterproductive. His thoroughness persuaded those who mattered that there was nothing more for a congressional panel to investigate or ascertain. His firm, calm, and steady hand had steered his profession through one of its worst crises of the twentieth century. Ray Billington, who had signed the Loewenheim letter that appeared in the *Times,* wrote at the time of Dick's retirement in 1980 to thank him for his "sane judgment," without which the episode "might have wrecked the profession."

In the end, Dick viewed the controversy as a sign of the times: "The committee believes that many of the misgivings about some of the complaints against the Roosevelt Library reflect the current suspicion of the national government. . . . This report also contains the *ad hoc* committee's views on how the AHA and OAH should, initially, approach any new charges and on the kind of machinery needed to investigate them." But he was pessimistic for the future, noting that the report's signers were "less confident about those recommendations. . . . They are well aware of the attacks on their personal and professional integrity which were begun at the outset of their labors and which have reached a crescendo in recent weeks. They greatly fear that, if this report is widely read, there will be few historians willing to accept a similar assignment in the future. Nor are they unmindful of the enormous drain on the financial resources of the American Historical Association and of the Organization of American Historians that this investigation has entailed. Whether this tremendous expenditure of time and money by men—and there are many besides the members of this *ad hoc* committee—who should be devoting their energies to pursuing scholarly research and by organizations which should be devoting their funds to promoting scholarly activities has been justified is not for the signers of this report to say. They can only profoundly hope that, for the good of the profession, there will never be another Roosevelt Library case."

The only real scandal involving the Roosevelt Library had been of Loewenheim's own making when he and his lawyer attempted to drag the AHA, OAH, NARS, and Dick personally through the mud long after the events triggering his original complaint. Dick made his most important personal point in the final report from his committee, "The members of the *ad hoc* committee, then, were not prepared in September 1969 to disqualify themselves on the basis of vague rumors and unsubstantiated charges. In retrospect, they wish they had; for theirs was an onerous assignment, involving an enormous expenditure of time and an inescapable threat to their personal and professional reputations, that no historian in his right senses would seek. . . . In sum, unless rules of conduct similar to those recommended by the *ad hoc* committee on March 30, 1970 are accepted, the profession will not be able to persuade experienced members to undertake, without fear of personal reprisals, the time-consuming and soul-searching task of investigating charges of the nature raised by the Roosevelt Library case."

Nevertheless, Loewenheim's assault did not end with the issuance of the ad hoc committee's conclusions. Rather, his systematic campaign to discredit individual members of Dick's committee continued through letters, telephone calls, and statements to the press. On September 9, Loewenheim wrote to Dick, complaining about a number of issues relating to the committee's work. One topic involved material that the committee had received from other individuals during its investigation. The committee had decided that, with limited exceptions, such correspondence would be made available for Loewenheim's review in the Library of Congress. Those exceptions involved letters the committee had received in strictest confidence; none had been used in its final report. These very few letters would be available to Loewenheim and the rest of the public only with the permission of their authors. Loewenheim was not satisfied with this resolution, but Dick set him straight. In his last missive to Loewenheim on this or any other subject, he wrote: "This case has brought enough grief to enough people without adding needlessly to the list. I forbear to quote at this point what Mr. Welch said, regarding Fred Fisher, to the junior senator from Wisconsin during the McCarthy-Army hearings in 1954."

Dick was referring, of course, to the famous televised remarks that attorney Joseph Welch had directed to Senator Joseph McCarthy: "You've done enough. Have you no sense of decency, sir? At long last, have you left no sense of decency?" Loewenheim had done enough. Dick told him to address all future correspondence concerning the work of the ad hoc committee to its lawyer.

* * *

One of the more appreciative members of the profession was Professor Natalie Z. Davis from the University of California at Berkeley. She was on the council of the AHA in April 1973 when she wrote to Dick, expressing her appreciation for his efforts after reading the final report: "So absorbing was it as a piece of historical research that I read it from start to finish. I was impressed both by the care with which the story was unearthed and the judiciousness and fairness of the comments. . . . All the way through, it seemed that one was caught in a drama that expressed many features of American life—the attitude that we scholars have toward our work as our private property, our overwhelming commitment to scholarly apparatus and reputation ('to our careers') as essential to our sense of well-being, the snobbishness of historians toward mere librarians, the proprietary attitudes of librarians, the political atmosphere of the '50s and '60s, the competitive structure of the publishing industry . . . and so on. The Report is among other things a fascinating historical document from the last twenty years. Since I could see from reading it that it was hardly an amusing task for you to have done the work, I want to express my appreciation for the Report and my personal thanks for the time and concern that went into the matter."

* * *

When I asked Dick how Loewenheim could have continued what became a thirty-seven-year career at Rice University, he replied, "You have to know something about Texas to understand that. The newspapers down there would print whatever he gave them." I did a quick online search to see he was right, and that Loewenheim's career continued for decades after the dispute was resolved. Three months before Loewenheim's death in 1996, the *Houston Chronicle* ran an article about the aging professor and "summarized" the Roosevelt Library controversy, albeit incorrectly:

"Loewenheim entered another storm in 1969 when he charged that archivists at the Franklin D. Roosevelt Library at Hyde Park, N.Y., a branch of the national archives, had concealed historic records from him. At issue were six crucial letters President Roosevelt had written the U. S. ambassador to Germany in the pre–World War II years. He contended that they were hidden so as to give Harvard University Press exclusive use of the documents in a book it published. This ultimately led to the rescinding of the Harvard copyright for the book in question, and a directive that documents in federal archives be available to all scholars on an equal basis. Making this protest got him branded a troublemaker, Loewenheim said. 'If my charges had been proved false, I would have been destroyed.'" .

The *Houston Chronicle* article was a travesty on many levels. First, Loewenheim's charges were proved false. Wholly apart from Loewenheim's discredited accusations that Roosevelt Library archivists had knowingly and deliberately withheld the infamous six letters, other researchers had previously used the very file containing those letters. Still others easily and quickly found another set of the supposedly "hidden" documents in the Library of Congress. Loewenheim could never acknowledge what Dick's committee had concluded: His charges had more to do with his own faulty research methods than any conspiracy against him. Second, Loewenheim's complaints did not produce any "rescinding" of a Harvard University Press copyright—no such copyright was ever given in the first place. Finally, Loewenheim's accusations did not produce any new "directive" about scholarly access to archived documents.

Especially for historians and journalists, the repetition of falsehoods should not succeed in creating what others come to regard as the truth. But when well-respected and widely read newspapers are willing to print—forty years later—that about which they do not know and are unwilling to investigate fully, the truth becomes much more difficult to find.

Dick said it best: "Welcome to Texas."

* * *

Pop's professional frustrations climaxed about five years after Dick's. A new chief of surgery took over at Mt. Sinai Hospital and refused to provide necessary medical staff support for Pop's area of specialty. In protest, Pop resigned as the director of otolaryngology at Cleveland's largest ENT department—the one he had built essentially from scratch. Thereafter, he systematically sent his patients to St. Luke's and University Hospitals, two institutions that had refused to consider him for an internship more than thirty-five years earlier. There is an ironic circularity in all of this, but the more important point is that by the early 1970s, Pop was grappling with problems having nothing to do with his Jewish background, just as Dick was. Both men had progressed upward in their respective professions, only to engage in the battles that all conscientious citizens mount against institutions, bureaucracies, and personalities frustrating a civilized person's efforts to make the world a better place. Once they were at the pinnacles of their respective careers, peers chose them to lead those fights. Jewish cream was finally getting its opportunity to rise to the top of America's melting pot, and the nation was becoming a better place for it.

Through it all, Pop never revisited what others might see as his own somewhat confusing view of his heritage, probably because he himself was not confused at all. From childhood, the trajectory of his life had directed him away from all things Jewish and any form of Semitic self-identification. He was a Jew only because others classified him as one. The times in which he had come of age created no incentive for him to pursue any different path. From his perspective and by every objective measure of a person's accomplishments in twentieth-century America, he had conquered anti-Semitism in the most definitive way: He was professionally successful and personally satisfied. He never looked back; there was no reason for him to do so. As he saw it, the best hope for a future that encompassed the very survival of his progeny lay exclusively on the secular path of assimilation ahead.

TWENTY

"When in Doubt,
I Didn't"

"How are you going to treat the Roosevelt Library investigation?" he asked me a few weeks after we first discussed it.

"Well," I answered, "at this point, I think it is an interesting story that should be told from the perspective of the hell it put you through for a year. But let me ask you, how should I treat it?"

"The difficulty," he explained, "is that we went through the entire process with the hope of setting up procedures to prevent that kind of thing from ever happening again. But complaints continue to be filed, and those kinds of investigations continue to occur. No one really seems to remember what I did. In a similar vein, a few years back someone from the Smithsonian Institution contacted me. I told the person that in 1940 I had published a biography of Robert Dale Owen—the man who had introduced and promoted the federal legislation creating the Smithsonian—and that an entire chapter of my book had been devoted to that topic. The caller was surprised to learn this and, a short time later, told me the Institution did not even have a copy of my book."

"So maybe a person can live too long?" I suggested with a smile. He seemed to be telling me that two important chapters of his life—his published dissertation and his leadership of the Roosevelt Library investigation—had been for naught or, at least as far as history was concerned, were becoming irrelevant.

"I think you are raising a very fundamental question," I continued, "namely, except for monumental figures in history—like presidents who start unjustified wars—what difference does any of us really make? In that sense, maybe nothing we do matters. Yet in another sense, everything we do can make a difference—although we cannot always see the final consequences. Sometimes things that seem important at the moment become less so over time. On the other hand, initially trivial matters turn out to be life-changing in their ultimate impact. I think that is true for everyone and everything."

At the risk of gilding the lily, as Dick would call it, I continued: "For example, my father-in-law devoted large portions of his life to establishing one of the first outpatient surgical programs in America. Yet within a few years of his retirement, both that specific program and the entire hospital itself were gone. Does that mean he made no contribution to lives of the people he treated, the doctors he trained, or the pioneering short-term hospital stay approach that has now become central to modern medicine? Certainly not. He did the best he could and the world is better for it. I think the same is true for you. How many people occupy your position, where national leaders publicly identify you among the handful of people who had a lifetime effect on them? Or where a tremendous number of ordinary individuals become better citizens because of your influence? In the end, it's all about the people you touch along the way. For most of us, it's one person at a time, and we can never be sure who we are reaching or how. You are more fortunate than many on that score. So was my father-in-law."

"Why would any of that cause anyone to be interested in a book about my life?" he asked, reiterating his continuing belief that I would have difficulty finding a publisher for the biography we were writing.

"Because your life may be more interesting than you think. All of us are simply collections of our own life's stories," I said. "You happen to have some very interesting episodes revealing themes and challenges. Some are unique to your century—the twentieth—and the historical events of your time; others have a universal application to the human condition. People are especially interested in stories with a familiarity to their own lives and something to help them through their own struggles. People are also fascinated by a person whose seemingly ordinary existence dramatically improved the lives of others. It is called living an inspirational life."

By this time, Shep Shanley had joined us as a regular participant in our Sunday morning sessions. Shep was the son of Dick's now deceased friend J. Lyndon Shanley. As another example of the historical circularity Dick loved to contemplate, Dick's fellow assistant basketball team manager at Princeton had a son who had been Shep's classmate there. As an instructor at Exeter, Shep had heard Ernie Gillespie's commencement address in 1967. Now he served as Northwestern's associate director of undergraduate admissions. "Surely, Dick," he said, "you are not questioning the value of this book-writing enterprise?"

"No, no . . ." Dick's voice trailed off. With renewed vigor, he changed to another subject. "Say, did I ever tell you about the time I almost left Northwestern altogether?" Once again and with very few words, he had captured my undivided attention as we moved forward.

* * *

While Dick had grappled with the Roosevelt Library investigation, student radicalism at Northwestern continued. When President Nixon announced America's incursion into Cambodia on April 30, 1970, protests erupted on campuses throughout the country. On May 2, the ROTC building was burned to the ground at Kent State University. The following day, Ohio governor James Rhodes sent the National Guard to the campus and personally appeared there to promise "every force possible" to maintain order. He denounced the protesters as worse than brownshirts—an allusion to Hitler's secret police—vowing to keep the Guard on site "until we get rid of them."

The next day, National Guardsmen suddenly shot into a group of protesters. Fourteen students were hit; five died from their wounds. Northwestern students responded with the erection of impromptu barricades blocking Sheridan Road, the main north-south artery connecting Chicago to its affluent North Shore suburbs. All traffic ground to a halt. Apart from a futile expression of angst associated with the killing of fellow students on another campus, the barricade itself could produce nothing meaningful. "Eventually," Dick told me, "five redbud trees—one for each of the fallen Kent State students—were planted on Deering Meadow to commemorate the tragedy there."

* * *

During the 1969–1970 academic year, relations within Northwestern's history department remained strained. As his sabbatical year ended in the spring of 1970, Dick received inquiries from The Johns Hopkins University, where the resignation of his fellow Roosevelt Library investigator Al Chandler had created an opening. Chandler had accepted Harvard's offer of a permanent position on the business school faculty and would go on to write *The Visible Hand,* a book that reshaped the approach to American business history. In a 1982 letter to Richard Russell, a former student and Adams House resident, Dick summarized in a single paragraph the circumstances causing him to consider for the first and only time the prospect of leaving Northwestern. He began with the crushing loss of Link to Princeton and the departmental turnover that followed shortly thereafter: "The years from 1960 to 1970 were ones of change. Link left in June 1960 to edit the Wilson Papers at Princeton. Billington resigned in 1963 to become a research associate at the Huntington and write a biography of Turner. Boyce retired in 1967."

Then came the turmoil during his three-year reign as department chairman: "I became chairman in 1966 as the department was doubling in size and unrest among students and faculty grew. Boyce had been chairman from 1948 to 1966. I had been acting chairman the one time he was on leave—in 1953–1954, and found I could run the department in my spare time. After 1966 it was very difficult." Not long thereafter was his successful advocacy on behalf of the NROTC: "I also threw myself, as a sort of one-man rear guard, into the defense of the NROTC program and managed to prevail, although the program disappeared at Harvard, Yale, Princeton, Dartmouth, and Stanford."

The culmination of the difficult decade came with the Roosevelt Library investigation. "In July 1969," he wrote, "I went to a conference in Japan and looked forward to a year's leave after my three-year stint as chairman. Instead I was drawn into the controversy over the Roosevelt Library and had to devote my year to that. If you want to read a 448-page report, of which I was the main author, on the meaning of paranoia and the folly of the profession, I would be happy to send you an autographed copy."

Dick gave only passing reference to his mother's death in 1969 and no mention at all of Ernie Gillespie's two years earlier. "It was then that, for the first and only time, I thought of leaving Northwestern," he concluded. "During the 1950s, I turned aside without investigating feelers from several institutions; Harvard was not among them. Now Johns Hopkins was interested in my replacing Al Chandler, Harvard class of 1940, as editor of the Eisenhower Papers and teaching half-time on foreign policy."

Dick thought seriously about accepting the Hopkins proposal. Editing the Eisenhower Papers would produce a major scholarly work. Another premier American historian, David Donald, encouraged Dick to join him on the faculty. He struggled with the decision and even made a trip to Baltimore to meet with Donald and other faculty members in November, but ultimately decided to remain at Northwestern. His explanatory letter to Donald focused on his concern that he not "repeat what Arthur Link has done" in devoting himself "entirely to editing and teaching in the years that remain." He hoped to complete books he had either already begun or "sketched out" in his own mind. He offered additional reasons in his 1982 letter to Richard Russell: "My closest friends were here. I was still very much part of Northwestern, though in 1960 I had given up the survey course and was beginning to cut back on key committee assignments."

He shared with me two more factors leading to his decision. First, Dick knew that Donald himself was planning to leave Johns Hopkins. "So much for the thought that I might become part of another premier collection of American historians," he told me. "Second and more importantly, I felt that I knew the Northwestern undergraduate student body. It was not that I knew everyone, but I had a 'feel' for who and what they were. By and large, I liked what I saw. I had developed a similar sense of Harvard's student population when I was there. In the end, I knew nothing about those who populated the Johns Hopkins campus." Once again, his fundamental aversion to risk drove his decision and he remained where things were comfortable, even if far from his idea of perfect: "When in doubt, I didn't."

* * *

Not long thereafter, one of his former graduate students, Senator George McGovern of South Dakota, secured the Democratic nomination for president. More than twenty years earlier, McGovern had been one of Dick's teaching assistants, whose duties included the grading of examinations in Dick's large survey class for the spring of 1949. McGovern had been eager to return to his South Dakota home in Mitchell to teach the summer session at Dakota Wesleyan, so he had made what he acknowledged to be an unusual request not likely to be granted: McGovern had asked Dick's permission to take the students' blue books to South Dakota, promising he would adhere to whatever deadline Dick imposed for the submission of grades. To McGovern's amazement, Dick approved the plan: "That was a testament to my assessment of George McGovern," he told me. "I can think of few others whom I would have permitted to remove blue book examinations from the campus."

Now as the November 1972 election drew near, McGovern tried desperately to focus more public attention on a story that *Washington Post* reporters Bob Woodward and Carl Bernstein had been covering about a break-in at Democratic National Committee headquarters in Washington's Watergate office complex. Although it would not be revealed until decades later, Nixon's October 19 taped conversation between himself and his chief aide, H. R. Haldeman, captured a conversation demonstrating that World War II and awareness of the Holocaust had not ended American anti-Semitism. Haldeman suggested to Nixon that the source of the leaks to the *Post* about the Watergate burglary and cover-up was the number two man at the Federal Bureau of Investigation, W. Mark Felt. When Nixon asked for a motive, Haldeman replied that Felt had wanted the top job at the FBI after J. Edgar Hoover's death, but the position had gone to Nixon's long-time political supporter L. Patrick Gray.

"Is he Catholic?" Nixon asked about Felt. Haldeman replied incorrectly that Felt was Jewish.

"Christ, put a Jew in there?" Nixon responded.

"Well, that could explain it, too," Haldeman said.

The percolating Watergate controversy did not affect the election's outcome and Nixon won in a landslide.

* * *

Meanwhile, Dick chaired the highly confidential ad hoc committee investigating a plagiarism accusation against a fellow departmental faculty member. Eventually, the case against the offender became so overwhelming that he quietly resigned. Whatever differences they otherwise had with Dick, his colleagues agreed on at least one matter: he could be trusted as a man of integrity, independence, and sound judgment in connection with the department's most sensitive issues and problems.

In 1973, Dick joined the Historical Advisory Committee of the Atomic Energy Commission, bringing to four the total number of governmental bodies now occupying his time: Department of State, Navy, Army, and the AEC. Eventually, he would add the Marine Corps (1975), National Archives (1978), Truman Library Institute (1978), and the CIA (1985). Outside government, he served on the advisory committees for The Papers of Woodrow Wilson and The Papers of J. Franklin Jameson. Dick had also participated in the establishment of the Society for Historians of American Foreign Relations (SHAFR) in 1967 and was one of two nominees to be its first president. "Can you guess who beat me in that election?" he asked. "Tom Bailey. Two years later, I became president."

Dick published numerous articles in professional journals throughout this period, including his presidential address for SHAFR that he spent six months preparing for publication. In his address, "A Crisis in Confidence: Foreign Policy Research and the Federal Government," he not only reviewed the state of the profession, but also alluded to the lessons of the Roosevelt Library case.

* * *

Such is the fate of a person who is gifted across a broad range of intellectual pursuits; something has to give. Dick excelled at everything he attempted. In times of trouble, professional organizations sought his leadership. At all times, governmental organizations sought his advice and colleagues sought his wisdom.

Pop faced increasing professional and personal demands, too. In addition to a medical practice that made him one of the nation's leading practitioners in otolaryngology, he had published numerous professional articles and taken on leadership responsibilities for his specialty at Cleveland's four major hospitals. He was also an assistant clinical professor of surgery at Case Western Reserve School of Medicine.

"A person can only do so much in life," both Dick and Pop told me at different times during their final years. For each of them, it was a lot, but they were never fully satisfied with their contributions. To Dick's own self-criticism that he should have written more books, the conclusive rejoinder must be: "And among the things you did accomplish, what would you have sacrificed to have become a more prolific author? What public service do you now view as having wasted your time? Inside or outside the classroom, whose life would you have chosen not to touch?"

TWENTY-ONE

Firsthand Experience—
Enter Steve Harper

"Sorry I'm late," I said, walking into Dick's room around 10:15 in the morning. Our normal Sunday morning starting time was fifteen minutes earlier; he had once chided me for being only six minutes tardy. My best strategy was a preemptive strike.

"I discovered something last week that might interest you," I told him, "especially in light of our conversation last week."

"And what is that?" he asked skeptically.

"I went to the Internet Web site for the Nobel Prize organization," I said. "It lists all of the Nobel laureates and, for each, provides a brief summary of the person's life. But here's the important point."

"Go on," he nodded.

"I went to the winner of the Nobel Peace Prize for 1912," I said as he began to smile. "You know who won that year." It was Elihu Root; now I knew I had his attention.

"Along with the brief biographical summary for Root, there are only two scholarly references listed for him. Yours is one of them," I said.

"Is the other Jessup?" he responded, asking about the two-volume biography published in 1938.

"Yes," I replied. "This goes directly to our discussion last week, when you were questioning whether your work had any lasting impact. Well, here is a pretty good example you cannot ignore."

"You know, Jessup had an advantage because Root was still alive and they spoke together while the biography was being written."

"Sort of like you and me," I interrupted. "But the point is—as I am sure you can see—your work is right up there with Jessup's as one of the two important treatments of Root. The two of you are all alone in that listing, and it has been fifty years since you published that book!"

"So, what you're saying is that this is the 'big leagues'?" he asked rhetorically in the language of America's pastime.

"Exactly," I concluded. "Your work has endured. At least as to Root, your work has endured in a profession where people seem to spend a lot of time reinventing the same wheels."

"Yes, they do, and I must say that I find this quite gratifying and pleasing."

Impact. We all want to have a lasting impact. As remarkable as it may seem, the continuing stature of Dick's short, interpretive fifty-year-old biography of Elihu Root may well be among his least significant contributions to the world. But it was one he could see and appreciate, and it brought an unexpected smile to his face when he first became aware of it.

* * *

We had finally reached the point in his story where I entered his life and, coincidentally, it was almost the same moment that Pop entered mine. I was supposed to meet Professor Leopold for the first time as my freshman year ended in May 1973. A friend and fellow student told me that the professor might attend an outdoor concert at Rebecca Crown Center. I had heard stories about him: how he maintained frighteningly rigorous academic standards in an era of increasing grade inflation; how his legendary class met all year every Monday, Wednesday, and Friday morning at eight o'clock; how he conducted the class discussion with a Socratic method that was both daunting and exhilarating.

I could not wait to meet him. Arriving at the appointed time, I found the university's most imposing faculty figure nowhere to be found. Somehow he later learned about my unsuccessful mission and followed up with a personal typewritten letter to my home that summer. He introduced himself and apologized for whatever miscommunication had caused me to assume he would attend an event that was never on his daily aide calendar of appointments. I kept his note, which read, in part, "I am sorry that I did not know in advance of your intentions, for I would have been very happy to meet and talk with you. . . . I am impressed by what Professor Breen has told me, for his standards are properly high. He mentioned your intention to pursue a reading schedule this summer. If there is anything I can do at this end, by way of advice or suggestions, I hope you will call upon me. If there is not, I shall look forward to making your acquaintance when you return to the campus in September." Professor Timothy H. Breen, an early American history scholar, had taught the first of my two freshman seminars; historian of modern Germany James J. Sheehan had taught the second.

I accepted Professor Leopold's invitation to recommend a summer reading list for me. Only now do I fully appreciate why Clarence Darrow's autobiography was among his suggestions. Later that summer, I received a handwritten letter from my freshman adviser, Ruth Bonde, stating she had "heard from Dr. Leopold that you had achieved a four-point average in your course work during the spring quarter." I was baffled that he somehow knew my grades. At that moment, I should have realized that his intelligence network was no match for any student who tried to elude its grasp.

* * *

I caught up with Professor Leopold during his office hours in the fall of 1973. Apart from our limited correspondence over the summer, I had no basis for any interaction with him. So I merely stopped by his second-floor office in Harris Hall to introduce myself and we had a brief conversation. I did not see him again until November when I attended the preregistration interview for his winter quarter course, "The Armed Forces in American History" (C-03).

During that remarkable autumn, I also met the eighteen-year-old freshman from Cleveland who would eventually become my wife. She introduced me to her mother during Northwestern's parents and families weekend in October. Two months later, I met her dad. She flew to my Minneapolis home over the New Year's holiday, after which I drove the two of us back to Cleveland before returning to the Evanston campus. My modest upbringing had not prepared me for the affluence I saw as we approached her Beachwood home on Duffield Road. Once inside, I was assigned to the twins' room, previously inhabited by the Loebs' earliest postwar baby boomers.

The next evening, Kit and I attended a casino-night party at her parents' Oakwood Country Club. The event was both interesting and foreign to me because I had never seen any such high-society functions. The fact that everyone there was Jewish made no impression on me at all. Kit referred to her upbringing as culturally Christian. Although I was not sure of her meaning, I took note of the illuminated aluminum Christmas tree on the second floor. Over the three days we were there, I met Kit's friends from high school. All were Jewish. Her life of apparent contradictions puzzled me.

* * *

Kit and I returned to Northwestern, where I eagerly awaited the beginning of my first class with Professor Leopold. Once it was under way, I decided that my best approach was to ready myself with three points I could make for each of the three questions for the day and then wait until discussion on a particular question was winding down before raising my hand. I hoped my concluding words might have their greatest impact after others had exhausted all aspects of an issue or argument. That positioning also challenged me to monitor all that had preceded whatever I might say so my words would not simply be "covering old ground," as Professor Leopold would sometimes remark gently to someone who repeated a point already amply made. By offering three items, I would also give him an opportunity to choose one as the basis for throwing things open for additional group discussion. The only risk in my plan was the possibility that the chair might not recognize me and, therefore, that my supposedly profound words would not be spoken. For some reason, that rarely happened, which I took to mean that I must have been doing something right on those occasions when I opened my mouth.

About three weeks into the quarter, I expressed concern that I was monopolizing his limited office hours as I beat a steady path to his door. The next day I received via university mail his letter to me, which read, "Apropos of your opening remark this afternoon, you do not have to apologize for frequent visits during my office hours or resist the impulse when you have something you wish to discuss. I am always glad to talk with you. Another approach is to collect a series of topics you want to probe and arrange in advance, by telephone (475-6337), to come and see me some evening for an hour or so. Under that format, I do not have to worry about keeping other students waiting."

I accepted his invitation immediately. Although the prospect of actually visiting Professor Leopold in his apartment was daunting, I steeled my courage and made the appointment. His most important requirement was that we meet after the *CBS Evening News with Walter Cronkite,* which he watched while eating dinner.

On the agreed date, I walked to the north lobby of the U-shaped Northwestern Apartments complex and pushed the button next to his name. He buzzed me in and I took the elevator to the sixth floor. I walked down the hallway until I saw him standing in the open doorway of his apartment. I think it was the first time I'd ever seen him without a necktie. We shook hands and he ushered me inside.

Predictably, the place was spotless. The furniture was worn, but comfortable and in good condition. We sat in his living room and he offered me a Coke, which I accepted. He asked about my family and my connection to the Minneapolis suburb that was also home to one of his longtime friends on the faculty, Ruth Bonde, my freshman adviser and home economics professor in a department that was being eliminated. Only years later—long after I had graduated and learned of the strong connection between Professor Bonde and Professor Leopold—did I fully appreciate the happy fortuity producing my assignment to her. After what felt like ten minutes had passed, I looked at my watch to see we had spent almost two hours together.

* * *

As C-03 continued, I found him to be as I had expected: demanding, but fair. He had told the students what they could expect and then made good on every promise. His masterful control of the discussions allowed the conversation to flow intelligently without letting a single person dominate the day. At mid-quarter, he gave each student a short typewritten strip of paper consisting usually of a sentence or two indicating the student's strengths and weaknesses in the class discussions, as well as a grade. Because class participation comprised a significant portion of the final grade, every student analyzed every syllable of the evaluative message. I still have all of mine, but I treasure most the first one because of its atypical length and because he obviously sensed that I did not function with the confidence others exuded as they spoke. In the longest by far of the mid-quarter assessments I would ever receive from him, he gave me necessary encouragement at a critical time.

"Your participation is not as frequent as I expected; but you always have something useful to say when you do speak and you state your piece in a manner conducive to provoking discussion not killing it," he wrote. "But I shall need your help as the quarter progresses and as my own expectations rise. Thus far I have been generally content if members demonstrated that they could speak and kept reasonably close to the issue at hand. But I will want more as they become more familiar with the main problems of the course and as they acquire more evidence and a better perspective with which to generalize. I shall also want more discussion between students and less between myself and individuals. With your forensic skills and beguiling smile, you can become an agent provocateur; and on your broad shoulders I lay that heavy burden, Sir. Grade: A."

His words inspired me to move beyond my own self-imposed limits. I certainly spoke more frequently in class thereafter. I am also sure I was not alone in the impact his insights had in encouraging his students to see their greater capabilities. Noted journalist Georgie Anne Geyer ('56) would write years later: "When I was long out of Northwestern, about 1985, I was about to begin work on my Fidel Castro biography. Frankly, although I was an experienced journalist and had already written three books, I called Dick and he invited me to the campus for a delightful lunch.... [W]e didn't talk that much about historiography or patterns of research; what I remember even now was that he gave me the confidence to do it. It was published in 1991, *Guerrilla Prince: The Untold Story of Fidel Castro*, and is now the standard work, which is what I dreamed of." I am certain I could fill another book with similar testimonials.

I had planned to major in history and eventually fulfilled all of its course requirements, but during the middle of my sophomore year I opted for the four-year combined bachelor of arts/master of arts degrees program in economics. During the summer after my sophomore year, I worked for Northwestern's nationally renowned macroeconomics professor Robert Eisner, who had served as George McGovern's principal economic adviser during the 1972 campaign. At that time, I learned that McGovern headed a long list of distinguished students who had studied with Professor Leopold. In the course of writing this book, I discovered that Eisner was also a New York Jew. Born in 1922, he died in 1998. Despite all the time we spent together, I never knew him very well. But I now wonder whether his journey through the twentieth century was in any way similar to Dick's.

During that summer of 1974, I also worked as a research assistant for Professor Breen, who was rapidly becoming a leading authority on eighteenth-century

America. Thanks to Breen, who would himself become the William Smith Mason Professor of American History after Dick retired, and Professor James J. Sheehan, who later moved to Stanford and became president of the American Historical Association in 2004, my writing vastly improved to the point where it could begin to withstand the scrutiny Professor Leopold would later give it. Professor Sheehan also gave me insights into Germany, Jews, Martin Luther, and anti-Semitism that my teachers had never revealed during my sixth, seventh, and eighth grade years at a Minneapolis Lutheran day school.

* * *

My work that summer kept me in Evanston, where I frequently spent a portion of my early evenings with Professor Leopold. Two weekends monthly, I drove to Cleveland for visits with Kit. Dick always wanted me to report my safe return from those trips; I now speculate that the specter of his cousin William's fatal automobile accident fifty years earlier might still have haunted him. My work ended in the middle of August and I spent two weeks prior to Labor Day living in Pop's home. Then we all traveled to a northern Minnesota cabin my parents had rented for our two-week family vacation. What I would now call assimilation came easily to all involved, although I had no awareness of the concept as I participated in it.

* * *

My "Leopold experience" continued throughout my entire junior year of 1974–1975. I had anticipated with delight Professor Leopold's yearlong sequence in American foreign policy. Of course, it met my highest expectations because it met his own higher standards. This time, I was among those who had experienced a taste of the Leopold approach in C-03 and held the psychological advantage over newcomers. His only concession to the eight-o'clock hour at which the American foreign policy class began was a coffee urn on a small table behind me. His other effort to keep everyone awake during class consisted of opening the large windows— even in the middle of winter—to maintain a constant temperature that felt no warmer than sixty degrees Fahrenheit. The lively discussions made the "walk-in freezer effect" superfluous. Reflecting on those days in Harris Hall 108, I now understand that Arthur Schlesinger Sr.'s early advice to a young Harvard instructor— to keep the windows open so students were not tempted to drowse—had never left Dick. On some days in January 1975, I could see my own breath as I sat in Harris 108 from eight to nine in the morning on Mondays, Wednesdays, and Fridays.

As for the early meeting time, he later wrote, "By setting the hour at 8:00 in the morning, I was not faced with the problem of admission but taught only 'the best and the brightest.' No one would try it today." This echoed a similar comment he had written in a lengthy letter to one of his former Harvard undergraduates and Adams House protégé: "In my teaching, I concentrated on the three-quarter history of American foreign policy; and in an era of declining standards and grade inflation, I managed to attract the very best, despite high standards and an 0800 meeting with discussion three times a week."

The course syllabus that Professor Leopold distributed at his individual pre-registration screening sessions set forth his expectations. In addition to the daily discussions accounting for one-half of the student's grade, written work included a short book report of no more than twelve hundred words and a final written examination of two hours' duration. If a student did not own Strunk and White's *Elements of Style*, he or she would be well advised to acquire it. Written final examinations consisted of several questions or statements from which the student would select two for response. Mastery of the factual material was essential, but rigorous analysis wrapped in graceful prose earned the greatest prize. He used different colored pens for comments on all written submissions: red was for content; blue was for style.

But the essence of the Leopold experience during my days as an undergraduate was the daily classroom discussion. Thirty years later, he told me that he graded each student at the end of each session. For the final grade, he used the combination of written and oral work to calculate individual rankings from the very top of the class to the very bottom. Among other purposes, his detailed records facilitated preparing the letters of recommendation he later wrote on behalf of those seeking admission to postgraduate programs in law, history, or other professions.

He never missed a class—ever. For a time during the winter of 1975, he walked with a noticeable limp and kept his left leg extended when he sat in his chair. I asked him what had happened and he replied, "Sciatica." Not knowing what that was, I inquired further and he explained it was some sort of unspecified nerve-related problem of unknown origin and caused shooting pains down his leg. I thought little of it until our more extensive conversations about his life in a wheelchair thirty years later.

Despite his best preregistration screening efforts, each academic quarter saw attrition from the original ranks of about forty, as fall became winter and winter became spring. In my year, the group of twenty-five who remained at the end constituted the survivors of the most rigorous class in the history department, if not the entire university. One would, perhaps, cede a single exception to the "gatekeeper" chemistry courses determining those who might advance to careers as medical doctors.

At the end of the spring quarter, the current C-13 survivors continued the tradition of playing a softball game against prior years' alumni in Deering Meadow, the site of the NROTC protests in 1969 about which I knew nothing as I fielded ground balls. I now realize the game was just one of his many personal efforts to link his large extended family of students across time. Dick was the umpire. I played second base both years and he called me "little Eddie Stanky"—a reference I assumed to be a function of my stature and/or intensity, although the truth was I had no idea who that ballplayer was. I now know Stanky played second base for the Brooklyn Dodgers from 1945 to 1947, was on the World Series team that included Jackie Robinson in his rookie-of-the-year debut as a first baseman, and moved to the Boston Braves in 1948. Robinson took over Stanky's second-base duties when Gil Hodges arrived that year to play first. Seven years later, my uncle, Frank Kellert, backed up Hodges at first and was standing at the plate when Robinson stole home in one of the more memorable events of the seven-game 1955 series the Dodgers won. I guess the circularity of history and life applies to me, too.

* * *

By May 1975, all of Vietnam had fallen unequivocally into communist hands. I used the topic to write a speech for which I won Northwestern's Kirk Oratorical Prize; it netted me some extra cash for the summer. I titled it "The Lessons of History" and cautioned my audience not to adopt the simplistic view that the recent "fall of Vietnam" into communism should somehow be viewed similarly to the "fall of China" that had produced a decade of recriminations twenty-five years earlier. One of the contest judges was my debate coach and a former Leopold student, Professor David Zarefsky ('68). I took two courses from him, too. Zarefsky once said that he would have taught a class at eight in the morning, but he did not want it to conflict with Dick's course. A few years later, he would become the dean of the School of Speech.

As my college career came to an end, Professor Leopold asked me if I wanted to attend one of the annual foreign affairs conferences sponsored by the three service academies and to which Northwestern sent only two student representatives. Having no idea what differences might exist among these events, I asked which one he would choose. After describing the beautiful mountains near the Air Force Academy and the unmatched setting of West Point, I now understand why he eventually said, "I would go to the Naval Academy at Annapolis." Once a Navy man, always a Navy man. I attended with a fellow student, David Klafter ('76), who was completing C-13 a year after me. The conference's keynote speaker was CIA director George H. W. Bush, who had played a peripheral role in the Roosevelt Library case and whose remarks to the assembly I found insightful and eloquent.

* * *

Professor Leopold remained a steady and growing influence in my personal life. At commencement exercises in June 1976, I proudly introduced him to my parents, and they to him. He was the famous Professor Leopold about whom I had spoken often. His letter of recommendation, I had told them, resulted in my admission to Harvard Law School. He roundly disclaimed any such responsibility and was quick to cite my overall academic record as the culprit.

If he ever made any judgments about my personal life, he never shared them with me. Nevertheless, I thought the tone of his limited remarks on the subject betrayed an implicit approval of my future wife. I am now certain it must have amused him that her surname was Loeb. In August of the year that became my Annus Mirabilis—1976—Kit and I were married in a civil ceremony conducted in her parents' suburban Cleveland home. Dick sent us a wedding present—a silver-plated bowl we still treasure, along with a note apologizing for his inability to send the gift he had intended: "a Revere bowl, in keeping with your future residence. . . . Neither the Cellini Shop nor Marshall Fields had any in stock or any expectations of an early shipment. Perhaps the denizens of the Middle West will not be able to tell the difference."

Kit and I spent our honeymoon driving a U-Haul truck with all of our worldly possessions from her parents' home to our apartment in Cambridge. Thanks to Pop's fortuitously timely retirement a few months earlier, we had furniture: a desk, waiting room chairs, medicinal waste baskets, and magazine racks from his two former offices. I now smile at the circularity of history that lies in the fact that, more than forty years earlier, our new hometown had been Dick's new hometown, too.

* * *

During the same year I started law school, Dick received one of his profession's highest awards when he became president of the Organization of American Historians. In that position, he followed luminaries including Thomas D. Clark (1956-1957), Fred Merk (1959-1960), Ray Billington (1962-1963), and, of course, Thomas A. Bailey (1967-1968). John Hope Franklin had been president during the 1974-1975 term.

Dick's OAH presidential address reflected his continuing mission to preserve for future historians the essential tools of their craft: primary source materials from the government. Three years earlier, Nixon had resigned in disgrace over the withholding, modification, and destruction of his Oval Office tape recordings implicating him directly in the Watergate scandal. Dick condemned the cynical arrangement Nixon had struck in 1974 with administrator of general services Arthur F. Sampson. It gave the former president the power to destroy incriminating tape recordings after five years and mandated their destruction by 1984 or after Nixon's death, if it occurred earlier.

Dick likewise cited Nixon as a living example of "how much the traditional system depended on the integrity of the man in the White House" as he lambasted him. "Even before he quit," he said, "Nixon caused alarm by telling the press that if the tax deduction for his vice presidential papers was disallowed, he would gladly take them back from the government since they were worth more than he had claimed. This remark led to the introduction of several bills in Congress declaring presidential papers to be public property. Then, on the day before Ford pardoned him, Nixon obtained from the administrator of general services the agreement described earlier. That document made the nation the eventual recipient of Nixon's papers but left to him the decision as to which would be donated and which withheld. It made virtually certain that the incriminating tape recordings would never be available to scholars."

Dick's career reached its zenith. As his former student and preeminent historian John Morton Blum later wrote, "Dick knew so many historians that he was constantly surrounded in the lobbies of the hotels where we met. 'There stands the ancient mariner,' it was said of Dick. 'He stoppeth one in three.'"

By then, as Dick described to me, Northwestern's history department had continued to grow and change. "In 1971, two new appointments had been Carl W. Condit, who wrote three excellent books on the railroads, an area outside his areas of art history and urban affairs, and Sterling Stuckey, who had been a Northwestern undergraduate before eventually returning to teach African American studies. Hanna Holborn Gray, a Renaissance historian who had completed her dissertation under the direction of my old friend, Myron Gilmore, became a department member by virtue of her position as the new dean of the College of Arts and Sciences in 1972; in 1974 she became provost at Yale. Henry C. Binford was hired in 1972, along with several others who subsequently departed.

"It would not be particularly interesting to discuss every personnel change in the department during the 1970s," Dick explained, "but one should be noted. In 1976, President Strotz was concerned that the history department faculty had too great a teaching load. Strotz approved the hiring of three assistant professors, each of whom would be employed for only three years and without any prospect of tenure. The first person chosen for such an appointment had recently completed his dissertation at Yale under the supervision of my former student John Blum. His name was Michael S. Sherry." Twenty years later, yet another circle of history in Dick's life would become complete when Sherry was named Northwestern's first Richard W. Leopold Professor of American History.

Apart from the prestige attending all of Dick's positions throughout the 1970s, the government-related service in particular presented a unique historical opportunity. As the American public viewed its government with increasing suspicion, attention focused more than ever before on documents that federal agencies might be withholding from the public. He devoted much of his effort, especially in connection with State Department records, to breaking loose the "classified" bonds preventing historians from developing a complete picture of recent historic events.

* * *

During our session in which we started to discuss his last decade as a classroom teacher, Dick told me, once again, that the most disappointing part of his life had been his failure to complete more books. The problem, as he explained it to me, was the time spent instead on various government committees over more than twenty years. That work was both personally enjoyable and meaningful in its impact, but it kept him too busy to research and write more scholarly works that would meet his high standards.

I found his views especially intriguing. He had also expressed a seemingly contradictory concern that no one had paid much attention to the several books he had written—his biography of Owen, the compilations he and Link co-edited, the Root volume, and the *Final Report of the Joint Ad Hoc Committee to Investigate the Charges Against the Franklin D. Roosevelt Library and Related Matters* (which was really a book, too). This led me to an important question: "What is the most important thing you have done in your life?"

Dick, Shep, and I were engaged in one of our regular Sunday lunches when I stopped all conversation with that inquiry. To facilitate the discussion, I volunteered to answer first, saying, "I have two answers. First, I do not think I have done the most important thing in my life yet. But my second answer assumes I might be wrong about that. If I am, then the most important thing I will have done will be whatever impact I have had on my children. If I have also influenced for the better some of my younger professional colleagues in the law, or the kids I coached in Little League, that will be a bonus. But for me, nothing is a close second to the importance that a parent should have to his or her child."

Shep wanted more time to ponder his response. Dick answered the question firmly and without hesitation, "Well, since I have no children, I would have to say that the most important thing I have done is the impact—however minimal—I might have had on those students with whom I have come into contact over the years."

* * *

At age sixty-three, Pop announced his retirement from the practice of medicine in 1975. He planned to retain his part-time university teaching position and travel with his wife of thirty-eight years in their motor home. He said they would be turtles—"carry our house on our backs wherever we go." Although they eventually made it to every one of the continental United States except Washington and Oregon, their principal destinations were the residences of their children and grandchildren.

His oldest daughter to whom he had written during the war had assimilated in a profound fashion: She had converted to Mormonism and lived in Provo, Utah. She and her husband eventually had nine children who likewise began having many children of their own. Pop's twin daughters had split the religious divide: one was a Protestant living in rural Illinois; the other married a conservative Jew and remained in Cleveland. Each of those daughters had two children. Pop's youngest child remained an enigmatic religious being.

In 1978, Kit and I returned to Evanston so she could take advantage of a

Northwestern University fellowship to pursue graduate study in learning disabilities at the School of Speech, where Professor David Zarefsky was her dean. We lived in a small Evanston apartment, and Professor Leopold eventually became "Dick" to me, although how and when that occurred I cannot remember. I do recall it took a long time for me to feel comfortable calling him that, just as it took me an even longer period to settle on "Pop" as the manner in which I would address my father-in-law. In fact, I studiously avoided calling him anything for years after Kit and I married, until I discovered that "Pop" was what he had called his own and clearly beloved father. I remember he responded with a wide grin the first time I used it.

PART FOUR

"After a stretch of forty-three years in the classroom, during which I enjoyed almost every moment, I do not miss it at all."

TWENTY-TWO

THE TWILIGHT YEARS OF A BRILLIANT CAREER

In January 1978, Dick testified before the Senate Foreign Relations Committee on the fate of the Panama Canal. The issue was whether to honor the earlier agreements requiring its reversion to Panamanian control in 1999. Both for his historical expertise and for his insight into a contemporary problem in American foreign policy, Dick was called to offer his views.

"David McCulloch was the star of that show because he had just written a book on the Panama Canal," Dick recounted. "But the committee was very cordial and basically said, 'We're with you. Tell us what to say.' I remember, in particular, Senator Dick Clark from Iowa treating us especially well. He lost his bid for reelection later that year, in large part because he favored allowing the Panamanians to control the canal. The way some people reacted to the issue, you would have thought that we were giving up Florida."

* * *

Dick was approaching Northwestern's then-mandatory retirement age of sixty-eight. Contemplating the next phase of his life, he turned to a practical consideration: where to live. The Northwestern Apartments, in which he had resided for thirty years, would no longer be available to him. As the summer of 1979 ended, I helped him move his belongings into a cooperative building called the Rookwood Gardens on the corner of Sherman Avenue and Noyes Street. He had hoped for a condominium a few blocks south of the campus because, among other reasons, it was closer to Northwestern's library and downtown Evanston's shops. But when a desirable unit in that building became available, he let his dear friend, retired Professor Ruth Bonde, have first shot and she took it. For him, chivalry was not dead.

The Rookwood was an acceptable second choice, situated near the north end of the campus. It had no elevator, but was sufficiently spacious to accommodate most of his extensive private library. It also helped that Shep Shanley already lived there. Familiarity with what might be coming next had always been an important element in Dick's ability to cope with life's transitions.

It was a bittersweet time as he began to accept awards for a lifetime of scholarly and personal achievement. In the same year Ronald Reagan defeated Jimmy Carter in the presidential election, Dick retired from teaching. As he reflected in his 1982 letter to a former Harvard undergraduate and Adams House resident: "The decade from 1970 to 1980 was a mixed bag." He described how he "ceased to exert a decisive voice in the department as younger men and newcomers began to play the role I had after 1948." By 1975, he had stopped teaching graduate students, mainly because he "did not wish to be burdened with directing dissertations" after his retirement. He also saw "a decline in the quality of the graduate students and the interests of the few good ones in fields other than" his own. He focused on his undergraduate three-quarter foreign policy course, set the class meeting time to weed out all but what he concluded were "the best and the brightest," and even added a freshman seminar to his teaching load for 1977: "Biography and the Study of History." He concluded, "All of this came to a predictable end in the spring of 1980, a most heart-warming season. . . . After a stretch of forty-three years in the classroom, during which I enjoyed almost every moment, I do not miss it at all."

On the heels of his retirement, Dick stayed with his cousin Alice in Highland Park to recuperate from cataract surgery on both eyes. He was still recovering in December 1980 when he started his annual newsletters to friends and former students. They substituted for the individualized handwritten notes he had included on his Christmas cards.

* * *

Despite all he was leaving, retirement seemed to invest him with new energy. He told the Northwestern Library Council in 1981 he would return to the Shaw Lectures he had never converted into a book; he wanted to finish that project, among many others. "Although I would like to finish the volume on the President and Congress and although I could be tempted to do another biography," he told his audience, "my main concern will be the historical profession and the writing of history. . . . Most of all, I want to write about my profession and the scholars under whom I have studied and with whom I have worked."

He developed a new routine, spending two hours every morning and two hours every afternoon in Northwestern's library. He continued to serve on numerous boards and committees, adding the last one five years after his retirement: In 1985 the CIA asked him to join its advisory committee relating to historical records. His most enduring memory of that service, which lasted only one year, involved a luncheon in which he sat next to CIA director William Casey: "Well," Dick said to me, "put it this way . . . he was not my favorite person."

Nor did he let up on his scholarly activities: "I regarded my chief mission in that regard as keeping the profession honest, and it needed someone to do that." He had actually started down that path in 1949, when historian Harry Elmer Barnes had become so outraged at one of Dick's articles involving Barnes' work that he refused to read Dick's letter of explanation and response to Barnes' counterassault.

"I sent him several letters and Barnes replied that, although received, the letters would remain unopened and unread," he told me.

"What did you do?" I asked.

"I sent him a postcard. He had to read that."

Dick solidified his position as what he called the "conscience of the profession" when he published two reviews on major treatises intended to be authoritative. He spent months identifying errors in *Encyclopedia of American Foreign Policy: Studies of the Principal Movements and Ideas,* a three-volume work edited by Alexander DeConde. He then wrote a review detailing the mistakes. After suggesting "the quality of the essays is generally high," he found that "only four" were "unsatisfactory." He criticized the editor for being "too gentle" with several essayists, noting one who "ignores the scholarship in the field since she published her own book in 1948. She cites outdated works, ignores the years from 1947 to 1967, and commits elementary errors." He then detailed some of them: "The Rush-Bagot agreement did not refer to battleships (p. 244). In 1921, Japan did not give up its British alliance of 1902; that pact had been changed in 1905 and 1911 (p. 245). It is not true that at the Washington Conference 'no attempt was made to provide machinery for the prevention or settlement of international disputes in the Pacific' (p. 246). The Four-Power Treaty was designed to do exactly that. Nor is it correct to say that the Nine-Power Treaty guaranteed the territorial integrity and independence of China (p. 246). The signatories agreed to respect, not guarantee—a major difference."

He dissected three other essays with similar precision. Then he turned his sights on the editor for "failure to exercise sufficiently rigorous control . . . and reluctance to insist on more exact phraseology, more factual accuracy, more consistent bibliographical citations, and more care in preparing the front matter, the appendix, and the index." Dick exposed all of the problems with the publication, large and small: "The main author of the four-volume *Neutrality: Its History, Economics and Law* was Phillip C. Jessup, not Francis Deák; the latter's name carries an accent (p. 102). Richard Hofstadter first presented his psychic crisis thesis in 1952, not 1965 (p. 136). Michael Usem should be Michael Useem (p. 157). Edward R. Stettinius was never a lawyer (p. 231). Zachary Taylor was ordered to the Rio Grande in 1846, not 1844 (p. 419). George W. Wickersham was Attorney-General under Taft, not Theodore Roosevelt, and the United States did not become a 'formal ally of the anti-Axis powers' after Pearl Harbor (pp. 449, 507).

Alfred Thayer Mahan published 'Looking Outward' in 1890, not 1897, while Dennis Hart Mahan was never a general, having retired as a second lieutenant (pp. 532, 549). It is not true that after 1909 American naval policy sought a fleet second only to England's; Richard Olney's assertion about being 'practically sovereign on this continent' occurred in 1895, not 1896 (p. 551). It is the Zimmermann telegram, not Zimmerman (p. 582). The Platt Amendment passed in 1901, not 1903 (p. 593)."

His detailed critique went on and on and on before concluding, "In short, as an imaginative and full-scale attempt to describe principal movements and ideas, as well as practices, in American foreign policy, the *Encyclopedia* registers some very real achievements. As a selective reference work—and the editor uses that term in the first sentence of the preface—it has some very serious shortcomings."

Richard Dean Burns' *Guide to American Foreign Relations since 1700* fared no better when Dick similarly revealed the errors he found in that 1,300-page book. "The book was written as a guide for members of SHAFR," Dick told me. "That context is important to understanding my effort. Unless it was reviewed critically in the sense of scholarship, it would become the unquestioned bible to which people returned. I wanted its flaws on the record for all to see."

In Dick's review, he wrote that in "the difficult area of finding aids there are, for major entries, too many glaring omissions, misleading descriptions, and outdated information." He then listed them over the succeeding seven pages, including, "Thus the entry for the *Dictionary of American Biography* [1:182] gives 1946, not 1928-1937, as the publication date of the first twenty-one volumes and omits Supplements 5-7, released in 1977, 1980, and 1981. The entry for the original annual *Writings on American History* [1:64] fails to note that none was published for 1941 through 1947. The entry for its successor [1:216] has only the four volumes covering 1962 to 1973 and not the subsequent yearly volumes issued in 1975, 1976, 1978, 1979, 1980, 1981, 1982, and 1983. The entry for the Council on Foreign Relations' annual *The United States in World Affairs* [1:147] does not warn that no volumes appeared for 1941 through 1944 and wrongly lists Simon & Schuster as the sole publisher."

He complained that "the handling of presidential papers is unsatisfactory," "[o]missions also detract from the value of a chapter on finding aids," "errors on documentary collections occur in later chapters," and "the main weakness of the compilation as a bibliography is the sheer number of petty errors . . . over 550 imperfections seem unacceptably high. That figure means that about 5.7 percent of the entries have some flaw." He provided numerous examples to support his conclusions.

The thoroughness of Dick's work continued to justify the high standards to which he held his colleagues. Even his old friend Tom Bailey could not avoid his candor. When Bailey published *The Pugnacious Presidents: White House Warriors on Parade* in 1980, Dick was dismayed to find numerous factual errors in the book. In his review appearing in the December 1981 issue of *American Historical Review,* Dick said specialists would find little new in a volume containing more errors than one might expect from so distinguished a scholar. In a 1985 article about the episode that followed, he described how his candor had almost cost him a lifelong friendship:

"Bailey wrote a nasty letter to the editor in which he distorted what I had said and insisted that he wrote 'for the general reader and not for disapproving pedants.' When Otto Pflanze [the *Review*'s editor] asked whether I wished to reply, I said I would be content with the following: 'Having published more than 140 reviews in scholarly journals since 1940 without previously eliciting a letter of protest, I do not wish to engage in a public debate with Professor Bailey, whose friendship I have valued for almost the same length of time. I do believe, however, that even if the book is written "for the general reader and not for disapproving pedants," it should be judged in the pages of the *Review* on the basis of its value for scholars.'

"I then did what I wish more authors would do today instead of exchanging recriminations in communications to the editor. I wrote Tom a five-page, single-spaced letter replying fully to his objections, reviewing our long friendship, and giving a complete list of the errors I had found. Tom responded graciously and at once, saying that he was overwhelmed by my letter and that he had instructed Pflanze not to print his protest. He admitted that he had left the proofreading to the publisher and ended with these words: 'On my next birthday I shall be eighty, and I have concluded that I am much too old to be writing books. Yet one advantage of a failing memory is that I shall soon forget that a cloud briefly darkened our valued friendship.' Fifteen months later he was dead.

"Thus ended the last of my life's circular connections to Tom Bailey," Dick told me. "It had begun in 1940 when I used his new textbook to teach my diplomatic history course at Harvard. In December 1941, I met him for the first time at the AHA's annual meeting; he was scheduled to teach at Harvard the following summer and we talked at length about the university. Then, unbeknownst to me, in 1945 Northwestern had invited Bailey to join its faculty as a full professor and chairman of the department. Fortunately for me, he preferred the West Coast. If Tom had accepted Northwestern's offer, he would have taken the position I eventually filled two years later. When he asked me to review two chapters of the manuscript for his forthcoming textbook *The American Pageant,* published in 1956, I told him that his scholarship was excellent, but I questioned the unsophisticated level of his language. He took my criticism well, but explained that he was writing for 'a generation being reared on comic books.' In 1958, I served with him and

James Phinney Baxter on the advisory committee that supervised the *Foreign Relations* documentary series for the State Department. In 1962, he congratulated me on the favorable reviews of *The Growth of American Foreign Policy*. After we worked together in founding SHAFR in 1967, Bailey trounced me in the organization's first presidential election, although I won the post three years later. He likewise preceded me by a decade as president of the OAH. And, finally, we participated in this concluding episode resulting from my candid review of his 1981 book."

* * *

In 1980, my in-laws bought a condominium in Chagrin Falls and moved out of their large, single-family home in Beachwood. Pop said they no longer needed all of the room that their five-bedroom residence had provided, and he was concerned that their extended travels away from Cleveland made their big empty house a target for burglars, who had already succeeded twice earlier. In their new residence, he built another photographic darkroom far superior to the one in his prior basement, as well as a workbench and model railroad layout that his grandchildren and I loved to run almost as much as he did. As he crafted small structures for his trains, he put to good use the woodworking skills he had first learned at his father's knee.

When Pop and Sue began spending their winters at a motor home campground near Naples, Florida, he bought a boat. He enjoyed the peaceful isolation of fishing and took courses in navigation so he would never become lost as he traveled the Intracoastal Waterway. "Retirement is akin to reading a book," he wrote. "When it is finished, it is put on the bookshelf and another is started. That is retirement. There's always another book to read. Many retirees find they can't, or won't, pick up the new book." He had it all figured out, or so he thought.

Pop's golden years did not work out as he had hoped. The Case Western Reserve University Hospital where he had labored for so long needed him for one more assignment—as director of the division of otolaryngology, head, and neck surgery. Even though it had been one of the hospitals that his Jewish heredity had rendered off limits when he had searched for an internship thirty years earlier, he answered the call. His "temporary" assignment lasted five years. By the time he disengaged professionally for the last time in 1980, he was sixty-eight and Sue's "smoker's cough" seemed to be getting worse.

TWENTY-THREE

Roll Call—Graduate Students

Dick continued to watch his closest friends leave forever. In 1977, Fred Merk died. When Myron Gilmore passed away in 1978, Dick lost a fellow member of his Harvard fist-ball group from half a century earlier and the man who had become his closest professional colleague from his Harvard days. Ray Billington died in 1981; Gray Boyce in 1982.

* * *

But accolades for Dick's distinguished career continued to accumulate. Prior to 1960, every Northwestern graduate student in American history and many others took his seminar "The Literature of United States History." To commemorate his retirement, the students whose dissertations he had directed—of whom there had been twenty—gathered at a Detroit dinner in April 1981 to present him with individual letters of appreciation. By then, Kenneth E. Shewmaker had become a professor of history at Dartmouth College. He wrote, "October 1961 was the beginning of a lasting friendship between us, and you have extended your characteristic graciousness and support to my son, who is a freshman at Northwestern University. I probably should emphasize more in this letter of appreciation how constructive your impact has been on my career and scholarship. With the benefit of hindsight, however, what I most want to thank you for is for being you: a brilliant scholar and teacher with the gift of sharing yourself in friendship with others."

Robert Moats Miller, professor of history at the University of North Carolina at Chapel Hill, had published biographies of three distinguished church leaders. He offered these words of praise: "For three score years Richard W. Leopold has remained for me and scores of his other students a model of the compleat historian, teacher, and man. We stand in awe of his honed mind, royal standards, absolute integrity, and sleepless industry. We salute his sacrificial service to our university, profession, and government. We are grateful for his wisdom and inspirational teaching. We are thankful for his many deeds of personal kindness, generosity, thoughtfulness. And if we fail to live up to his example, I, for one, will not fret overmuch, for few students were ever graced by such an unflawed mentor as Dick Leopold."

James C. Curtis had become professor of history and director of American studies at the University of Delaware by the time he had been selected to speak on behalf of all of Dick's graduate students at a 1980 retirement dinner. The following year, he wrote, "How does one thank a mentor for inspiration and encouragement throughout the most important part of an education? I tried in my remarks last spring to sum up my feelings about you as a teacher and it is as a teacher that I will always remember you. To me, the essence of great teaching, like the essence of friendship, is a fundamental concern for the individuality and humanity of a student. I felt that regard the first evening that I met you, when as a prospective graduate student, fresh out of Naval service, I inquired about the nature of the program and even went so far as to solicit advice on the proper attire for the classroom. You greeted these questions with a kindness and encouragement that I felt throughout my years as a student. . . . As a teacher, you set the highest possible standards and held us to them. You did so not out of the desire to point up our shortcomings, but in the firm belief that we had potential. . . . I feel extremely fortunate to have worked with you."

He received similar letters of praise from the others whose dissertations he had supervised and who had since scattered to the four winds—most in teaching, but a few outside academia. Richard A. Andrews was working for the California Seismic Safety Commission; David H. Culbert was associate professor of history at LSU; Gerald A. Danzer was teaching at the University of Illinois at Chicago Circle; Frederick S. Harrod was at the Naval Academy at Annapolis; Edward J. Kallina Jr. was at the University of Central Florida; Warren F. Kuehl was at the University of Akron; Barry F. Machado was an assistant professor at Washington and Lee University; Richard A. Matre was provost at the Loyola University Medical Center in Maywood, Illinois; Richard Megargee was professor of strategy at the Naval War College in Newport, Rhode Island; Charles G. Sadler was associate professor at Western Illinois University; William B. Skelton was teaching at the University of Wisconsin at Stevens Point; John R. M. Wilson was chairman of the department of history and political science at Mid-America Nazarene College in Olathe, Kansas; Fred H. Winkler was professor of history at the University of Idaho; Benedict K. Zobrist was the director of the Truman Library; Laurence H. Shoup was in California; and James Tillapaugh was an educator at the University of Texas of the Permian Basin.

Robert L. Tree of Iowa Wesleyan echoed the views of all when he wrote: "His impeccable scholarship over these many years has been instructive to his students and to the profession. His fine qualities as a teacher, leader and person have been an inspiration to all who have known him. There are many of us who are forever in his debt."

In 1984, his former Northwestern doctoral students honored him with their sponsorship of the OAH Richard W. Leopold Prize. Awarded biannually, it recognized the best book written by a historian associated with federal, state, or municipal government and covering foreign policy, military affairs, activities of the federal government, or related biography. That was also the year his closest friend Arthur Link served as president of the American Historical Association and the Organization of American Historians.

Beyond the relatively few whose dissertations he had supervised, other graduate students felt his influence. Former senator and Democratic presidential candidate George S. McGovern reflected on Dick's significance to his life: "I believe every thoughtful student who studied under Professor Leopold's direction would agree that this country has produced no more dedicated and competent professor. He has not only mastered his own field, but he has had a lifetime passion to convey his knowledge and insights to his students."

Another early graduate student was Jack Blacksilver, later a professor of economic history at Georgia State University, who wrote of the "profound impact of Dr. Leopold as an educator upon a very large number of undergraduate and graduate students over four decades." He continued, "The meticulously organized, effectively presented lectures highlighted the evolving role of the American society within a broad global setting. In his seminars and advanced graduate courses, Dr. Leopold initially inspired awe and fear, followed by grudging admiration and finally by great respect and deep affection. For the fortunate core in my class who could rely upon Dr. Leopold as their major thesis adviser . . . a superior dissertation was virtually assured. For remaining graduate students, Dr. Leopold served as a lodestar of scholarly achievement and dedication to the profession, a late-twentieth-century reincarnation of 'Mr. Chips.'"

William Bruce Catton, the son of a famous historian, eventually became a professor of history at Middlebury College, but in 1952 he was a Northwestern doctoral student. In 1990, he wrote, "It is no exaggeration to say that Professor Leopold could do all of the many things a teacher-scholar is supposed to do, and that he consistently did them—all of them—extremely well."

Arnold Schrier went on to become the Walter C. Langsam Professor of European History at the University of Cincinnati and described the impact of Dick's "filled-to-capacity" course in American foreign policy in 1949: "In all the years I spent in graduate school I don't recall another faculty member who so struck me with the precision of his lectures and the organization of his presentations. Each was a stirring performance, rich in the insight and interpretation that derives from a thorough mastery of the field. I learned from him the meaning of superlative teaching. Indeed, Professor Leopold became and has remained my role model. In the thirty-four years that I have myself been a faculty member I have tried to emulate the high standards Professor Leopold embodied as a master teacher. For me, at least, his influence has been a lasting one."

Likewise, Dick's remarkable success during his early years at Northwestern echoed in the subsequent careers of other students, including D. A. Miller (professor of history and comparative religion at the University of Rochester), Thomas N. Bonner (distinguished professor of history at Wayne State University), and William H. Harbaugh (Langbourne M. Williams Professor of History at the University of Virginia). Walter L. Arnstein would one day become the Jubilee Professor of the Liberal Arts and Sciences in History at the University of Illinois, but in 1956 he was one of Dick's graduate students: "Of the numerous teachers of history whom I encountered during my undergraduate and graduate years, none ranks above Professor Leopold. He proved a hard taskmaster, but I can think of no teacher who perused his students' work with greater care or provided more helpful criticism, nor can I think of any who prepared more carefully for the classes he taught. When I first began supervising graduate seminars myself, I modeled their organization in large part on Richard Leopold's."

These tributes recognized an approach Dick had begun at Harvard, where he had a strong impact even on those for whom he was not a formal dissertation supervisor. Marc Raeff, a graduate student in government, went on to become professor of Russian history at Columbia University; he still recalled his experience in Dick's lecture class forty years earlier: "I remember Professor Leopold's lectures quite well. They were models of the genre: clear, well organized, given with restrained brio, full of information and—most important of all—stimulating comments and general reflections on the forces and dynamics of foreign relations. . . . Professor Leopold's course left a long lasting interest in foreign affairs and a sober and better understanding of the diplomatic issues faced by the United States."

Long before Arthur M. Johnson became a professor of history and, thereafter, the president of the University of Maine, he was one of Dick's early graduate students at Harvard: "Of all the professors that I had both as an undergraduate and graduate student, I can honestly say that Professor Leopold stood out as a teacher. His scholarship, reflected in his enthusiasm for his subject, made a major impression on me. But above all it was his organization of lectures and his obvious effort to ensure that time spent in his classroom would be productively utilized to the fullest set an example that influenced my own teaching for nearly four decades. . . . His greatest contribution, I suspect, was in influencing graduate students like me to seek a career in teaching and research in emulation of what he did for us."

Philip K. Lundeberg was a curator for the National Museum of American History at the Smithsonian Institution when he wrote, "As a graduate student at Harvard early in the postwar decade, I was struck by both Dick Leopold's impeccable scholarship and inspired teaching. . . . Leopold conveyed the ideals of rigorous, impartial scholarship in a manner both effective and humane, making a strong impression in a department whose senior contingent, then including Morison, Schlesinger, Langer, and Merk, was in many respects unrivaled in the annals of American historiography."

Philip C. F. Bankwitz became professor of French history at Trinity College, but he, too, gained his historical footings in Dick's diplomatic history course at Harvard: "Professor Leopold is unique . . . in the power of his teaching."

Another testimonial came from a man who exemplifies the circularity of Dick's life. Donald B. Cole wrote several books, including *Martin Van Buren and the American Political System, A Jackson Man: Amos Kendall and the Rise of American Democracy,* and *The Presidency of Andrew Jackson.* He is now professor of history emeritus at Phillips Exeter Academy—the institution where another gifted teacher had first instilled in Dick a love for studying the past.

Cole drew his inspiration to pursue a career in that profession in 1946: "I was enthusiastic about history but had not decided whether I wanted to teach in secondary school or go ahead with a scholarly career. After completing Dick's course, there were no doubts remaining; I wanted to do both. What I remember most clearly about Dick that year was the care with which he prepared his lectures. . . . I also remember the enthusiasm with which he delivered those lectures. I was enthralled with diplomatic history ever since. The personal interest that Dick had for his students also remains in my mind. . . . It is clear to me that I am only one of hundreds of students who have been won over to careers in history because of this fine man."

* * *

During the Reagan administration, George F. Kennan's earlier predictions that Soviet communism was sowing the seeds of its own destruction came true. Not long thereafter, what would have been unthinkable only a decade earlier became a reality when Germany was reunified and the Berlin Wall came tumbling down. In 1988, George H. W. Bush became president after one of the ugliest political contests in history. I remember thinking his 1988 campaign bore no resemblance to the intelligent keynote address he had offered as CIA director during the Naval Academy's student conference in 1976. The transformation of George H. W. Bush between 1976 and 1988 would make an interesting subject for some other book; I suspect there is a story there.

* * *

Meanwhile, Pop suffered a crushing blow in August 1982 when Sue died of lung cancer. Six months later, he married a Cleveland nurse whom he had first met on the transport ship taking them both overseas during World War II. Since then she had married and divorced twice, maintaining periodic contact with Pop as she sought medical assistance for her son. When she read Sue's obituary in the *Plain Dealer,* she gave him a call because, as she later told me, "I was sick of taking care of old people in the nursing home where I worked, and I was sick of working." I wish I could say she was joking. It was no accident that her prior marriages had failed; Pop was not equipped to deal with her complex psychological baggage. Even worse, he was emotionally vulnerable to her tactics taking him farther away from his daughters and grandchildren. Among other tragic ironies, she was anti-Semitic. In that sense, perhaps Pop's acculturation had been too complete.

At her urging, he sold his motor home and replaced it with something called a Park Model, which was stationary manufactured housing. She said she needed the additional space the new accommodations provided at their Naples campground. The sad truth was that she did not enjoy their trips to visit his children and their families. Taking away his wheels brought Pop's travels to an abrupt halt. Not long thereafter, he sold his Chagrin Falls condominium, as well as the Park Model, and purchased a single-family home located in a former military officers' retirement community near Melbourne, Florida.

Pop had begun planning ahead for a time when he might need assisted living. The developer of the real estate project where he bought his final home had promised construction of a progressive care facility that any and all residents would use as the demands of an independent existence became too great. When I reviewed with Pop the legal papers for his purchase, I warned him that the developer had no legal obligation to build such a facility and that he faced great risk if that element was important to his decision. The bigger problem, I suggested, was that his proposed new home was a long way from any family support if his health failed.

He proceeded with the acquisition and, consistent with his finest attributes, soon found himself surrounded with new friends who elected him to leadership positions. The infirmary that was supposed to accommodate the development's residents never materialized in any way close to the manner described in the initial sales pitches. Eventually, Pop's frustrations led him to resign from his elected posts in the residents' organization. He stayed in Melbourne and, to the great regret of everyone except his second wife, physical distance facilitated his emotional isolation from those who loved him most. During the final decade of his life, his daughters traveled to Florida with their families as often as their time and money permitted, but that usually meant no more than once annually per daughter.

Through it all, Pop remained active. He served as surgeon general of the Military Order of the World Wars, traveled to medical conventions, established blood pressure checkup sessions, ran health screening programs, continued old hobbies, started new pursuits, read constantly, and, when he had the chance, entertained his grandchildren in the way that only he could.

TWENTY-FOUR

A PRISONER OF HIS WHEELCHAIR

It was New Year's Day 2005. Dick's phone rang shortly after I had seated myself for one of our regular two-hour morning sessions. My holiday activities did not matter to anyone but Dick and me because the other members of my household were still asleep—and for him the days were all pretty much the same.

I answered the phone for him: "Dick Leopold's room."

"Who is this?" said the female voice on the other end of the line.

"I'm one of Dick's former students."

"Well, this is Dorothy Ver Steeg, the wife of one of his former faculty colleagues. I'm calling to wish him a happy new year and a happy birthday," she responded.

I handed him the phone and tried to make myself invisible, but could not help overhearing his side of the conversation. Dorothy's husband, Clarence Ver Steeg, was the fourth member of Northwestern's famous American history quartet. Dick's discussion with Dorothy about Clarence's unspecified health difficulties prompted Dick to say at one point: "I hope it is nothing so serious that it will require a wheelchair." Although it was his only source of mobility, Dick clearly regarded his wheelchair as his prison.

His other memorable comment came as he tried to recall for Dorothy the specific details of some earlier event in his life: "If I had my files here, I could be as sharp now as I was then."

If I live to be ninety-four, I hope I am half as sharp as he was at that age.

* * *

After nearly a decade at the Rookwood, including a term as its president, Dick became concerned that his advancing age made it unwise to live alone. As he described his situation to me, "It is not realistic for one not to consider the inevitable effects of age as a person reaches his mid-seventies. It is far better to anticipate that time before it is too late."

On November 16, 1989, he moved into the Georgian, a retirement community with options for long-term care. The desirability of the housing created a waiting list; those who already had apartments in the building received preference as vacancies became available. J. Lyndon Shanley and two other Northwestern faculty members—Moody Prior, who had been dean of the graduate school, and Rudy Goedsche from the German department—had already preceded him to the Georgian; that certainly made Dick's decision easier. Taking two steps backward in the hope of someday taking a giant step forward, he took up residence in a one-room apartment on the fourth floor. With this move, he would have to part with most of what remained of his vast personal library. Exeter was the beneficiary of his largesse; he donated 111 cartons of books to his alma mater. In 1993, he acknowledged "the order of my current loyalties . . . Northwestern, Exeter, Harvard, and Princeton."

The most important attractions of his new environs lay in the essential features of life at the Georgian. The transition was easier because he already knew a number of the current residents, "but what surprised me," Dick said, "was the number of new friends I made, including Harold Blake Walker and Bea Elbel, who had no connection to Northwestern." Although he had not mentioned it to me, I later discovered he had remained at Elbel's bedside during her final hours, comforting her with readings from the Bible.

All meals were served in the Georgian's elegant dining room. By virtue of the requirements for independent living in that particular facility, all residents were able to care for themselves. The discussions were lively and the food excellent. Of course, the residents immediately saw what everyone had seen in Dick for his entire life: They elected him three times to two-year terms as president of the residents' council.

Life was as good as it could be for someone approaching eighty. Within a year of moving into the Georgian, he received the SHAFR's Norman A. Graebner Prize for his outstanding contributions to teaching and scholarship. Benedict K. Zobrist, director of the Truman Library, had organized other former fellow Leopold graduate students to provide supporting letters. That was also the year—1990—when his former Northwestern undergraduates established the annual Richard W. Leopold Lectureship under the leadership of Ralph Zarefsky ('72), Lee Huebner ('62), and John C. Roberts ('61) (who had attended Loewenheim's 1970 appearance before Dick's ad hoc committee on the Roosevelt Library investigation). As Zarefsky said at the time, "He had a kind of old-fashioned approach to some things, especially the emphasis on rigor and civility. . . . What you're seeing is a return of what people felt he gave to them." The lectureship was also a natural progression from the annual year-end softball games Dick had umpired between teams comprising his current C-13 students and alumni from the prior year.

He attended an important family event on March 24, 1990, when his nephew John married. John's new wife was Terry. Dick was delighted to see his nephew avoid Dick's "unfortunate example of bachelorhood."

After about two years, a spacious unit overlooking Lake Michigan and offering a view of the Chicago skyline became available. Dick moved into the best housing he had known since childhood. His eighth-floor apartment benefited from cool lake breezes on hot summer days; it was a short walk to the university library and downtown Evanston. Once the added benefits associated with the Georgian's dining experience were added, there was no comparison to any of his prior residences. He hoped to spend his remaining days there, but it was not to be.

* * *

For a decade beginning in the mid-1980s, Kit and I continued to entertain Dick in our home. After the first few visits, he suggested we might consider including Ruth Bonde in the festivities. By then we had three children—the oldest was nine; the youngest was three. Ms. Bonde added a new dimension to our periodic gatherings and we shared many pleasant and humorous times together, especially as our playful ninety-pound Labrador retriever flopped herself wildly in Ms. Bonde's vicinity, on one occasion long enough for a glass of sherry to spill onto her lap. But Ruth had an infectious belly laugh easily covering the animal's gaffe.

When I drove Dick and his date back to their respective abodes, he always insisted that we drop off "Ruthie" first. He would escort her to the front door and then return to my car so I could complete the evening's rounds. As the years passed, the six front steps of our front porch became more difficult for the two of them to navigate. The absence of a handrail did not help. Dick always instructed me to hold Ms. Bonde's arm as she walked down the stairs; he said he could manage just fine without any assistance. On one such occasion, one of my sons followed along as we headed outside. His strong interest in history had enhanced his relationship with my former professor. As we approached the front door, he asked Professor Leopold if he wanted to use a young shoulder to steady himself for the walk down the approaching stairs. Dick smiled with gratitude and placed a firm hand on the lad's shoulder; he also commented for years thereafter on how impressed he had been with the child's thoughtfulness.

* * *

Professionally, Dick gradually took himself out of the game. In November 1991, he attended the final meeting of the editorial advisory committee of The Papers of Woodrow Wilson. In the newsletter of Northwestern's history department, which he edited for twenty-five years prior to relinquishing the role in 1988, he noted that the first such meeting "was held in Washington in 1960 with Mrs. Wilson present." In April 1992, he received the OAH's Distinguished Service Award.

Later that year, on November 9, 1992, Harry Leopold Jr. died. It was a difficult blow. Dick and his brother had been close from the beginning. As a child, he vacationed with Harry and Ethel throughout the American West and the Canadian Rockies. He had followed Harry to the Franklin School, Camp Koenig, and Exeter. Together, Dick and his brother had dealt with their father's untimely death and the continuing challenges their mother had presented. When she had died, Harry, his wife, Lucy, their son, John, and eventually John's wife, Terry, became his only nuclear family. Now Harry was gone, too.

A month later, Dick lamented to Michael Barnhart ('73), a former student who had become a professional colleague, about the growing "compartmentalization" and "balkanization" of the profession: "We now have separate societies not only for women's studies, urban studies, immigration studies, etc., but also chronological groups such as early America, Gilded Age, etc." Such trends certainly ran counter to the assimilation themes of his personal existence. He took even more personally "a continuing prejudice among many leading scholars against international relations," but felt increasingly powerless to remedy it. In 1994, he wrote: "*Who's Who in America* dropped me from the annual volume three or four years ago." By then, Bill Clinton had made George H. W. Bush a one-term president.

Dick continued corresponding with those who wrote to him; he also retained his sharp editor's pencil. In a letter to Edmund T. Delaney, he generally praised the author's manuscript of his autobiography, but could not resist critical comment: "As I warned above, I cannot read books without acting as editor, and I now list a few inevitable and insignificant slips. On page 14, the *Leviathon* should be the *Leviathan*. I was never in Claverly [in Adams House], but I am certain that the swimming pool to which you referred (29) was in the Westmorely section of Adams House, facing the Bow Street Catholic Church." Dick knew that one for sure; it was where Paul Buck had first told him in 1938 about the remarkable offer Harvard was going to make, allowing him to remain there for another five years after the expiration of his three one-year terms.

"On page 37," he continued, "Stamford should be Stanford. The Anschluss occurred in March 1938, not 1937 (43). It is Adolf Hitler, not Adolph as you wrote in a contemporary letter (52). It is Harold Macmillan, not MacMillan (65). Ernest J. King insisted on being called COMINCH, not CNO (70) and technically speaking, Mac Bundy's book on Stimson was not a biography (71). On page 107, incumbant should be incumbent. On pages 120 and 149 Henry Hope Read should be Reed. On page 125 memoriable should be memorable; on page 128, synpathetic should be sympathetic. It was not the Bricker Amendment that lost by one vote in the Senate (136). Over the years Bricker had watered down his text, but even the weakest version could muster only 42 votes on February 25, 1954, with 50 voting nay. The next day an even weaker substitute by Walter F. George resulted in a 60–31 vote. Lastly, the name of Felix Rowayton (204) does not look right; I could not find such a name in *Who's Who in America.*"

He was eighty-three years old when he wrote that letter.

* * *

Dick had just completed his written comments on the manuscript of former Harvard undergraduate student John Morton Blum's autobiography when Jean Demos, the wife of the acting master who had welcomed him to Adams House in 1937, died after sustaining a fall in June 1995. He wrote a stirring letter of tribute to her son and daughter, whose mother "played an indispensable role" during his war years: "Clean sheets and a warm bed never looked so good as they did around midnight on December 18–19, 1942, when I arrived from Jefferson Barracks with an honorable discharge from the Army and a commission pending in the navy. . . . God bless a wonderful woman whose courage, wisdom, and love enriched all our lives. *Ave atque vale.* Hail and farewell." The letter was typed, except for his hand-written final line: "We shall not see her likes again."

* * *

"I completed the two-mile walk to my doctor's office for my annual physical examination during the fall of 1995 in record time," he told me as we resumed his story. "I was in good health and the doctor told me so. I likewise made the return trip to my apartment at the Georgian in record time."

But 1996 turned bad in a very big way. On May 22, he wrote Arthur Link a letter he had been hoping he "would not have to write" when Arthur's wife Margaret died a day earlier. It climaxed "two years of farewells" to some of his "dearest friends—Jean Demos, Sheila Gilmore, Elting Morison, Ruth Bonde."

After describing the highlights of their times together, he offered a fitting conclusion: "Through all those tumultuous forty-seven years, Margaret stood above the fray—a devoted wife, a caring mother, a loyal friend, a source of wisdom and common sense. Her kindness knew no bounds; her charity had no limits. You'd have gone far without her; you went much farther because of her. In my remarks at your retirement dinner on May 19, 1991, I saved for the last of your nine characteristics of love. 'Central to that love,' I concluded, 'is Margaret, who has read and criticized with an editor's skill every word that Arthur has written, who has ministered to him in sickness and in health, and who has offered sage counsel on every occasion. . . . The old adage is apt; behind every great man stands a great woman." He closed with a line similar to the one he had handwritten in his condolence note to the Demos children on the death of their mother, Jean. This time, he typed it: "We shall not see the likes of her again." He signed the letter to his best friend, "Yours in sorrow."

Not long thereafter, he gave another eulogy. This time it was for his friend J. Lyndon Shanley, who died in October 1996.

* * *

A short time earlier, Dick had awakened with severe pain on his left side. He self-diagnosed the sciatica afflicting him earlier in life and so informed his physician, who accepted the assessment without seeing him. The doctor prescribed rest and over-the-counter pain relievers. Dick began to use a cane to steady his walk.

While president of the Georgian's residents' council in January 1997, Dick gave a lecture on the history of the facility. Afterward he realized he had used the lectern to steady himself for the entire speech. The nurse suggested he should use a walker, rather than a cane, on a regular basis. With the pain on his left side continuing, Dick took a trip to see his doctor. By then, he had another physical issue that did not fit his earlier self-diagnosis, although it was not actually a problem for him. Dick knew that most other men of his advancing years rarely completed an evening's sleep without at least one nighttime bathroom trip to urinate. For some reason he ascribed to good fortune, he did not have that difficulty.

His doctor ordered a CAT scan, and the results were twofold. His uninterrupted nights were the result of an enlarged bladder not functioning as it should; that condition could be cured with a catheter. The pain on his left side had a more problematic origin: spinal stenosis. Although cortisone shots provided temporary relief from the discomfort, only surgery would offer any chance for permanent relief. Soon thereafter, specialists reviewed all of the tests and came to the conclusion that the stenosis was so widespread that surgery would not likely result in improvement. Although a former student in Tennessee told Dick that he knew a specialist who might help, Dick was so fed up with medical tests he decided enough was enough. He would allow nature to take its course; it became a rough trip.

Through the fall of 1997, the Georgian had met his every physical and psychological need beautifully. In addition to having spacious living quarters, he took all of his meals in a common dining room where the fellow residents were alert and the mealtime conversations lively. It was only a short walk to all of downtown Evanston's amenities and an even briefer journey to Northwestern's library, where he still maintained a reserved research carrel. But all of that came to an end when doctors could not stop the continuing disintegration of his spine and the resulting compression of his spinal cord. By September, he had lost the use of his legs. The first time he entered the Georgian's dining room in a wheelchair, with former student Jim Eckelberger ('60) pushing him, his fellow residents gave him a standing ovation.

Even so, the rules of his residential community were clear and, as the current president of the residents' council, he felt especially obligated to respect them. Only fully independent dwellers were allowed to remain in the building that housed him. Although the next stop on a typical resident's life-ending journey was to a "partially independent" facility across the street, where help was provided on a periodic schedule, Dick opted for an immediate move to the final stop. The Wagner Health Center would become his new home.

Wagner was divided according to its five floors. Those living on the top two floors were more independent than those on the second and third. As a result, the staffing for each floor varied according to its residents' needs. The upper floors required fewer nurses and related support personnel than those immediately below. The first floor was the intensive care unit. It housed those requiring the most attention, as well as those who were recuperating from acute medical problems before they returned to their permanent rooms after a hospital stay. He obtained the best room with the best view on the fifth floor. He could look to the east and see the treetops, but little else. The dining area was immediately outside his room across the hallway.

His annual newsletters had continued without interruption until December 1997, when tremors in both hands rendered him unable to type or write and he declared that year's missive to be his last. The uproar of protest among his readers was deafening, so for December 1998 and each year thereafter, he enlisted the aid of former student and practicing attorney Betty Olivera ('77) to transcribe his still eloquent words for mass distribution. At the end of each letter, he listed those close friends and former students in the historical profession whom he had outlived— all of whom he would miss in the coming year. Arthur Link graced that section of his 1998 Christmas letter because he had died in March of that year.

*   *   *

Pop remained in relative seclusion from his family during the 1990s because he was unwilling to deal with his second wife's hostile reaction to his progeny; however, he attended two family reunions that became highlights of his final years. On those occasions, as he surveyed his four daughters' families, including thirty grandchildren and great-grandchildren, he joked with obvious pride more than once: "Just think of it—all of this is my fault!" His second wife ended those reunions with an emphatic "Will is getting too old to travel." Her statement was wrong, but he did not have the stomach to fight her on it. In his defense, I became personally convinced that Sue's death had left him so devastated that, whatever problems his second marriage otherwise presented, it prolonged his life by many years. Some people need to be married; he was one.

TWENTY-FIVE

Nearing the Final Station
on the Schedule

Dick and I had been working on his biography for about four months when I received a phone call from John Leopold, a chief judge in Colorado's most populous state court district. He had heard that I had been spending Sundays with his uncle and invited me to join him and Terry for lunch. They were planning one of the three visits they made to Chicago each year.

Two weeks later, I met Terry when I arrived at Dick's room. John was in the hall on one of the occasional cell-phone calls he took throughout the day. Eventually, he joined us and started to tell a story about a 1961 dinner including Dick, Harry, John (who was fourteen), and the Links. As John was about to relate a remark that Link had supposedly made about the recent presidential election, his cell phone emitted an otherworldly sound, causing Dick to say without hesitation: "Now Arthur is going to correct you." Dick's mouth opened wide in an enormous grin. No one else in the room noticed the joke premised upon his deceased friend's intense religious views, but I laughed aloud with him.

We retired to a conference room on the first floor for our luncheon because Dick "hated eating in the bedroom." The meal was appropriately simple. Dick had a toasted cheese sandwich—John called it a panini, to which Dick furrowed his brow while responding, "a what-what-ee?" Joining us was Shep Shanley, who was Dick's second most frequent visitor after me. As a matter of arithmetic truth, a person should always be adding people to one's life as he or she gets older. But as fewer make their presence known, it seldom seems that way.

* * *

When he needed it most, Dick's students unknowingly came to his rescue. The year 1997 had been a terrible and depressing setback for him, but with one notable exception. In May, David Klafter called me. He was a former C-13 student whom

I first met when Dick paired us for the Naval Academy's student conference on foreign policy issues in 1976. After graduation, he had gone on to law school at NYU, then into a law firm, and, finally, into business. He asked if I would join him and Aaron Marcu ('77), a fellow C-13 alumnus who had graduated from Harvard Law School in 1980, as the founding committee to establish a Richard W. Leopold Professorship in American history. I agreed immediately. I had asked the university about such a venture a few years earlier, but settled for establishing a modest Richard W. Leopold Scholarship when I learned about the daunting seven-figure amounts required to endow a chair.

At the annual Leopold Lecture in the fall of 1997, we formally announced the effort to raise more than a million dollars for the chair. We had a head start because provost Lawrence B. Dumas had generously committed Northwestern as a major founding contributor. Only six months later, sufficient funds had been pledged to make the professorship a reality. On May 15, 1998, Weinberg College of Arts and Sciences Dean Eric J. Sundquist presented Dick with the Northwestern University Medal of Merit at a formal dinner in his honor. In attendance were several hundred distinguished guests—trustees, current deans, faculty, and the college's board of visitors. After I spoke on behalf of those whose generosity in tribute to him had made the evening possible, he addressed the assemblage in his clear, strong baritone—without notes and with an eloquence none in the room could have matched. How he managed to maintain his composure throughout the event I will never know; I and many of his former students in attendance certainly could not. The following evening, he called me on the phone with only three words of reaction: "What a high!"

Seven years later, he explained his feelings more fully to me: "One of the worst times of my life was followed by one of the best. The creation of the professorship made a tremendous difference in my outlook. It raised me from the depths of depression to one of the high points of my life. In some ways, it will sustain me to the end." So, in the final analysis, all he had invested in his own students came back to reward him at a crucial time. What went around, came around. Yet again, the circularity of history revealed itself to him.

* * *

As Dick's 1962 book had predicted, by the end of the century the hotbed of international controversy was the Middle East; that situation was not likely to change any time soon. As he and I completed this book, another George Bush resided in the White House after losing the popular vote but prevailing first in the United States Supreme Court and then in the Electoral College in 2000. After the nightmare of September 11, 2001, and *Le Monde*'s declaration on that newspaper's front page "We are all Americans," Bush squandered a unique opportunity to enhance America's international stature. Directly contrary to Dick's advice that

Americans "not attempt to remake mankind in their own image," Bush pursued preventive war and nation building.

Conducting a politics of fear, Bush avoided his father's fate and won a second term running as a "war president" in connection with a conflagration he had initiated based on faulty intelligence and in defiance of America's finest historical traditions. After the invasion of Iraq, the absence of advance planning and inept leadership revealed itself for years thereafter. Every day there was worse than the day before—for the region, that country, and ours. Catering to conservative Christian extremists in the pursuit of his domestic agenda that similarly exploited Americans' fears and differences, the president's resulting inattention to social programs embarrassed the nation when Hurricane Katrina decimated New Orleans in 2005. The rich got richer as his tax policy redistributed wealth from the poor and the middle class to the most affluent. By the middle of 2006, serial scandals were rocking the administration, most of the world seemed unhappy with the United States, and more than seventy percent of Americans had finally grown weary of their own president as his approval ratings dropped to the historically low level last seen when Richard Nixon resigned the office. Even Bush's supposed political base was abandoning him.

Like many of us, Dick felt helpless to stop our blundering national leaders during these difficult times. In contrast to his time as a classroom teacher, he had grown comfortable discussing his personal politics with me. After all, during our conversations, he had now revealed his vigorous support of Franklin Roosevelt during the 1930s and 1940s; that historical fact could not have been discerned from the neutrality with which he had conducted his college courses through 1980. So as the congressional elections approached during the middle of George W. Bush's second term, I asked Dick if he thought history would judge Bush to be America's worst president ever.

"Well, that would be quite a feat," he said after a brief pause, "because it would mean he had surpassed Warren Harding and James Buchanan for that dubious honor." I knew that Harding's Teapot Dome scandal, among many other failures, had made his administration one of the most corrupt, but I had not recalled enough about Buchanan to know what had so distinguished him. I laughed when I later learned that he had presided over the disintegration of the Union immediately prior to the Civil War.

"Even so," Dick continued, "I think Bush is well on his way to that unfortunate distinction."

* * *

Dick continued to focus on those things he could influence, like the annual task of trying to determine who should be invited to the lectureship that bears his name. Dick was unfamiliar with noted political commentator Fareed Zakaria when his name surfaced as a candidate to become the fifteenth Leopold Lecturer in 2004. But Zakaria, who had also earned his doctorate at Harvard, had heard of Dick.

"As I worked on my dissertation on American foreign policy between the Civil War and World War I," Zakaria said during informal remarks at the dinner preceding his lecture, "I was haunted by the magisterial treatment that my topic had already received in the 1962 treatise that Dick had written. So my appearance tonight is something of a payback."

Arthur Schlesinger Jr. was quite direct in expressing his admiration prior to giving the fourteenth annual Leopold Lecture a year earlier: "Dick Leopold is among my oldest and dearest friends. I could think of no higher honor than the invitation that has been extended to me to stand before you tonight as a Leopold Lecturer."

As to such lecturers, Dick always had views about those under consideration, but was careful never to let his personal feelings overshadow the desires of the next generations empowered to extend the invitations. He attended the dinners preceding the Leopold Lectures, although his immobility presented logistical problems. Fortunately, the able assistance of Scott Martin ('84), who became a Leopold loyalist after Dick's retirement without ever having taken a class from him, overcame it. Before Dick lost the use of his legs, Martin escorted him on several trips, including a visit to the site of what had been Camp Koenig, now overgrown, as well as other locations of many cherished childhood memories.

"Those are trips I will always value and never forget," he told me. "Scott has always performed above and beyond the call of duty when it comes to me. He has been a great friend." Dick was also sustained by regular visits from Shep Shanley, who became a more frequent guest as he participated with me in the two-year journey retracing a remarkable life. Dick always anticipated with great enthusiasm the visits from his closest relatives, John and Terry Leopold, and he eagerly awaited the round of former students who typically came calling in connection with university reunions and the annual Leopold Lectures.

As the end drew near, Dick's tremor made the task of eating a continuing challenge, but his mind remained crisp and his analytical strengths fully intact. When asked after each Leopold Lecture how he thought it went, he provided an honest, candid, and completely accurate assessment of the speaker's strengths and weaknesses—both substantively and as to presentation.

For as long as he could, he continued to review manuscripts of distinguished colleagues. John Morton Blum wrote that in editing the Theodore Roosevelt letters, Elting Morison relied on Dick, "whose meticulous professional standards he valued, as did I. Indeed we asked Dick to review the early volumes of the letters for style and content, and we would not have gone to press without Dick's approval." Blum also acknowledged that his Wilson manuscript "profited from the generous readings and suggestions of both Link and his Northwestern University colleague,

Dick Leopold, a good friend but also a strict critic." It was no accident that Blum, one of the most prominent of twentieth-century American historians, signed the copy of his autobiography that he sent to his old friend in Evanston: "For Dick: Tutor, friend, professional model.... Affectionately, John."

Shortly after Dick's eighty-ninth birthday, someone typed up his reactions to Arthur Schlesinger Jr.'s manuscript of his forthcoming autobiography. After two single-spaced typewritten pages of praise, Dick identified "some inevitable slips" that should be corrected before the book went to print: "Your father was an [Adams House] Associate, not a Fellow; we never put five people in C-57; Hicks was not a Tutor but a Counselor in American History; Harvard's undergraduate enrollment in your day was 3,500 so that 500 could not have been one-fourth; Agar and Bingham are both given as editor of the *Courier-Journal;* King during the war was known as COMINCH rather than CNO; Gleason ended his career as editor of the *Foreign Relations* series; and the *Queen Elizabeth* could not have out-run the modern destroyers. And in fairness to FDR, his Boston speech on October 30, 1940 was the only one in which he failed to include the saving words 'unless we are attacked.'" Schlesinger's handwritten note on Dick's copy of the finally published book read: "For Dick Leopold, with regard and affection across many years."

Dick continued to teach. On January 26, 2005, he conducted a discussion for the residents of the Mather Pavilion on "The Presidents." The crowd demanded an encore performance, so on February 23 he spoke on "The Presidents and Their Families" and followed with additional monthly installments thereafter, starting with "The Presidents: James K. Polk, The Forgotten President." When I asked him about the Polk lecture shortly before the designated date, he said, "It was supposed to be 'Woodrow Wilson, the Tragic President.' He will be much more interesting to the residents than Polk, but we'll do Wilson after Polk."

"It seems that you are so popular that you have been engaged for an indefinite run," I responded.

"You know," he continued, "the thing that impresses the audience most is that I do not use any notes for my presentations."

"Well," I said, "that's impressive."

For as long as he was able, he continued to lead. In his final years, he was president of his facility's residents' council.

Even to the end, he continued to laugh. After spending about two hours with me and Shep Shanley, Dick was preparing himself for lunch and checked the menu. "Prime rib—heh-heh-heh-heh-heh-heh—that's a joke. Boy, I just hate this. Why don't the three of us go out someplace?" he mused. The closest we could arrange was a lunch in the room downstairs for the following Sunday. I promised to bring the sandwiches. His request in that regard was always the same: "Plain Swiss cheese on honey-wheat. Nothing else. Nothing." When Shep and I left him that day, he wore a wide grin and promised to reserve the downstairs room where we would dine.

He offered his friendship and advice to all who sought it. I consulted with him on a wide range of issues. His advice was always sound; wisdom knows no age. He heard periodically from friends and colleagues throughout the country. He and John Morton Blum spoke regularly. W. Duane Benton ('72), who had been in the NROTC program and then went to Yale Law School, offered to send Dick the tape of his swearing-in ceremony as chief justice of the Missouri Supreme Court (he was appointed to the United States Court of Appeals for the Eighth Circuit in 2005). Michael A. Barnhart ('73), who went on to do postgraduate study with Ernest May at Harvard, dedicated one of his books to Dick and taught at State University of New York at Stonybrook. Former student Phyllis Elliott Oakley ('56) periodically stopped by to see him during her return to Northwestern as a visiting professor of political science during the spring of 2002 and 2005. In 1999, she retired after a long and distinguished career in the foreign service, including jobs as assistant secretary for intelligence and research; assistant secretary for population, refugees, and migration; and deputy spokesman under Secretary of State George Schultz. She and her husband Robert—a Princeton graduate from the class of 1952, career foreign service officer, and former ambassador to Zaire, Somalia, and Pakistan—were the joint Leopold Lecturers in 1994.

* * *

Unless you live in a body like Dick Leopold's, it is hard to imagine the difficulty of his final years. He retained virtually all of his mental acuity; whether that made his existence more or less difficult is an interesting question. He would have said that he spent his final years waiting to arrive at the last station on the schedule. But until he got there, he entertained all who visited him. For the out-of-towners, he always answered his voice-activated phone—a gift from Northwestern's Weinberg College of Arts and Sciences Dean Daniel Linzer in 2005—unless the caller made the mistake of interrupting his afternoon nap between two and four o'clock, or his five to six o'clock news hour immediately before dinner. Anyone who participated in the conversations that followed was the better for it.

Of that, as Dick would have said, there can be no doubt.

* * *

After Pop's second wife died suddenly and unexpectedly in January 2000, he and I made arrangements for him to move to Chicago. He spoke of it enthusiastically as a return to his second home—the city where he and Sue had been newlyweds; where he had a medical residency with one of the top specialists in his field; where he still laughed about the howling winds that whipped past his small but solid frame as he stood at the 55th Street station on the Illinois Central Line in Hyde Park. I had found the perfect place for him: the Georgian in Evanston. Dick no longer lived there because his physical condition had required a move three years earlier to what was now called the Mather Pavilion. But both men would be part of the Mather organization, and I knew they would be in sufficiently close proximity that they would find each other. I was eager to introduce Dick to Pop and Pop to Dick. It would be a remarkable meeting of Leopold and Loeb.

But it never happened. A cancer in remission for almost ten years resurfaced and moved swiftly to end Pop's life in May 2000, shortly before his eighty-eighth birthday. All of his daughters were with him. When it became my turn to speak at the well-attended memorial service in the Florida retirement community he and his second wife had called home for more than fifteen years, jaws dropped throughout the audience as I described how he had overcome quotas against Jews to gain Yale admission in 1929 and a place at Western Reserve Medical School four years later. He had assimilated so completely that his best friends in his final neighborhood had never known of Pop's Jewish background at all.

My words were followed by military trappings that his daughters knew he would want and that befitted a "full bird colonel," as my former "pfc" father would say with a lingering awe even forty years after his own service as a paratrooper had ended. Uniformed officers gave a twenty-one-gun salute and then followed with the folding of an American flag presented to his oldest daughter "with thanks from a grateful nation." The ceremony ended with one of his grandchildren playing taps on a trumpet the young man had not held since high school. We sent Pop off in style.

When I returned to his home and began reviewing his personal papers, I noticed near his recliner three books he had been reading simultaneously before the final onset of his terminal illness. One was a mystery novel; another was on a science subject that I cannot recall; the third was a history of World War II. The next day, his daughters divided his effects in a most civilized way: They took turns making their selections. Fortuitously and without any comprehension of its significance, Kit chose her great-great grandfather Joseph Mellor's microscope. It now sits proudly on display in our living room, and it still works. She also selected the Mason's gavel Pop's father received in commemoration of his service as worshipful master. And she selected his Army mess kit, including an old canteen and medical supplies dating from the war. No one else was interested in his college yearbooks or diplomas from Yale and Western Reserve Medical School, so they were given to me as the family custodian of historical artifacts.

TWENTY-SIX

THE MEASURE OF A MAN

Faithful historian and accomplished teacher that he was, Dick permitted me no shortcuts in my quest to learn his story. He guided me to particularly useful sources along the way, including an article on his Indiana encounter with Maurice Cuba, his remarks to the Massachusetts Historical Society about his Harvard years, his Arthur Link tribute describing their relationship and his effort to keep the Wilson scholar at Northwestern, and his 448-page report on the Roosevelt Library investigation. He also provided helpful direction to personal papers housed in Northwestern's Archives.

But he saved the best for last. Only as we neared the end of a purely chronological exploration of events and people in his life did he reveal that he had compiled "a collection of autobiographical letters." They were located in a folder among his 182 boxes in the Northwestern University Archives.

"I am sure that if you call Kevin Leonard, he should be able to find the file for you," he told me.

The following day, I placed that call and, by the end of the week, I had a copy of the entire collection. Although it would have been interesting to read the file earlier in our project, he must have known that a certain depth to my experience would have been lost if I had. Incremental discovery and revelation along the way had made our journey together dramatically interesting to me; the trip itself had become as captivating as the destination.

For more than a decade after his retirement in 1980, Dick had begun organizing his personal papers in a subterranean room that Northwestern Archivist Patrick Quinn had set aside for him. What he now called his autobiographical letters consisted of a tiny subset of his extensive correspondence between 1957 and 2001. As he personally culled them from among the thousands he had sent during his lifetime, he had made copies so each original "cc" would remain in the respective file for the correspondent to whom the letter had been addressed. He had placed each extra copy in a single separate folder I now held.

As I had expected, the letters contained some straightforward biographical facts, but there was much more. Although I had already read many of the letters in the individual correspondent files from which he had copied them, collectively, they also revealed dimensions of the man that, I suspect, very few had ever seen. I knew immediately that only his own words could properly bring his story to a close. Now they will—with a little help from Pop.

* * *

On April 13, 1995, Dick sent Edmund T. Delaney editorial comments on the manuscript of Delaney's autobiography. They had been Princeton classmates, but only passing acquaintances while at school together. "Henry Hammond—one of the three Hammond boys with whom I shared a home in Washington during the war—called me to say that he had run into Delaney, who had written an autobiography," Dick recounted. "He told me about it and Delaney sent me a copy at Henry's suggestion. I felt obliged not only to read it, but also to comment upon it."

His critique closed with a suggestion that might tempt Delaney to pursue a biography of Dick: "I have done some autobiographical writing but have rejected the notion of attempting a full-length volume for several reasons, including the absence of a publisher. Most of what I would say would deal with the universities of which I have been a part, teaching and writing, historians I have known, and the relations between the historical profession and the federal government. My correspondence files starting in 1948 are exhaustive; before that date they are spotty. I never kept a diary, but I have all my engagement books starting in 1940, except alas from October 5, 1942 (when I entered the Army as a private) until March 1946 (when I was released as a Lieutenant in the Navy). I kick myself for not resuming the engagement books when I reported to the Office of Naval Records and Library on December 24, 1942." He warned Delaney that additional materials about Dick's life were on the way to him, "[h]oping you may be interested . . ."

Delaney did not take Dick's bait, and for that I am very grateful. Although not trained in historical research methods, I told my former professor at the outset that I wanted to understand his story because I knew just enough about him to suspect he had one. I assumed he would guide me as necessary to assure the integrity of our enterprise as a historical work. In that sense, as I sometimes told him, he had reentered the profession to direct one final dissertation—this one. When he suggested that no one would be interested in the resulting book, I responded that my job was to write it so the reader wanted to continue. As we progressed, I also opined that the more I learned about him, the more certain I became that others would develop my enthusiasm for understanding him, the events shaping his life, the people who had made all the difference, and those to whom he had made all the difference. We would write a historically accurate account and let others decide the nature of its appeal. His own words now frame the closing discussion.

* * *

Perhaps more central to Dick's story than he realized when our project began was his journey as a nonpracticing Jew through twentieth-century America. A better articulation might be—and these are my words, not his—the journey of a person who never regarded himself as Jewish in any way, but who went through life with a Jewish identity that others gave him for a sinister and discriminatory purpose. In a sense, I think he and Pop were suspended between two worlds and may have felt fully integrated into neither. Although Dick wrote in 1995, "I have no religion myself," it is now clear to me that his statement alone could not dictate how others viewed him.

In important respects, his course was charted long before he was born. A predominantly Jewish community that was the childhood home of Dick's mother centered itself on Chicago's south side during the late 1800s and early 1900s. When Ethel Kimmelstiel moved to New York City and married Harry Leopold Sr., she entered an even more secular world, although her family had already been nonpracticing. "My parents' marriage ceremony," he told me, "was probably performed by a rabbi, but in a proceeding that was almost certainly without any religious aspects."

Dick grew up in an ethnically diverse upper-class Manhattan neighborhood. When limited educational options propelled him and his older brother into the predominantly Jewish Franklin School, he became part of what would be his one and only Jewish cohort—if I can call it that—in his life. It was an imperfect fit because his family continued the nonpracticing approach of his grandparents' households. Although his peers respected him for his intelligence and interpersonal skills, he did not identify with any of their Semitic beliefs or traditions. He had no reason to do so.

"I was always moving the other way," he told me. "That was my protective armor—to do everything I could to avoid being identified as Jewish because I did not think there was anything Jewish about me. I remember an incident when I went to school on one of the Jewish holidays; I stopped at the deli to buy my lunch. Maybe I was just rebellious, but on that particular day, I bought a ham sandwich."

Rebellious against whom or what? He certainly was not challenging his family's attitudes, which reinforced assimilative behavior already under way for at least a generation before him. Nothing he encountered as a young child caused him to reconsider his direction. To the contrary, personal experiences reconfirmed, for him, the wisdom of a secular approach as a matter of survival and success in an anti-Semitic land. He discovered that when his Aunt Blanche married, she had traded her obviously Jewish maiden name—Kimmelstiel—for the more distinguished-sounding Churchill; her new husband had adopted the latter in abandoning the German-Jewish name of Kirshberger.

"The name changes were a reaction to anti-Semitism and American animosity toward Germany during World War I," Dick explained. "Lots of people did that at the time."

The 1920s were worse for those "identified as Jewish," to use Dick's phrase. After the notorious Leopold-Loeb killing in 1924, the insidious underlining of the name Leopold in Boston newspaper articles at the Exeter school post office when Dick was twelve reinforced his need to distance himself from anything Semitic. His early childhood had made that a short and easy distance to travel. Exeter was a predominantly white Anglo-Saxon Protestant institution when Dick was there from 1926 to 1929. Its exclusive fraternities and mandatory chapel sessions reminded Dick to maintain his secular path if he hoped to move from the second- or third-class citizenship that still seemed to persist because he was "someone identified as Jewish," even though he never so regarded himself. The Princeton eating clubs reminded him that the issue of anti-Semitism would endure, regardless of his continuing inability to determine exactly why others labeled him a Jew.

He knew that the criteria being used to classify him could not have been religious. As Dick told me, he was unfamiliar with Jewish religious traditions. Like Pop, Dick came from a family that acknowledged Christmas and Easter, not Rosh Hashanah and Yom Kippur. Yet he certainly developed an awareness of unique barriers to his success, as a letter to his mother during his senior year at Princeton revealed. In it, he questioned whether he could make a career in history, despite his "racial handicap."

More remnants of his ethnic baggage—the origins of which he himself could not pinpoint—would follow him to Harvard. At the time, Dick did not know that the university's only Jewish tenured faculty member, a Semitic studies professor named Harry A. Wolfson, had written in 1922 that Jews should "submit to fate" rather than "foolishly struggle" against prejudice. "Some are born blind, some deaf, some lame, and some are born Jews. To be isolated," Wolfson wrote, "to be deprived of many social goods and advantages," was the Jews' common lot. Although Dick favored President James Bryant Conant's new national scholarship program for undergraduates and a new examination—the SAT—being used to select winners, he was unaware that only "western" applicants were eligible for the scholarships, thereby excluding less affluent Jews from the large population centers of New York and Boston.

But he did have firsthand experience with anti-Semitism at Harvard. As an assistant senior tutor at Adams House, he learned about the classification of "stars" who were spread equally among the Harvard residential houses. However distant his internal connection to being Jewish was by then—and it was very distant indeed—he seems not to have lingered over the possibility that those in Cambridge making decisions about his future may have labeled him a "star," too. Yet, he certainly must have realized that granting tenure to a Jew at any Ivy League institution would be unprecedented at that time, especially in his chosen field of American history.

Hope must have triumphed over reality. Perhaps he concluded by 1938 that any ethnic impediment did not apply to him because he had finally shed the last of his Semitic residue, whatever it might have been. If his hypothesis were correct, only objective merit would have mattered to his advancement. Tangible supporting evidence would have been his selection as assistant senior tutor at Adams House and his appointment to a five-year position following three years as an instructor. Even though that was the end of the academic road for him in Cambridge, he never asserted that those responsible for foreclosing his long-term future at Harvard acted in bad faith, and it is certainly not for me to say they did. But as Dick himself observed, Harvard "fumbled for six years over the field of diplomatic history" after losing Dick in 1948. It did not have a tenured faculty member in that field until 1959, when Ernest May became an associate professor after teaching Dick's old course for more than ten years.

Notwithstanding Harvard's shortcomings, Dick found it to be a vastly superior environment to Princeton's. As he wrote to a college classmate in 1990, "[A]fter I came to know Harvard College and House system from 1937–1942, I rather think I might have been even happier on the banks of the Charles." Those words speak volumes about the problems that must have plagued him as an undergraduate.

A similar distance from Judaism would accurately describe Pop's viewpoint as well: "The truth is, we were in no way truly Jewish, but were always Jews to the rest of the world." The most important part of that statement is the first half: "The truth is, we were in no way truly Jewish . . ." Because of the households in which they were raised, neither Pop nor Dick could identify what it was about them or their personal histories qualifying them to be "Jewish" in the first place. As Dick told me, "I was trying to move away from whatever all of that was."

One of Dick's early Harvard undergraduates, John Morton Blum, may have experienced a similar socialization away from his Semitic origins. He, too, had no childhood connection to anything Jewish: "Both my parents rejected Judaism and never practiced it. My mother found a substitute for spirituality by joining the Ethical Culture Society, an essentially secular organization that endorsed the Ten Commandments." Even so, his family "was no less Jewish for its rejection of Judaism."

Certainly in their early years, it must have been confusing for Dick, Pop, John Blum, and similar nonpracticing Jews when others saw them differently from the way they saw themselves. The conundrum must have become more acute as they made their way to Ivy League schools and beyond. They traveled a difficult road, overcoming quotas, prejudices, and systematic discrimination against a group that, in their minds, should not even include them. In addition to obvious episodes like the verbal and physical abuse Blum withstood during his first year at Andover, more subtle forms of exclusion sometimes blocked opportunities for advancement in ways that could not be known at the time and even to this day cannot be proven conclusively.

But many things became a matter of a public record that cannot be ignored. Harvard president Lowell's anti-Semitic sentiments have survived him, as have similar views that led Columbia to impose the Ivy League's first informal quotas limiting Jewish attendance. Ironically, Harvard and its fellow elite colleges accomplished anti-Semitic discrimination through the introduction of new criteria having a much different use and purpose today: personal recommendations, considerations other than purely academic achievement, and evaluation of "character."

Long-standing practices and attitudes persisted beyond the introduction of the supposedly objective SATs and related inroads into the discriminatory use of subjective admissions criteria. In his 1938 inaugural address upon his ascent to the Yale presidency, Charles Seymour said, "Yale was dedicated to the upraising of spiritual leaders. . . . The simple and direct way is through the maintenance of the Christian religion as a vital part of university life."

In this fuller historical context, it becomes easier to see why, in such a hostile world, Dick would not have departed from his own family's non-Jewish traditions to reclaim a long-lost identity as a Jew: Things always became worse when others placed him in that category. Even so, his fundamental belief in fair play eventually caused him to view his own disappointment in the junior year assignment of a Jewish roommate at Exeter as a source of personal shame. When he later came to that realization, it burdened him for a long time.

But he took advantage of subsequent opportunities to atone for his childhood act of self-preservation—the maintenance of what he called his "protective armor"—when he helped to break down other barriers of prejudice and discrimination at Harvard and Northwestern. Three examples reveal the profound potential of a single person to rise above his own disadvantages and improve the world. Before the war, he helped Lucien V. Alexis become the first African American undergraduate student to be admitted into the Harvard house system. At Northwestern, Dick battled a racist admissions director who imposed discriminatory policies during the 1950s. On Northwestern's Council on Undergraduate Life, he fought to eliminate provisions in fraternity and sorority charters that imposed prohibitions based on racial, religious, or ethnic grounds—including bans on Jews. He was, in other words, the kind of crusader who reformed institutions over a period of time from inside them. He built slowly while standing on the shoulders of giants as he himself became one.

* * *

That Dick, Pop, John Blum, and others sharing similar backgrounds overcame the unique obstacles confronting them says much about their character. They had some help after 1945 because the outcome of World War II and the horrified response to the Holocaust began to change things for the better, although the job took a while and is still not complete. Even as the war ended, Dartmouth's President Ernest M. Hopkins declared, "Dartmouth is a Christian college founded for the Christianization of its students." In September 1945, John Blum heard directly from Elliot Perkins—master of Lowell House, lecturer in eighteenth-century history, and Dick's former War Service Information Bureau colleague—that Blum should pursue a career in law rather than history because, Perkins said, "Hebrews can't make it in history." Fortunately for the profession, Blum disregarded that advice.

Disabling barriers to a Jew's advancement fell as the generation including Dick, Pop, and John Blum came of age. As their opportunities increased, they took full advantage and succeeded in the ways most important to each of them. Pop rose to the top of the medical profession. Among his many other accomplishments, Blum became the first Jewish Fellow on the Harvard Corporation Board (although, ironically, fellow Jews Oscar Handlin and Robert Lee Wolff jealously urged him to decline the invitation on the grounds that Harvard had never offered Blum a tenured appointment on its faculty). Dick's remarkable career speaks for itself.

The statistics prove that others must have had similar experiences. In 1940, only two percent of professors were Jewish. By 1975, although comprising only three percent of the population, Jews comprised one-fifth of the faculty at major universities and one-fourth at Ivy League schools; a higher percentage taught at the nation's top medical and law schools. Although there is no evidence as to the number of these new educators who were nonpracticing, my suspicion is that such men quietly comprised most of the movement's vanguard.

Wholly apart from the discrimination they faced and overcame before World War II, one can reasonably ask how, if at all, the war and the Holocaust shaped the way Dick and Pop viewed themselves as a matter of their Jewish identities. To me, the answer is simple; however, not everyone will like it. Neither man had any internal Jewish identity at any point in his life, so there was nothing for either man to revisit after the war. From childhood, they were Jews only because others so labeled them. From an early age, they developed survival mechanisms allowing them to distance themselves from that identification—Dick actually called it his "protective armor"—to blend in so that no one would notice Jewish ethnicity lurking in their family backgrounds. But in no sense did they regard being Jewish as part of their personal histories. Maybe they should have, but they did not—any more than I feel any kindred with my German forebears whose descendants down a much different branch of my large family tree may have been Nazis from 1933 to 1945.

So when I asked Dick how the war changed his self-identity as a Jew, he answered immediately: "Not at all." Pop's biography and postwar life confirm his similar view. By the end of the war, the two men were in their thirties; their approaches to life and those around them were fully established. Their efforts had produced success eluding many of their Jewish counterparts—whether practicing or not. Because both men found their lives to be personally and professionally satisfying, there was no reason for them to reconsider the manner in which they had already navigated through severe anti-Semitic shoals. That they benefited from the heightened awareness of anti-Semitism's evils following the Holocaust was, in a sense, simply a happy fortuity for them. They had already set their courses when it came to their ethnicity—or internally perceived lack thereof—and nothing about the war caused them to change direction.

Many practicing Jews may find offensive the lack of Jewish self-identity that defined Dick and Pop. In that sense, both men were trapped in an untenable middle ground: non-Jews regarded them as Jews; Jews regarded them as traitors to their heritage and, therefore, non-Jews. I think they properly belonged in neither camp; they themselves comprised part of a transitional generation. Dick had no offspring, but three of Pop's four children continued his assimilative path. Others may criticize their decisions, but Dick and Pop would say that they simply functioned as they thought they should in a secular society—and maybe the world would be a better place if everyone did likewise. Hence Pop's overriding theme: "People is people."

Others may view all of this differently, but that is how all of this looks to me, a person who wandered into this minefield without any particular awareness of the surprises that awaited. It has certainly become clear to me that these issues are far more complex than I could have imagined when Dick and I began this project, and they are profoundly sensitive for almost everyone on every side of the controversy.

* * *

Of course, it is always the personal dimension that makes any discrimination real, and individual attitudes sometimes seem hopelessly intractable. Until my conversations with Dick, I had not thought about the extent to which I had already received a limited firsthand exposure to the power and endurance of anti-Semitism. In the 1910s, Dick's Aunt Blanche joined many other Jews in moving to the south side, not far from the University of Chicago's campus. By 1924, her family lived at the Ambassador West on the near north side. In the succeeding generation, many Jews (including Dick's cousin Alice) skipped over the other northern suburbs along Lake Michigan before finding in Highland Park a community that would accept them. As the twentieth century unfolded, many Chicago Jews migrated northward from the city into Evanston and southward from Highland Park into Glencoe, which got its first synagogue in 1920 and an extraordinarily grand one on Lake Michigan in 1964. Immediately north of Evanston, Wilmette gradually added Jews to its population. Immediately to the south of Glencoe, Winnetka did the same.

By 1983, the small, affluent suburb of Kenilworth found itself between two communities that had a significant Jewish presence—Wilmette on the south and Winnetka on the north—while it had very few such families. (Ironically, though, Dick's 1929 Exeter class yearbook notes that John P. Spiegel, his second-year roommate who took the bed Dick had planned for Stewart Cort, was from Kenilworth.) At the time, Kit and I were searching for our first house after living for three years in an Evanston condominium. A well-meaning real estate agent discouraged us from becoming too interested in a Kenilworth home because it would "not be the right community" for us. The agent knew that Kit was of Jewish descent (whatever that now meant), and we all understood immediately the meaning of her comment. From that moment, we had no interest in Kenilworth.

Similarly, as I finished this book, I recalled the wife of a partner in my law firm reporting on her interview with the admissions committee at a Chicago country club during the mid-1980s as intended principally "to make sure that I was not Jewish or anything." She and her husband remain our friends and we know the comment intended no offense, but the incident helped me to understand the proliferation of Jewish-only country clubs resulting from the non-Jewish clubs preceding them. Even one of our elderly next-door neighbors, who has since died and who lovingly watched our kids grow up, once remarked offhandedly that "*those* people" possessed undesirable qualities apparent to the rest of us. He had forgotten that Kit and our children were among "*those* people," although the connection was neither religious nor cultural.

As someone wiser than I once said, "The thought is the father to the word, and the word is the father to the act." It is one thing for people to view others as being different from themselves; it is something else to use stereotypes in placing a rank order on the value of diverse cultures inhabiting a single planet. Any one of us can, at any time, find ourselves among "those people" for some purpose others might find convenient. It is a dangerous game, but I now wonder if it will ever end.

* * *

Another aspect of Dick's journey was the importance of public service. He proved it first with his choice of a profession. Scholarship and teaching should be among the most valued of any civilization's pursuits because they are critical to the future. Unfortunately, free-market capitalism rarely so rewards those activities. In that respect, a person's most important impact is usually a personal one. Dick symbolized those who gave much of themselves to enlighten America's youth while seeking little in return. Pop likewise regarded his most important contributions as his impact on those whom he touched along the way—children, grandchildren, patients, friends, medical students, professional colleagues, and others whose lives he brightened simply because he was there for a time.

But I now better understand that for Dick, Pop, and many of their generation, one event bound them all together in tasks that transcended their individual acts and transformed them forever: World War II. Fully one-third of Pop's 1996 autobiography is devoted to the period from 1937 to 1946. This book likewise includes a disproportionate number of pages discussing that period of Dick's life. I now have a new appreciation of how the war became and remained a prolonged defining moment in the lives of Dick, Pop, and millions of others who served their country during freedom's greatest challenge. I now know why Pop never missed an opportunity to watch any movie or documentary about the war. I also realize why Dick bristled at the Bush administration's use of the word *war* in the aftermath of 9/11, because that terminology cannot properly occupy the same rhetorical space describing the world between 1939 and 1945.

In the most important lines on this topic in his autobiography, Pop wrote: "The relating of life's experiences is supposed to be in chronological order, but the war calls for a difference. As this is written, more than a half century after that coming home day, the total experience has not faded. The recollections are much clearer than much that has happened in those succeeding fifty years. The stresses were much greater. But then so was the accomplishment. We were parts of history; we were doing things of importance to millions of people; we worked not for personal gain but for world changes. . . . Yes, there was personal competition for status and position; there was guaranteed food and lodging—of a sort which we would not repeat by choice. We existed in a way we had never thought we could do, way beyond anything we might have envisioned possible. And we accomplished the goal; we won the war. We were soldiers of the United States. And everybody with whom I speak these days feels the same way. Keep in mind that at all memorials—Fourth of July, Memorial Day, Veterans' Day, and more, every veteran whom you see is reliving those days of sacrifice combined with accomplishment."

After Dick read Pop's remarks for the first time as he and I worked on an early draft of this book, he said, "That is a very good paragraph."

* * *

Like the wartime experience itself, Dick's public service did not end when the war was over. He continued to serve his country and his profession for years thereafter and well into retirement. He could have relaxed and led a more leisurely existence after he turned seventy, eighty, or even ninety, but he never did.

Yet for all he accomplished, it was never enough for him. As his own harshest critic, he would occasionally say he should have done more in the way of scholarly activities.

"How do you respond to those who say that I am not particularly distinguished because I wrote only three books—four if you count the Roosevelt Library investigation report?" he asked near the end of our discussions.

"I say everything depends on how you measure a man," I replied. "You are a living example of the stone cast into the pond; it creates concentric ripples beyond your own ability to see them and long after the stone is thrown." He nodded in understanding, if not complete acceptance.

Pop's life tells a similar story. In the postscript to his autobiography, he wrote, "What does all of this mean? . . . To me it means a life in which there was service to my country, sufficient income to have a comfortable home for my family, 44 years of wedlock producing four offspring—each being a totally self-sufficient adult . . . A life spent caring for the sick, and reaching a position in academia. Personally, I find this satisfactory, although there is certainly room to say that all of this might have been more productive to society. But in my view, it represents the old teaching of personal responsibility and caring for one's fellow man."

* * *

Dick was always clear and unambiguous in emphasizing the importance of integrity in a person's life. It was no accident that Paul Ward called him when Francis Loewenheim and his lawyer began their assault on the profession and important government institutions in 1969. Ward told him the controversy required a man of Dick's stature and unquestioned character to take command of the situation. Despite the tremendous personal cost to him at an already difficult time in his life, Dick saw the matter through to its end in the hope that future generations of historians would benefit from his sacrifices. When his profession and his government continued to call on him during the decades thereafter, he always answered with his best effort.

Nevertheless, skeptics will always walk among us. When a would-be author on Northwestern's undergraduate life during the 1960s and 1970s asked about "an allegation" that Dick had "provided information to military intelligence about colleagues and/or students during the Vietnam-era protests," his response was firm and direct: "The answer is an unequivocal no. The question is both insulting and stupid. My sole contacts with the Army were ten weeks as a private from October–December 1942 and a five-year membership from 1966–1971 on the Army's Historical Advisory Committee. That group was concerned with the volumes on the Army in the Second World War and the Korean War and had nothing to do with military intelligence or the conflict in Vietnam. Further, if I had reported on my colleagues, they would hardly have lived with me in harmony until my retirement in 1980 and since. Further still, if I had been guilty as alleged, it is unlikely that I would have admitted it now. Hence I find your question stupid.

"If there is anything in my professional life that I have guarded scrupulously, it is my honesty, fair-dealing, and integrity. That I succeeded, at least to a large degree, should be evident from my election as president of the Organization of American Historians, from the overwhelming endorsement of our findings in the troubled Roosevelt Library case, and from the prize established in my name with the OAH."

He went on to explain that the allegations about which his correspondent inquired arose from his attempt to manage a divisive department, his resistance to radical revisions to the graduate curriculum, and his successful one-man defense of the NROTC as various faculty, student, and administration forces sought to banish it from Northwestern. He closed his missive with a passage demonstrating his indefatigable commitment to civility and self-control: "I wish you success in your book and can only hope that it is based on solid historical evidence and not rumor, hearsay, or vile slander. You may use this letter as you wish."

He signed the letter "sincerely yours," which others will recognize as a sharp divergence from his typically warm "faithfully yours." In that sense, you had to know Dick Leopold very well to have any idea when he was angry, disappointed, or hurt. At a tender age, he chose for himself the middle name of William as a tribute to a beloved cousin who had died tragically, but "Eminently Civilized" would have been a more descriptive moniker.

As an undergraduate, I heard from a faculty member that he thought Dick had been a member of the Spartacus Youth League during his early years. When that remark was uttered, I did not know that the SYL was a communist organization. A similarly absurd comment was once made that Dick had "emerged from Schlesinger's red cell" in Cambridge, which, of course, never existed. But the words wrapped the famous historian's liberal politics in colorful rhetoric.

So in a sense, Dick could not win. At various times in his life, political extremists at both ends of the spectrum accused him of being something he was not. It was not that the truth was somewhere in the middle; it was that the truth was nowhere to be found in such "vile slander," as Dick would call it.

Of course, all of the allegations were false, but there is a lesson to be learned about the power of accusation and the danger of gossip, even when a man of great stature is the target and even when the speaker's motive lacks any malice. Historical accuracy remains central to any pursuit of the truth. Dick properly realized that continuing diligence is absolutely essential to the success of that mission; historians more than others owe a special duty to all of us in that regard. When one of my children opined that "history is irrelevant," I responded, "In most important respects, history—accurately told—is more relevant than anything else a person could study. If you do not understand correctly where you are from, your effort to keep track of where you are going becomes hopeless. It is true for individuals and it is true for civilizations."

Dick's colleague Arthur Schlesinger Jr. said it best at one of the recent Leopold Lectures: "History is to a nation what memory and conscience are to an individual."

* * *

Then there is the matter of Dick's profoundly sentimental side as it has manifested itself in his pervasive attachments to his former students and professional colleagues. He grew up and lived in a time when men simply did not reveal emotional reactions; however, a 1933 letter to his mother is telling: "You know my character well enough—old in a few respects, but a kid in most ways. You know how sensitive I am, how easily hurt."

Twenty years later, he urged Arthur Link to reject Princeton's offer and remain at Northwestern. Dick wrote that he would make "no appeal . . . on grounds of friendship and emotion," but his own words then betrayed him. He described the prospect of Link's departure as imposing "a personal and professional loss, the extent of which I shudder to contemplate."

He certainly realized he needed physical proximity to a "family," because he created one wherever he went. Although he maintained ties to each former family after he moved away, no person's emotional requirements can be met exclusively through the mailbox. When he left the Gilmores, the Littles, and the Demoses in Cambridge, he forged a new family with the Wilds, the Links, the Shanleys, and Ruth Bonde in Evanston. I now think everyone needs a family wherever he or she is. Certainly the nuclear unit into which a person is born is sufficient for many purposes and for a long time. But it alone cannot take any of us across life's finish line.

Dick's students were a unifying presence permeating all of his transitions; they comprised a different kind of family for him. Because he maintained personal privacy under such close guard, it was sometimes easy to miss the magnitude of his deep sensitivity, but it was there. For example, in 1982, he wrote what he called a "hail and farewell" note to a former Adams House student, who had been one of those helping to get Dick "off to war" in October 1942, but from whom he had heard nothing for thirty years. In response, he was pleasantly surprised to receive a telephone call, followed by a long letter.

Dick answered the letter within twenty-four hours: "I am most grateful for your response to my 'hail and farewell' note of the 3rd—your prompt telephone call on the 6th and your long letter of that same date, with its many interesting enclosures, which arrived yesterday. I dispatched that note with a heavy heart. Admittedly, there had been more than a thirty-year lapse in our correspondence and, even, direct contacts; but I could not, or would not, believe that the old friendship was gone."

He then described a more general anxiety relating to correspondents who had come and gone: "If I seemed edgy about not receiving a prompt reply [to a letter Dick had written four months earlier], there is a good reason. Over the years my extensive correspondence with former students, colleagues, and academic associates has occasionally come to an abrupt close. I always regret those endings, some of them explicable and some not. Being without progeny, I value the friendships of many years ago and, where they are truly meaningful to me, try to keep them in repair. . . . It is even more distressing when I attempt to resume and renew—without results."

His 1995 letter to a former Exeter classmate who had become his mother's physician in the 1950s continued this theme: "Writing to someone with whom you have not been in touch for many years is a tricky matter. If there is no answer, you are unsure as to whether the letter miscarried, the addressee is dead or incapacitated, or whether he or she does not give a damn."

"I am not really in any position to initiate contact with people who have dropped away," Dick explained to me. "But even when I do not receive a note or card in response to my annual Christmas letter, I continue sending one out to that person for several years thereafter. But after five years, I cross them off my mailing list."

Dick knew that his former students, regardless of whether they maintained contact, honored him most in the conduct of their lives. From his early Adams House days, he had always enjoyed his special relationships with undergraduates. That tradition continued at Northwestern. In 1992, when asked to name those individuals who had exerted the most significant influence on his life, aspiring presidential candidate Richard Gephardt ('62) identified his parents and continued his answer to the national television interviewer: "I had a history professor at Northwestern—named Richard W. Leopold." Congressman Gephardt had been Dick's student during the final year that "The History of American Foreign Policy" was taught as a lecture course.

Among the earliest participants in his newly developed C-13 discussion class was Nicholas Chabraja ('64), who needed a spring class that met at eight in the morning so he could practice with the Northwestern golf team during the afternoons. He circled back to take the fall and winter sessions the following year, persuaded Dick to write his recommendation to Northwestern Law School, and eventually became chairman of General Dynamics Corporation and a Northwestern trustee.

The more than three hundred contributors to the Leopold Lectureship and Professorship include, in addition to those previously mentioned, accomplished citizens in diverse professions: former NBC newsman John S. Palmer ('58); Hank Reiling ('60), who became the Eli Goldston Professor of Business Administration at Harvard; NROTC midshipman Jim Eckelberger ('60), who made a career in the Navy and retired as a two-star admiral; Mark Feichtinger ('70), who achieved that rank as a reservist; commander Dan Moore ('77), who returned to the campus as a professor of naval science and tactics at Northwestern.

Jack Guthman ('60) went on to Yale Law School and became one of the most influential attorneys in Chicago. It says something about Dick and his students that as I was finishing the first draft of this book, Kit and I encountered Jack and his wife just steps from the River Seine in Paris. The initial subject of our conversation and the only point of connection between us was, of course, Dick Leopold, but Jack eventually gave us several fine restaurant recommendations and I gained a new friend.

As Guthman once said, "We call ourselves Leopold people. We were adopted." He also correctly observed, "Aside from substance, you came away from [Dick's] course with a great desire for striving toward excellence. He demanded of you what he demanded of himself—a lot of intense work and analysis. I think it prepared you for challenge." Guthman's classmate, Philip W. Stichter ('60), went on to Harvard Law School. Returning to visit as often as he could during Dick's final years, Stichter wrote, "You personify the best in being a scholar, a teacher, a gentleman, and a friend."

Mary Livingston Peterson ('62) had a son who attended another college; she sent Dick his 150-page senior thesis. Dick read it, checked every reference, and wrote that his comments should be taken as "the counsel of perfection." She continued, "I think that summarizes his standard. He felt that there was something perfect you could work for. . . . The thing about Dick Leopold is that you're not just a student while you're there. You're a student for life."

Another former student from the class including Reiling, Eckelberger, Guthman, and Stichter was Gordon Segal ('60), founder of Crate & Barrel. He and his wife Carole ('60)—also a former Leopold student—have consistently supported the Lectureship and Professorship. In a recent *Chicago Tribune* profile, a reporter asked Gordon, "I hear you like hiring people from academia?"

"We like teachers," he answered. "Many of our senior executives . . . come from teaching because part of what we believe is important is educating our staff, and our staff is available to educate our customers." I think I know where Segal received some of his early inspirational insights on the seminal importance of a great teacher in a person's life. As he later wrote, "Richard Leopold was one of the most supportive and nurturing teachers I've ever met. He spent most of his time pointing out what we'd done *right*, rather than what we'd done *wrong*. Then, he'd add just enough criticism to let us know we could do even better."

Dick also accommodated unique requests in his effort to get the best from his students. Entertainer Garry Marshall later noted, "I personally had trouble answering the long essay questions in the blue books. [Professor Leopold] allowed me to answer with dialogue scenes rather than prose writing and graded me on content rather than style. It helped me tremendously and I think my early Bismarck dialogue aided me in writing sitcoms and movies for a living."

The list of similarly grateful alumni goes on and on and on—educators, lawyers, judges, government servants, businessmen, diplomats, doctors, mothers, fathers, and ordinary men and women who became better writers, speakers, thinkers, and citizens as a direct result of time with him. To discuss all of them would require another book; to those whose names and accomplishments I have omitted, I can offer only my apologies.

At the time of Dick's retirement in 1980, several former undergraduate students from the 1950s and 1960s organized a tribute dinner in his honor. When someone asked Marshall Randall Hall ('60) if the gathering was a family one, he replied, "Yes, sort of . . ."

"That is the most one could hope for—that is as good as it gets," Dick told me, as he recounted the episode during one of our final conversations about this book.

* * *

Fortuity was one of Dick's favorite themes. Throughout our discussions, he remarked how life took some turn "by chance," dictating the course of events that followed. Paul Buck was one of his favorite examples: "A fortuitous connection to a famous writer helped Buck win a Pulitzer Prize," Dick summarized. "That led to tenure. An automobile accident that took the life of another Harvard colleague led to his becoming the dean of the Harvard College faculty of arts and sciences before he was named provost."

Other illustrations pervade this book, including Arthur Schlesinger Sr.'s invitation to a 1937 fist-ball game that led Dick to Adams House, an initial encounter with Walter Muir Whitehill that ultimately kept him from active duty in the Pacific Theater during World War II, Thomas A. Bailey's refusal of Northwestern's offer to teach diplomatic history that left the position available to Dick two years later, and many others.

I now see the phenomenon more clearly with respect to Pop's life and my own. Tragic fortuity in the form of his father's sudden death in 1941 kept Pop and Sue from accepting an assignment in the Philippines that would probably have led to their demise during the Japanese invasion. But for the suggestion of Joseph U. Schorer ('75), my former high school debate partner, and his advice that I consider Northwestern for my own higher education because it had the best intercollegiate debate program in the country, I surely would have attended the University of Minnesota. I accepted Joe's suggestion, visited the school, and continued debating in college under the tutelage of Dick's former student David Zarefsky ('68), who was finishing his doctoral dissertation on his way to becoming dean of the School of

Speech. Needless to say, any number of other paths available to me at the time would have led to a place that could not have produced this book. Even more importantly, I would not have met a young freshman who eventually became my wife and the mother of our three children. Stated differently, my life has been charmed from almost the same moment that I began my "Leopold experience" in college.

Dick would never have suggested that an awareness of fortuity should diminish the role of personal responsibility and sound judgments in contributing to a satisfying life. But it is always helpful to remember that sometimes things beyond a person's control can be decisive in the journeys we take.

* * *

The circularity of history was another of Dick's favored topics. He saw it often in his own life in ways recounted in this book. They included places and people who have entered, exited, and reentered—sometimes repeatedly, including the city of Chicago, James Phinney Baxter, Thomas A. Bailey, Payson S. Wild, J. Lyndon Shanley, and Gray Boyce, among many others.

It was true for Pop, too. It would take another volume to describe all of the people who circled back to his life, including the Cleveland doctor whose own father had been sponsored in private practice by Pop's grandfather, Felix Rosenberg, and who was finally able to return the family favor two generations later when he similarly sponsored Pop's postwar career. Geographic circularity is also evident in Pop's life. Born and raised in Cleveland, Pop found himself periodically drawn to Chagrin Falls, where he attended Boy Scout summer camps in the mid-1920s, met Charles Lindbergh at the estate of his best friend's uncle in 1927, was a summer camp doctor during 1936, and eventually bought his first retirement residence in 1980. Likewise, he completed his residency in Chicago—a city he loved—and looked forward to spending his final years there until an aggressive cancer ended that dream forever.

* * *

Finally, Dick's later years offer another lesson all should find inspiring. Spinal stenosis confined him to a wheelchair. The tremors in his hands made even the simple task of raising an eating utensil to his mouth difficult; shaving became impossible. Moving into or out of a wheelchair required assistance from at least two people. His body was at the mercy of others, but his mind remained his own to the end. Like all of us, he occasionally struggled with loneliness and isolation, yet somehow he never despaired. With all he could not do, he focused instead on all he could.

During our discussions, I witnessed one incident in particular that said much about his fortitude and persistent good humor. Shortly after I had seated myself in front of him, his favorite nurse's assistant Lynn Cotto knocked on the door and opened it.

"Come in, my dear," he beckoned with a lilt in his voice.

"I'll come back," she said.

"No, sweetie," he replied. "Please go ahead and do it now."

I was not sure what the "it" was, but I interjected myself anyway, "No, please go ahead."

"I'll come back," she responded.

"No, please do it now. Now is a fine time," he said.

She continued to resist, "No, I can come back."

"I do not know what it is that the two of you have in mind," I began, "but please, do not let my presence here interfere with whatever he wants you to do. I've known him long enough to know that when he says, 'Now is fine,' that is as forceful as he will get and he means business. So we had better not cross him."

Dick was grinning at Lynn, who was clearly devoted to him. She returned his smile. "Okay," she said as she went back into the hall and returned with a large contraption, the purpose of which I would soon learn as I saw a demonstration.

"It's for lifting me from the chair," he explained. His mental acuity was so great that it was sometimes easy to forget that he was a prisoner of his wheelchair.

She wheeled the mechanism toward him, and he placed its attached harness around his shoulders. As soon as he was set, she started to turn the crank at the front of the device and raised him about three inches from his chair.

"Ahhhhhh, that feels good," he sighed.

"It looks like an uplifting experience for you," I mused as both Dick and Lynn humored my terrible pun with a chuckle. With such encouragement, I had no choice but to continue.

"Are you getting high?" I asked as the laughter continued.

"Is this the high point of your day?" I said as Lynn became downright giddy. It was clear that the environment and its patrons afforded only limited opportunities for humor.

"All right, that's it. Three strikes and you're out," he said as he smiled at me.

After a few minutes, she lowered him to within an inch of the chair, where he rested before his next ascent. Then she turned the crank and raised him back up for another three or four minutes, as he explained that the process helped both to remove pressure on his bottom (from constantly sitting in the chair) and to stretch his spinal column. After the second round, he said he was done for now—but made her promise to return in an hour as they blew kisses to each other from across the room.

Every day he watched and waited for the circularity of history and the fortuity of events to take him someplace both familiar and unexpected. He looked for ways to make the world a better place. And he found them.

* * *

Without intending offense to the dean, I decided it was more important to spend two hours of my Saturday morning with Dick than attend the final session of the annual Northwestern University Weinberg College of Arts and Sciences board of visitors meeting on May 14, 2005. It was, as Dick would say, fortuitous that I did so. At 9:45 A.M., I exited the elevator at the fifth floor of the Mather Pavilion. As I approached Dick's room, two nurse's assistants stopped me.

"The paramedics are with him," one of them said with a look of alarm. Fortunately, my regular visits had made me a familiar figure and they spoke to me as if I were a family member: "He won't let the paramedics take him to the hospital. We called his nephew and his doctor. Everyone has told him that he needs to go to the hospital because we cannot help him here. His heart rate is down and has been dropping. Can you help?"

I walked into the room where he lay on the bed. "Dick, what's going on?"

"Steve, you are just in time," he said as he barely opened his eyes. "It appears that I am in the process of dying."

"Well, you can't do that yet, because we're not finished with the book," I said jokingly. "Besides, aren't we all in the process of dying?"

He laughed and told the paramedics with complete lucidity who I was: "This is Steve Harper. He is a close friend and is writing my biography. I would trust his judgment, perhaps irrationally so, more than anyone else around me at the present time."

Then he looked at me as I asked what I could do to help. He explained that he was quite weak and had become progressively more so since the prior evening. He suggested I speak with the doctor on call to see what I could learn. He did not want to go to the hospital unless the doctor insisted because, as he put it, "The last time I was there, I waited around for hours and accomplished nothing." After conferring with others outside his room, I learned that the doctors had already been consulted and were of the unanimous view that the hospital was his next logical step. He seemed to be improving with the oxygen paramedics had administered, but that was only a temporary solution to an unknown problem.

I returned to his room and explained that the doctors agreed he should go to the emergency room. I told him I would meet him there. He acquiesced and, as we left the fifth floor, all of the nurse's assistants and other workers gathered to wish him a speedy recovery and a prompt return home.

His earlier assertion of his imminent demise turned out to be premature. I waited with him in the emergency room while doctors and nurses examined him. When they removed bandages covering his left foot, which he had told me several weeks earlier was afflicted with "ulcers and some kind of infection," the source of his current difficulty became obvious. The foot had swelled significantly and become bright red halfway to his knee.

"That foot is out of control," the doctor said. "We're going to admit him and get some antibiotics going on it."

He obtained a private room and regained his strength throughout the day. I left him at five in the afternoon so he could pursue his sole daily television viewing activity—watching the local and national news for an hour. We had spent the immediately preceding two hours resuming our work on his biography. We were nearing the last phase as we conducted a forced march through his detailed index of papers to make sure I had not missed anything important. Proceeding alphabetically, we had advanced as far as the letter E. I returned on Sunday, when we got through the letter F.

He was hospitalized for the next two weeks as specialists moved to different areas of potential concern throughout his body. As a result, his scheduled lecture to the Mather Pavilion residents on the James K. Polk presidency had to be postponed, but our mission continued, as it would until he alone decided we were done. It turned out to be longer than I would have predicted.

By the summer of 2006, the collective contributions of his friends and former students to the Richard W. Leopold Professorship in American history reached the two-million-dollar mark, making the chair permanent. On the day he received that news, we were working on remarks the OAH had asked him to submit for its annual meeting to celebrate the organization's centennial in March 2007. The OAH wanted to hear from its oldest living former president, along with other past presidents, including his old friend from Harvard, John Hope Franklin. Dick decided the initial part of his paper would describe the first meeting he had been invited to attend in 1938, when registration was five dollars, his single room was two dollars and fifty cents, and lunches cost fifty cents. Earlier in our session that day, I had told him that Northwestern might be interested in publishing the biography on which he and I had labored over the prior two years.

"Well," he said, "that comes as a pleasant surprise. I think there have been 250 contributors to the professorship and lectureship, so I'd expect there might be 75 who might actually buy the book." He had underestimated the total number of contributors—it was actually 350. I was also pretty sure he had also misjudged the interest that even those who had never known him might have in his twentieth-century journey. Time will tell.

* * *

On October 19, 2006, Dick gathered with one hundred friends and former students to celebrate the Richard W. Leopold Professorship's milestone funding achievement. He had been in the hospital with a pesky infection only a few days earlier, but this was an event he was determined to attend. Appropriately, he closed out the proceedings by first correcting certain factual inaccuracies in prior speakers' comments and then offering reminiscences. His strong baritone on full display, he scanned the audience for faces prompting stories unique to each. I sensed that he did not want the evening to end.

"Well," he said, "I think it's time to bring these proceedings to a close. Is there any food left?" The audience laughed as all rose spontaneously to give him one final standing ovation.

A week later, infections returned and he went back into the hospital. I was one of the many visitors who greeted him daily. He had hoped to return to his room at the Mather Pavilion in time for the annual Leopold Lecture on November 13 and, failing that, to give his planned November 29 lecture to fellow residents on Andrew Jackson's presidency. Although he was discharged from the hospital a few days after Samantha Power delivered the first ever Leopold Lecture for which he was not present, his health continued to fail and his strength waned. On the day before Thanksgiving, I began to read to him the many letters of tribute submitted in connection with the October celebration of the permanent Leopold chair. I completed the task on Thanksgiving morning, November 23, 2006—with all of the letters having been read. Eleven hours later he died peacefully, secure in the knowledge he was loved and his extended family of friends and former students would endure.

In a circularity of history that Dick would have truly enjoyed, David Zarefsky's son, Marc, a Northwestern student and reporter for *The Daily Northwestern*, called me on the Monday after Dick's death. He had been assigned the task of writing an article about one of Northwestern's most eminent professors, Richard W. Leopold.

On the first Sunday after Dick's death, I met with John Leopold and Shep Shanley for lunch in the Evanston Room of the Mather Pavilion. John was seeking our thoughts concerning a memorial service. Kevin Leonard joined us because we were also planning to clear out Dick's room. Many of his papers were destined for the Northwestern Archives.

"Well," John began after asking each of us how we were coping with our significant loss, "any thoughts on what we should do for a memorial?"

"The planning for that might be easier than you expected," I volunteered. "I discussed the issue with Dick, and he had very definite thoughts on the matter."

I then read to them the final pages of my manuscript. Dick had thought the book's ending "quite appropriate under the circumstances," explaining that it would have greater impact if he were not still alive when it was published. Always eager to solve potential problems with a flair for the dramatic, he handled that one, too. So I now conclude my journey with Dick in the way I now realize he had always expected it to end, namely, with one of our private conversations about a year before he died.

* * *

"We have to return to the subject that started all of this," I told him. "Remember Labor Day 2004, when you asked me about what might be appropriate for a memorial service upon your death. Have you given any thought to that?"

"Yes, I have," he responded immediately. "I accept your earlier advice that I cannot require that nothing be done. So, I think if someone wants to take the ball and run with it, that will be fine with me. It will also be fine if that person gets tackled behind the line of scrimmage."

"A football analogy? I thought for sure you would use the language of trains or baseball," I interjected.

"But I think it would be a mistake to leave this in the hands of the Northwestern history department," he continued, "because there is no one left there who really knows me anymore. Letters like Ray Billington's to me upon my retirement are meaningful because Ray really knew me. But you can't just read letters at a memorial service. When last I was thinking in these lugubrious terms, I told the Northwestern archivist that I wanted him to write up a description for use in response to inquiries from professional historical journals."

His last point I already knew. The university archivist had told me that Dick had been urging him to prepare an obituary, but he had refused because he feared that it would somehow hasten Dick's death.

"Let me press you a little more. If you could script and stage it, what would the service look like?" I asked.

"I would have an undergraduate, a graduate student, and my biographer," he said with a wry smile. "I would try to stay away from any religious aspects. The rest would be music. Mozart and Beethoven—and school songs from Exeter, Harvard, Princeton, and Northwestern. And maybe a reading from Mr. Dooley."

Mr. Dooley was Finley Peter Dunne's character in a series of columns appearing in the Chicago newspaper more than a hundred years earlier. Dick quoted from them, beginning with his Harvard lectures, and he sometimes read them to our C-13 class in 1975.

When I smiled at the thought of the Exeter school song in his memorial service, along with humorous words from a political commentator from the 1890s, he smiled back and said, "Well, this has been my life. At one point, I owned all of the Mr. Dooley volumes."

"Which symphonies?" I asked.

"Beethoven's Ninth—*Choral*—or the Sixth—*Pastoral*—or the Third—*Eroica*. For Mozart, the *Gran Partita*."

"But they could not all be played," I said. "That would take hours. Would you want portions of each, or emphasis on a single one?"

"Certainly not the former," he said. "I think Beethoven's Sixth."

"What school songs are you thinking of?" I continued.

He then recited lines from "Old Nassau" and directed me to Samuel Eliot Morison's volume on the shelf, *Three Centuries of Education at Harvard: 1636–1936.* Inside was a program from a gathering of the Harvard Alumni Association in 1947. I then read aloud the words of "Fair Harvard," written in 1811:

> Fair Harvard! thy sons to thy jubilee throng,
> And with blessings surrender thee o'er,
> By these festival rites, from the age that is past
> To the age that is waiting before.
> O relic and type of our ancestors' worth,
> That has long kept their memory warm,
> First flow'r of their wilderness! star of their night!
> Calm rising thro' change and thro' storm.

Farewell! be thy destinies onward and bright!
To thy children the lesson still give,
With freedom to think, and with patience to bear,
And for right ever bravely to live.
Let not moss-cover'd error moor thee at its side,
As the world on truth's current glides by,
Be the herald of light, and the bearer of love, . . .

He then said the final line with me as I read it:

Till the stock of the Puritans die.

When I asked him about the Exeter song, he said, "Non Sibi," which had been written a few years before his 1929 graduation. He then started singing ever so softly:

Exeter fair, O mother stern yet tender,
Born with our land and loyal now as then,
Long have you stood, unchanged, our youth's defender,
Bidding us hither that we may be men.
Men's eyes may dim with losing or with winning,
Faithful in all, you still see clear the end,
Teaching us here each fair and wise beginning,
On which the sum of life must yet depend.
Here at your hearth, still safe within the portal,
We light the torch and hear the world's far call;
Into our hands you give the flame immortal,
And, by God's grace, we vow it shall not fall.

I looked up the phrase *non sibi*. It means "not for oneself."
To steal one of the lines Dick reserved for a cherished few:

"WE SHALL NOT SEE THE LIKES OF HIM AGAIN."

The personal papers of Richard W. Leopold are located in the Northwestern University Archives, Evanston, Illinois. In addition to his private papers and correspondence, all of his published articles and manuscripts are included in that collection. Together with his oral amplifications, those materials comprised the principal original sources for this book. Assistant Archivist Kevin Leonard provided continuing and invaluable assistance in accessing those materials for this project. Dick reviewed the draft manuscripts of this book several times to assure the accuracy of words specifically attributed to him and of the events depicted. He remained a very tough critic to the end.

The unpublished autobiography of Dr. William J. Loeb and my recollections of conversations with him and his daughters comprise the source of information about his life.

For factual background concerning anti-Semitism in higher education during early-twentieth-century America, I relied principally on the prior work of two scholars: Jerome Karabel and Edward S. Shapiro. Karabel's important and comprehensive volume, *The Chosen: The Hidden History of Admission and Exclusion at Harvard, Yale, and Princeton* (Boston and New York: Houghton Mifflin, 2005), was a source of statistical information and primary historical material, including the statements from various Ivy League faculty and administrators quoted in chapters 2, 3, 4, 5, and 26 of this book. Shapiro wrote on that subject in "The Friendly University: Jews in Academia since World War II," *Judaism* (Summer 1997); *A Time for Healing: American Jewry since World War II* (Baltimore and London: The Johns Hopkins University Press, 1992); and *We Are Many: Reflections on American Jewish History and Identity* (Syracuse, N.Y.: Syracuse University Press, 2005).

Information about the origins of Harvard's house system comes, in part, from Samuel Eliot Morison's *Three Centuries of Harvard: 1636–1936* (Cambridge, Mass.: Harvard University Press, 1936).

Finally, John Morton Blum's autobiography, *A Life with History* (Lawrence: University Press of Kansas, 2004), illuminated periods of Dick's life from the perspective of a contemporary, as did *Mirror to America: The Autobiography of John Hope Franklin* (New York: Farrar, Straus & Giroux, 2005) and Arthur M.

Schlesinger Jr.'s *A Life in the Twentieth Century: Innocent Beginnings, 1917–1950* (Boston and New York: Houghton Mifflin, 2000). The information about J. Robert Oppenheimer appears in K. Bird and M. Sherwin, *American Prometheus: The Triumph and Tragedy of J. Robert Oppenheimer* (New York: Random House, 2005).

NOTES

PROLOGUE

4   *Yet another lecturer and former student was Republican Congressman:* Debra Shore, "Making History," *Northwestern Perspectives* (Winter 1991), p. 9.

4   *He later continued:* Rep. Jim Kolbe to Dr. Richard W. Leopold, October 19, 2006, Richard W. Leopold Papers, Northwestern University Archives ("Leopold papers").

4   *She credited her former professor, Richard W. Leopold:* Georgie Anne Geyer note in commemoration of the Richard W. Leopold Professorship, October 2006, Leopold papers.

5   *One former student observed:* Dave Corbett ('60) note in commemoration of the Richard W. Leopold Professorship, October 2006, Leopold papers.

5   *As television and motion picture writer/producer/director Garry Marshall ('56) would later describe:* Garry K. Marshall letter to Dr. Richard W. Leopold, October 2, 2006, Leopold papers.

5   *With the publication of his seminal treatise:* Richard W. Leopold, *The Growth of American Foreign Policy: A History* (*"Growth,"* New York: Alfred A. Knopf, 1962).

8   *Dick and I had discussed the* Times' *lukewarm review:* Arthur M. Schlesinger Jr., *War and the American Presidency* (New York: W. W. Norton & Co., 2004).

CHAPTER 2: "THE FIRST TEST: THE GREAT CRUSADE"

17   *His earliest days coincided with the time:* Leopold, *Growth*, p. 237.

18   *When Germany failed to respect Belgian neutrality:* Id., p. 297.

19   *Current events associated with the ongoing European war:* Id., p. 296.

20   *Nevertheless, what Dick would later call "Wartime Diplomacy":* Id., p. 338.

20   *The Kaiser's days were numbered, and the "Preparations for Peace" began:* Id., p. 352.

21   *Dick's 1962 book would subsequently describe these monumental international events:* Id., p. 379.

21   *He wrote seven decades later:* Richard W. Leopold letter to Edmund T. Delaney, April 13, 1995, Leopold papers.

22   *Pop's first memories were of weekly sessions:* William J. Loeb's unpublished autobiography, *A Twentieth Century* (1998) ("Loeb autobiography"), pp. 1, 4.

23 *"Great Grandpa Joseph Mellor was a physician":* Id., p. 15.

23 *In fact, Pop's family moved:* Id., p. 4.

23 *Their new home was in Cleveland Heights, which was becoming:* www.jewishvirtual library.org; www.jewishcleveland.org.

23 *Pop's forebears had emigrated from an anti-Semitic Western Europe:* Id., p. 13.

24 *By the mid-1910s, about 40 percent of Columbia's undergraduates were Jewish, prompting its dean, Frederick P. Keppel, to ask:* Edward S. Shapiro, *We Are Many: Reflections on American Jewish History and Identity* ("*We Are Many*," Syracuse, N.Y.: Syracuse University Press, 2005), pp. 128–29.

24 *It became the first major private college:* Id., p. 129; Jerome Karabel, *The Chosen: The Hidden History of Admission and Exclusion at Harvard, Yale, and Princeton* ("*The Chosen*," Boston and New York: Houghton Mifflin, 2005), pp. 129–30.

CHAPTER 3: "THE INTERWAR COMPROMISE"

25 *"Here is to the boy with a thousand smiles":* Leopold papers.

26 *As for then-current events:* Leopold, *Growth*, p. 390.

26 *Dick's 1962 book would later describe:* Id., pp. 406–07.

27 *The Immigration Act of 1924 reduced the annual quota:* Karabel, *The Chosen*, pp. 47–48, 103–05.

27 *Franks had disappeared when nineteen-year-old Nathan Leopold:* www.encyclopedia .chicagohistory.org; *The Encyclopedia of Chicago* (Chicago: University of Chicago Press, 2004), p. 475.

30 *As he approached his teenage years:* Loeb autobiography, pp. 9–10.

31 *Pop reported seventy-five years later:* Id., p. 13.

31 *But the Boy Scouts accepted him:* Id., p. 7.

31 *Pop remained only one medal short:* Id., p. 7.

CHAPTER 4: EXETER AND PRINCETON

33 *It became easy to understand why:* Richard W. Leopold to Ethel Leopold, January 6, 1933 (containing reference to letter written six years earlier), Leopold papers.

35 *In the preface, Dick would write:* Leopold, *Growth*, p. xi.

36 *As he later wrote, he chose that school:* June 10, 1996, Princeton questionnaire, Leopold papers.

36 *Although he was unaware of the statistics at the time:* Richard W. Leopold to Edmund T. Delaney, March 7, 1995, citing Marcia Graham Synott, *The Half-Opened Door: Discrimination and Admissions at Harvard, Yale, and Princeton, 1900–1970* ("*The Half-Opened Door*," Westport, Conn.: Greenwood, 1979), Leopold papers; see also Karabel, *The Chosen*, p. 127.

37 *Dick wrote sixty years later, "I have no religion myself"*: Richard W. Leopold to Edmund T. Delaney, March 7, 1995, Leopold papers.

38 *In the 1932 Princeton straw vote:* Richard W. Leopold to Edmund T. Delaney, March 7, 1995, citing November 2, 1932, issue of *Alumni Weekly*, Leopold papers.

39 *In the faculty voting, Hoover won by a smaller margin:* Id.

39 *By his own account, he was "sensitive":* Richard W. Leopold to Ethel Leopold, January 6, 1933, Leopold papers.

39 *In a Princeton alumni questionnaire sixty years later:* June 10, 1996, Princeton questionnaire, Leopold papers.

39 *Also important to him was the second recipient:* Leopold, *Growth,* p. xi.

40 *"After one semester of kindergarten":* Loeb autobiography, p. 3.

41 *During summers between his high school years:* Id., p. 5.

41 *University Secretary Varnum Lansing Collins wrote in November 1922:* Karabel, *The Chosen,* p. 124, citing V. L. Collins' letter to Henry Canby, November 23, 1922, Princeton University Archives.

41 *In 1918, Yale College Dean Frederick S. Jones said of the Jews:* Karabel, *The Chosen,* p. 75, citing "Meeting of the New England Deans Held in Princeton," minutes, May 9–10, 1918, Yale University Archives, pp. 21–22.

41 *Four years later Robert N. Corwin, chairman of Yale's admissions committee, wrote:* Shapiro, *We Are Many,* p. 130, citing Synott, *The Half-Opened Door,* p. 150.

41 *In May 1922, Roswell Angier, a psychologist and the freshman class dean, asserted:* Id., citing Synott, *The Half-Opened Door,* pp. 17, 130, 155, and Dan A. Oren, *Joining the Club: A History of Jews and Yale* (New Haven, Conn.: Yale University Press, 1985).

41 *Jewish enrollment at Yale reached its high point in 1923:* Karabel, *The Chosen,* pp. 114–15.

42 *In the fall of 1926, Yale Dean Clarence W. Mendell wrote:* Karabel, *The Chosen,* p. 109, citing Clarence Mendell, "Harvard," December 8, 1926, Yale University Archives.

42 *In a 1926 editorial entitled "Ellis Island for Yale":* Shapiro, *We Are Many,* p. 131.

42 *Admissions reflected those attitudes: by 1931, Jews accounted for:* Karabel, *The Chosen,* pp. 114, 115, 117.

42 *Jewish enrollment at Yale would not reach its record 1923 level:* Karabel, *The Chosen,* p. 115.

42 *Pop described his life at the college:* Loeb autobiography, p. 14.

42 *During his junior and senior years:* Id., p. 15.

42 *"The 'club' of teenagers," Pop wrote:* Id., p. 10.

42 *During the summer between his junior and senior years:* Id., p. 15.

43 *Although he could not afford the weekend journeys:* Id., p. 15.

43 *Named after socialist Eugene V. Debs:* Karabel, *The Chosen,* p. 118, citing *Yale Banner: Class of 1933,* Yale University Archives; and Todd Purdum, "Eugene V. Rostow, 89, Official at State Dept. and Law Dean," *New York Times,* November 26, 2002; and Eugene Rostow, "The Jew's Position," *Harkness Hoot,* November 23, 1931, Yale University Archives.

43 *Eugene's younger brother Walt Whitman Rostow: New York Times,* February 15, 2003.

CHAPTER 5: HARVARD

46 *Schlesinger suggested that Robert Dale Owen:* Richard W. Leopold, "The Adventures of a Novice in Research: New Harmony and Indianapolis, 1935," *Indiana Magazine of History,* vol. 74 (March 1978), pp. 1–22.

48 *"I am very anxious":* Richard W. Leopold to Lewis Perry, February 21, 1936, Leopold papers.

48 *Along the way, he wrote to Ethel:* Richard W. Leopold to Ethel Leopold, September 25, 1936, Leopold papers.

49 *In 1995, Dick would write, "I have no religion myself":* Richard W. Leopold to Edmund T. Delaney, March 7, 1995, Leopold papers.

49 *"By some decision it had a limit of 10 percent Jewish students," Pop later wrote:* Loeb autobiography, p. 16.

49 *"We graduated 68 of the 83 admitted students":* Id., p. 16.

49 *Pop's rigorous schedule left little leisure time:* Id., p. 16.

CHAPTER 6: "ANNUS MIRABILIS"

52 *One of Dick's illustrious professors on the Harvard faculty was Samuel Eliot Morison, whose history of the university:* Samuel Eliot Morison, *Three Centuries of Harvard: 1636–1936* (Cambridge, Mass.: Harvard University Press, 1936).

53 *Even decades later, Roosevelt would describe the event:* Karabel, pp. 16–17, citing G. C. Ward, *Before the Trumpet: Young Franklin Roosevelt, 1881–1905* (New York: Harper & Row, 1985), pp. 217–22, 235–36; T. Morgan, *FDR: A Biography* (New York: Simon and Schuster, 1985), pp. 81, 155–56.

53 *Needless to say, Jews were not welcome, either:* Mary Dearborn, *Mailer: A Biography* (Boston and New York: Houghton Mifflin, 2001), p. 23.

55 *In 1922, Lowell, who also served as vice president of the Immigration Restriction League:* Karabel, *The Chosen,* p. 86.

55 *In fact, Lowell actually believed Jews lacked:* Shapiro, *We Are Many,* p. 127.

55 *In 1926, chairman of Harvard's admissions committee Henry Pennypacker stated his concern:* Shapiro, *We Are Many,* pp. 127–28, citing Louis Joughlin and Edmund

M. Morgan, *The Legacy of Sacco and Vanzetti* (Chicago: Quadrangle, 1964), pp. 39–40; Alan M. Dershowitz, *Chutzpah* (Boston: Little, Brown, 1991), pp. 66–67.

55 *His national scholarship program was available only to "western applicants":* John Morton Blum, *A Life with History* (Lawrence: University Press of Kansas, 2004), p. 22; Karabel, *The Chosen*, pp. 175–78.

55 *Many colleges followed Harvard's lead:* Karabel, *The Chosen*, p. 178.

57 *He later wrote that, although future Nobel laureate Bridgman (age fifty-three) was the eldest member of the group:* Richard W. Leopold to Maila L. Walter, July 17, 1992, Leopold papers.

57 *But forty years after their last game, Scott would remember:* Austin W. Scott to Richard W. Leopold, September 25, 1974, Leopold papers.

57 *In the preface of his published manuscript:* Richard W. Leopold, *Robert Dale Owen: A Biography* (Cambridge, Mass.: Harvard University Press, 1940), x.

57 *Merk would be thanked again:* Leopold, *Growth*, p. xi.

59 *In a letter almost sixty years later:* Richard W. Leopold to George M. Elsey, January 3, 1995, Leopold papers.

59 *Summarizing President Conant's new limits on nontenured faculty:* Richard W. Leopold to Dr. Peter Carroll, November 22, 1989, Leopold papers.

59 *In April 1938, Elting Morison sat through a rehearsal:* Richard W. Leopold to Elting E. Morison, January 10, 1992, Leopold papers.

60 *Still, the prospect of a strong Harvard foundation:* Richard W. Leopold to Professor E. D. Salmon, April 24, 1938, Leopold papers.

60 *Some of his classmates were married by then:* Richard W. Leopold to Arthur M. Moody, February 27, 1990, Leopold papers.

60 *Many more engaged in "excessive drinking":* Id.

61 *Selig Perlman, a labor economist at the University of Wisconsin, advised Jewish graduate students in history:* Edward S. Shapiro, *A Time for Healing: American Jewry since World War II:* (Baltimore: The Johns Hopkins University Press, 1992), p. 105.

61 *A 1937 report of the American Jewish Committee:* Shapiro, *We Are Many*, p. 134.

61 *Throughout the 1930s, Harvard's only Jewish faculty members were:* Karabel, *The Chosen*, p. 94.

61 *He went to Mt. Sinai:* Loeb autobiography, p. 17.

61 *She was a direct descendant of Simson Thorman:* www.jewishvirtuallibrary.org.

61 *By then, the next major wave of Jewish immigration to Cleveland:* Id.

62 *In contrast to these more conservative and orthodox Jews:* Loeb autobiography, p. 13.

62 *After eight months in a small furnished Oak Park apartment:* Id., p. 18.

CHAPTER 7: "GROPING FOR A POLICY"

63 *He refused, affirming in a letter:* Richard W. Leopold to Ethel Leopold, April 25, 1940, Leopold papers.

64 *Because he did not favor maintaining the stock exchange seat:* Id.

64 *An important teaching aid arrived in 1940 when Thomas A. Bailey's new textbook:* Thomas A. Bailey, *A Diplomatic History of the American People* (New York: Crofts, 1940).

65 *As he wrote five decades later:* Richard W. Leopold to Marcia G. Synott, February 3, 1986, Leopold papers.

65 *As he described the episode in a letter to Ethel:* Richard W. Leopold to Ethel Leopold, December 4, 1940, Leopold papers.

66 *"I do not know when anything has hit me harder":* Id.

67 *G. Wallace Chessman ('41) told me more than sixty years later:* Steven J. Harper interview with G. Wallace Chessman, September 11, 2004.

68 *According to Franklin, Dick asked him:* John Hope Franklin, *Mirror to America: The Autobiography of John Hope Franklin* ("*Mirror to America,*" New York: Farrar, Straus & Giroux, 2005), p. 96.

68 *Blum later described Dick's lectures:* Id., pp. 34–35.

68 *As Blum observed about his days at Andover:* Id., p. 4.

68 *He was subjected to aggressive anti-Semitic attacks:* Id., p. 8.

68 *There were no Jews or Catholics:* Id., pp. 8–9.

69 *As an African American working his way:* Franklin, *Mirror to America,* p. 64.

69 *"After I made the nomination," Franklin later reported:* Id., p. 65.

CHAPTER 8: "THE SECOND TEST: THE STRUGGLE FOR SURVIVAL"

73 *Most Americans still preferred neutrality:* www.charleslindbergh.com/americafirst/speech.asp.

74 *He wrote to Ethel the following day:* Richard W. Leopold to Ethel Leopold, December 8, 1941, Leopold papers.

74 *In January 1942, he explored briefly:* Richard W. Leopold to Laurence B. Packard, January 13, 1942, Leopold papers.

76 *That evening, he wrote to Ethel:* Richard W. Leopold to Ethel Leopold, October 3, 1942, Leopold papers.

76 *On his daily calendar, he made the last entry:* Richard W. Leopold daily aide, 1942, Leopold papers.

77 *Dick assumed his chances for a commission were gone:* Richard W. Leopold to Ethel Leopold, December 7, 1942, Leopold papers.

77 *Dick responded immediately:* Richard W. Leopold to Walter Muir Whitehill, December 8, 1942, Leopold papers.

77   *Whitehill's telegram awaited him:* Walter Muir Whitehill telegram to Leopold, December 10, 1942, Leopold papers.

77   *A longer letter followed on December 15:* Walter Muir Whitehill to Richard W. Leopold, December 15, 1942, Leopold papers.

78   *"When we were ready to finish school in 1937," he later wrote:* Loeb autobiography, p. 20.

78   *On a visit from Chicago to Cleveland over the Labor Day weekend in 1940, Pop's mother handed him a letter:* Id., p. 20.

78   *Pop's status removed the kind of uncertainty:* Id., p. 21.

79   *"One's decisions are frequently formed":* Id., p. 23.

CHAPTER 9: INTERLUDE

82   *Eventually, I reviewed the letter:* Richard W. Leopold to Ethel Leopold, March 28, 1943.

86   *In February 1946, he wrote to Ruth:* Richard W. Leopold to Ruth Delano, February 11, 1946, Leopold papers.

86   *He also reported:* Richard W. Leopold to Ruth Delano, February 8, 1946, Leopold papers.

86   *The first was dated April 20, 1944, in which he wrote:* William J. Loeb to Sue G. Loeb, April 20, 1944, Loeb papers.

87   *On his daughter's first birthday, he wrote:* William J. Loeb to Joan Elizabeth Loeb, June 3, 1944, Loeb papers.

87   *A year later, he wrote from Italy:* William J. Loeb to Joan Elizabeth Loeb, June 1, 1945, Loeb papers.

87   *In 1991, he wrote:* Richard W. Leopold to Sylvia Riggs Liroff, July 30, 1991, Leopold papers.

87   *Concluding his 1945 V-Mail to his daughter on her second birthday, he wrote:* William J. Loeb to Joan Elizabeth Loeb, June 1, 1945, Loeb papers.

CHAPTER 10: CASUALTIES OF WAR

90   *Two months after his mentor boarded a train:* Dana Reed to Richard W. Leopold, November 18, 1942, Leopold papers.

90   *By January 1943, Dick had received his commission, and Dana wrote:* Dana Reed to Richard W. Leopold, January 5, 1943, Leopold papers.

90   *In February, Dana was "drilling" at Brigantine Field:* Dana Reed to Richard W. Leopold, February 18, 1943, Leopold papers.

90   *In April, Dana wrote from Meadville:* Dana Reed to Richard W. Leopold, April 11, 1943, Leopold papers.

90   *By May, he was in Nashville:* Dana Reed to Richard W. Leopold, May 23, 1943, Leopold papers.

90 *Two weeks later, he was at Maxwell Field:* Dana Reed to Richard W. Leopold, June 8, 1943, Leopold papers.

91 *At Dorr Field in Arcadia, Florida, Dana was thrilled:* Dana Reed to Richard W. Leopold, July 30, 1943, Leopold papers.

91 *In September, Dana responded to what must have been:* Dana Reed to Richard W. Leopold, September 8, 1943, Leopold papers.

91 *In October, Dana was at Gunter Field:* Dana Reed to Richard W. Leopold, October 17, 1943, Leopold papers.

91 *In early December, Dana was at twin-engine advanced school:* Dana Reed to Richard W. Leopold, December 9, 1943, Leopold papers.

91 *A month later, Dana wrote from Smyrna Army Air Field:* Dana Reed to Richard W. Leopold, March 16, 1944, Leopold papers.

92 *On the subject of American politics, he expressed disappointment:* Dana Reed to Richard W. Leopold, April 13, 1944, Leopold papers.

92 *From there, Dana went to Westover Field:* Dana Reed to Richard W. Leopold, May 23, 1944, Leopold papers.

92 *On D-Day, June 6, 1944, "the greatest amphibious force ever assembled stormed ashore in Normandy":* Leopold, *Growth,* p. 603.

92 *On October 31, Dana sent him a notice of change of address card:* Dana Reed to Richard W. Leopold, October 31, 1944, Leopold papers.

92 *Dick immediately shot off a "prompt reply to the postal":* Richard W. Leopold to Dana Reed, November 14, 1944, Leopold papers.

93 *Twenty years later, Dick learned from William Witkin:* William Witkin to Richard W. Leopold, November 7, 1995, Leopold papers.

94 *His accompanying note was straightforward:* Richard W. Leopold to Harley P. Holden, March 18, 1982, Leopold papers.

94 *In a 1995 letter expressing gratitude to Witkin:* Richard W. Leopold to William Witkin, November 16, 1995, Leopold papers.

CHAPTER 11: "THE UNITED NATIONS AND THE PEACE"

96 *"In the fall of 1945, Arthur Schlesinger Jr. had been made a full professor with tenure":* Arthur M. Schlesinger, Jr., *The Age of Jackson* (Boston: Little, Brown, 1945).

97 *In a 2001 letter to Arthur Jr., Dick would write:* Richard W. Leopold to Arthur M. Schlesinger, Jr., February 8, 2001, Leopold papers.

97 *The final result remained unchanged:* Richard W. Leopold to Ethel Leopold, November 3, 1945, Leopold papers.

97 *Quite the contrary, as he wrote to Merk in 1945:* Richard W. Leopold, "'Not Merely High Scholarship but High Character and Personality': The Harvard History De-

partment a Half-Century Ago," *Proceedings of the Massachusetts Historical Society*, vol. 95 (1984), p. 125.

98 *After Ruth Delano bade him farewell at Union Station in March of that year:* Ruth Delano to Richard W. Leopold, April 6, 1946, Leopold papers.

98 *A month later, she wrote that she was "at a complete stalemate":* Ruth Delano to Richard W. Leopold, May 1, 1946, Leopold papers.

98 *On June 10, Ruth sent him a typed letter of thanks:* Ruth Delano to Richard W. Leopold, June 10, 1946, Leopold papers.

98 *On July 15, she wrote that she would "become a civilian on July 17":* Ruth Delano to Richard W. Leopold, July 15, 1946, Leopold papers.

98 *By August 15, she was back in her native Minnesota:* Ruth Delano to Richard W. Leopold, August 15, 1946, Leopold papers.

99 *In 1952, he won the Pulitzer Prize:* Oscar Handlin, *The Uprooted: The Epic Story of the Great Migrations That Made the American People* (Boston: Little Brown, 1952).

99 *Forty years after the events, Dick wrote to a former Northwestern graduate student:* Richard W. Leopold to Dr. Peter Carroll, November 22, 1989, Leopold papers.

99 *Insofar as Arthur Schlesinger Sr. had any role:* Shapiro, *A Time For Healing*, p. 105, citing Peter Novick, *That Noble Dream: The "Objectivity Question" and the American Historical Profession* (Cambridge, UK: Cambridge University Press, 1988), pp. 172–74.

99 *Their grandson, Arthur Jr., would later write:* Arthur M. Schlesinger, Jr., *A Life in the Twentieth Century: Innocent Beginnings, 1917–1950* (Boston and New York: Houghton Mifflin, 2000), p. 1.

100 *It remained severed when a Congregationalist minister:* Id., p. 15.

100 *In the 1950s, a newspaper reported:* Id., p. 5.

Chapter 12: A Loss in the Family

104 *On January 31, the day after a Hindu extremist killed pacifist Mahatma Ghandi, Dick wrote to Ethel:* Richard W. Leopold to Ethel Leopold, January 31, 1948, Leopold papers.

105 *Then senior tutor Frederick L. Gwynn observed:* Fred L. Gwynn remarks, May 21, 1948, Leopold papers.

106 *He reminded his audience:* June 24, 1948, Leopold remarks on May 21, 1948, Leopold papers.

106 *In the fall of 1946, she began study at Yale:* Ruth Delano to Richard W. Leopold, October 20, 1946, Leopold papers.

106 *She was still there in March 1947 when she wrote:* Ruth Delano to Richard W. Leopold, March 28, 1947, Leopold papers.

107 *In December 1947, Ruth was working in Washington and wrote:* Ruth Delano to Richard W. Leopold, December 27, 1947, Leopold papers.

107 *The next letter in Dick's "Ruth Delano" correspondence file:* Richard W. Leopold to Ruth Delano, June 19, 1948, Leopold papers.

107 *She answered him a month later:* Ruth Delano to Richard W. Leopold, July 31, 1948, Leopold papers.

107 *Their next and final communication is dated December 27, 1950:* Richard W. Leopold to Ruth Delano, December 27, 1950, Leopold papers.

107 *Especially in later years, Dick identified himself in his writings:* Richard W. Leopold to Dr. Arthur W. Seligmann, March 15, 1995, Leopold papers; Richard W. Leopold to Arthur M. Moody, February 27, 1990, Leopold papers.

CHAPTER 13: NORTHWESTERN

111 *James had been a faculty member from 1896 to 1935:* Dick's recollections of the exact years in which various history department faculty members joined the university from 1945 through 1980 were aided by the *Northwestern University History Department Newsletters* that he prepared during the first five years after his retirement in 1980. They are among the Leopold papers. Along with recent developments, his annual *Newsletter* for the academic year 1980–81 described the department from 1935 to 1950. Thereafter, his *Newsletters* covered 1950 to 1960 (1981–82 issue), 1960 to 1970 (1982–83 issue), and 1970 to 1980 (1983–84 issue).

CHAPTER 14: BUILDING THE HISTORY DEPARTMENT

115 *Link was born in 1920 and raised in a rural area of North Carolina:* George B. Tindall, "The Formative Years," in John Milton Cooper Jr. and Charles E. Neu, editors, *The Wilson Era: Essays in Honor of Arthur S. Link* (*"Wilson Era,"* Arlington Heights, Ill.: Harlan Davidson, 1991), pp. 7–29.

116 *"I had first heard of Link":* Arthur S. Link, *Wilson: The Road to the White House* (Princeton, N.J.: Princeton University Press, 1947).

116 *In May 1948, Dean Leland informed me of Strevey's resignation:* Richard W. Leopold to Ray A. Billington, May 20, 1948; Ray A. Billington to Richard W. Leopold, May 25, 1948; Richard W. Leopold to Ray A. Billington, May 29, 1948, Leopold papers.

117 *Dick later learned that Link's conversation with Northwestern's dean:* Richard W. Leopold, "Arthur S. Link at Northwestern: The Maturing of a Scholar," in *Wilson Era*, p. 32.

117 *He reported to Arthur Schlesinger Sr. his surprise:* Richard W. Leopold to Arthur M. Schlesinger, March 21, 1949, Leopold papers.

119 *"No active duty for my unit":* Loeb autobiography, p. 40.

CHAPTER 15: THE LEOPOLD-LINK DECADE AT NORTHWESTERN

121 *They agreed to the enterprise:* Richard W. Leopold and Arthur S. Link, eds., *Problems in American History* (Englewood Cliffs, N.J.: Prentice-Hall, 1953).

122 *Originally, the Links had planned to take their children:* Richard W. Leopold to Ethel Leopold, May 19, 1953, Leopold papers.

124 *Dick produced his second book in 1954:* Richard W. Leopold, *Elihu Root and the Conservative Tradition* (Boston: Little, Brown, 1954).

124 *Arthur published four major books:* Arthur S. Link, *Woodrow Wilson and the Progressive Era: 1910–1917* (New York: Harper & Brothers, 1954); *American Epoch: A History of the United States Since the 1890s* (New York: Alfred A. Knopf, 1955); *Wilson: The New Freedom* (Princeton, N.J.: Princeton University Press, 1956); and *Wilson the Diplomatist: A Look at His Major Policies* (Baltimore, Md.: Johns Hopkins Press, 1957).

124 *As soon as he hung up, he wrote Link a letter:* Richard W. Leopold to Arthur S. Link, February 6, 1955, Leopold papers.

127 *In 1982, he wrote to a former Harvard undergraduate:* Richard W. Leopold to Richard H. Russell, August 10, 1982, Leopold papers.

128 *Meanwhile, Pop saw the orders that would have activated his reserve unit:* Loeb autobiography, p. 40.

128 *"In 1959," Pop explained:* Id., p. 41.

128 *Professionally, he was a pioneer in his field:* Id., p. 36.

CHAPTER 16: ARTHUR LINK LEAVES EVANSTON

131 *He titled the last section:* Leopold, *Growth,* p. 709.

131 *He concluded the book with a prescient paragraph:* Id., p. 810.

133 *When he related the saga in a letter to Blum:* Richard W. Leopold to John Morton Blum, December 13, 1959, Leopold papers.

133 *After the Northwestern board of trustees:* Leopold, "Arthur S. Link at Northwestern: The Maturing of a Scholar," in *Wilson Era,* p. 46.

134 *In November 1959, more than five years had passed:* Alfred A. Knopf to Richard W. Leopold, November 11, 1959, Leopold papers.

134 *As Dick and I read the most recent Oppenheimer biography:* K. Bird and M. Sherwin, *American Prometheus: The Triumph and Tragedy of J. Robert Oppenheimer* (New York: Random House, 2005), pp. 11–15, 16, 21, 27.

135 *Bridgman's letter of recommendation described Oppenheimer:* Id., p. 39.

136 *Dedicating the treatise to his history teachers:* Leopold, *Growth,* p. xi.

136 *The text received favorable reviews and, as Dick explained in 1981:* Richard W. Leopold, "The Writings of a Teacher-Scholar: Aspirations Versus Achievements," *Northwestern University Arts and Sciences,* vol. 4 ("Aspirations Versus Achievements," Fall 1981), pp. 16–19.

137 *In the alumni magazine, Billington explained: Northwestern University Alumni News* (February 1963), p. 10.

138 *He also collaborated with Link in producing the third edition:* Richard W. Leopold and Arthur S. Link, eds., *Problems in American History* (Englewood Cliffs, N.J.: Prentice-Hall, 1966).

138 *"With the inevitable guilt accompanying such a move":* Richard W. Leopold to David E. Kyvig, November 27, 1991, Leopold papers.

139 *On June 11, Ernie summoned the strength to deliver a commencement address:* W. Ernest Gillespie remarks to Exeter graduates, June 11, 1967, Leopold papers.

139 *On October 30, 1967, Ernie wrote his last letter:* W. Ernest Gillespie to Richard W. Leopold, October 30, 1967, Leopold papers.

140 *In anticipation of his sixtieth class reunion in 1989, Dick wrote:* Richard W. Leopold, "W. Ernest Gillespie: A Memoir," *The Phillips Exeter Bulletin* (Winter 1989), p. 26.

140 *"This was THE social club of the community":* Loeb autobiography, pp. 9–10, 37.

Chapter 17: 1968

144 *He wanted Dean Robert Strotz to appoint a committee:* November 7, 1968, Meeting of the Faculty of the College of Arts and Sciences, Leopold papers.

144 *He immediately wrote to Strotz, expressing his concerns:* Richard W. Leopold to Robert H. Strotz, November 7, 1968, Leopold papers.

145 *He had exploded onto the scene:* Robert H. Wiebe, *The Search for Order, 1877–1920* (New York: Harper Collins, 1967).

146 *Dick had the last word:* Richard W. Leopold to Robert H. Wiebe, November 12, 1968, Leopold papers.

146 *"To maintain my balance I did more teaching than any chairman":* Richard W. Leopold to David E. Kyvig, November 27, 1991.

147 *Yet, as Dick would write more than twenty-five years later:* Richard W. Leopold to Edmund T. Delaney, March 7, 1995, Leopold papers.

Chapter 18: The Assault on the NROTC

150 *Dick thought that* The Daily*'s "blatant misrepresentations":* Richard W. Leopold, "The NROTC Issue, 1968–1969" (June 15, 1969), p. 5, Leopold papers.

150 *Dick's position was straightforward:* Richard W. Leopold remarks to the Faculty of the College of Arts and Sciences of Northwestern University (June 1969), Leopold papers.

153 *Shortly thereafter, he addressed the new naval officers:* Richard W. Leopold, remarks to midshipmen (June 14, 1969), Leopold papers.

153 *On October 2, 1969, the "Report of the General Faculty Committee on the NROTC":* "Report of the General Faculty Committee on the NROTC" (October 2, 1969), Leopold papers.

154　*When Dick spoke to the University Senate:* Richard W. Leopold remarks, October 9, 1969, Leopold papers.

154　*Although on sabbatical, Dick returned to speak:* Richard W. Leopold remarks on January 29, 1970, Leopold papers.

155　*In October 1969, Duffield found himself in the Army:* John W. Duffield to Richard W. Leopold, October 2, 1969, Leopold papers.

CHAPTER 19: THE ROOSEVELT LIBRARY INVESTIGATION

157　*Even so, in August 1969, he wrote to a colleague:* Richard W. Leopold to Allen S. Hussey, August 19, 1969, Leopold papers.

158　*The letter summarized Loewenheim's charges:* Joint AHA-OAH Ad Hoc Committee [on issues raised by Mr. Loewenheim], *Annual Report of the American Historical Association for the Year 1969,* vol. 1—Proceedings (*"Initial Report,"* Washington, D.C.: Smithsonian Institution Press, 1970), pp. 129–31.

158　*Library archivist Edgar Nixon had subsequently included the documents in question among fourteen hundred items in a three-volume book: Franklin D. Roosevelt and Foreign Affairs, 1933–1937* (Cambridge, Mass.: Belknap Press of the Harvard University Press, 1969).

159　*Zabel's subsequent telegram remained conspicuous in its omission: Initial Report,* p. 123.

159　*Yet for more than two months, Ward and Loewenheim jousted with Dick over the role of the Leopold committee: Initial Report,* pp. 123–24.

159　*In that letter, Loewenheim described a telephone call: Final Report of the Joint AHA-OAH ad hoc Committee to Investigate the Charges Against the Franklin D. Roosevelt Library and Related Matters (*"Final Report,"* August 24, 1970), p. 86.

160　*At the end of October 1969, the AHA reaffirmed the charter of Dick's committee: Final Report,* p. 195.

160　*On November 17, Dick's committee sent initial letters of inquiry to the signatories of the* Times *letter. On December 2, the administrator of the General Services Administration sent Bush a lengthy rebuttal: Initial Report,* pp. 125–26, 134–38.

160　*Characteristically, Dick responded immediately: Final Report,* p. 208.

160　*Among the materials was a statement: Initial Report,* pp. 143–44.

160　*It was always best to start with basic facts and then work outward from there: Final Report,* pp. 13–44.

161　*Loewenheim also asserted that the supposedly withheld letters:* Id., pp. 56–101.

161　*In a letter to Dick dated February 28: Final Report,* pp. 260–61.

162　*The extraordinary session convened at the AHA offices:* Id., p. 285.

162　*In a remarkable testament to Dick's interpersonal skills:* Id., p. 287.

162　*Dick announced that the record of the investigation would be closed:* Id., pp. 297–99.

163 *Meticulously researched with every available source consulted and referenced:* Id., p. 427.

163 *In fact, the report found:* Id., p. 424.

163 *The report also concluded that Harvard University Press:* Id., p. 426.

163 *In fact, the committee found "impressive":* Id., p. 428.

163 *The report described miscommunications:* Id., p. 428.

164 *Ray Billington, who had signed the Loewenheim letter that appeared in the* Times, *wrote:* Ray A. Billington to Richard W. Leopold, May 19, 1980, Leopold papers.

164 *In the end, Dick viewed the controversy as a sign of the times:* Final Report, pp. 439–40.

164 *Dick made his most important personal point in the final report from his committee:* Final Report, pp. 331, 340.

165 *In his last missive to Loewenheim on this or any other subject, he wrote:* Richard W. Leopold to Francis L. Loewenheim, September 21, 1970, Leopold papers.

165 *She was on the council of the AHA in April 1973 when she wrote to Dick:* Natalie Z. Davis to Richard W. Leopold, April 10, 1973, Leopold papers.

166 *Three months before Loewenheim's death in 1996, the* Houston Chronicle *ran an article:* www.chron.com/content/chronicle/metropolitan/96/07/07/loewenheim.html, displaying article by Bob Tutt, *Houston Chronicle,* July 5, 1996.

CHAPTER 20: "WHEN IN DOUBT, I DIDN'T"

171 *Chandler had accepted Harvard's offer:* Alfred D. Chandler, Jr., *The Visible Hand: The Management Revolution in American Business* (Cambridge, Mass.: Belknap Press of the Harvard University Press, 1977).

171 *In a 1982 letter to Richard Russell, a former student:* Richard W. Leopold to Richard H. Russell, August 10, 1982, Leopold papers.

172 *His explanatory letter to Donald:* Richard W. Leopold to David Donald, November 30, 1970, Leopold papers.

173 *Although it would not be revealed until decades later:* Robert Woodward, *The Secret Man* (New York: Simon & Schuster, 2005), p. 86.

174 *In his address, "A Crisis of Confidence":* Richard W. Leopold, *American Archivist,* vol. 34 (April 1971), pp. 139–56.

CHAPTER 21: FIRSTHAND EXPERIENCE—ENTER STEVE HARPER

176 *I kept his note, which read, in part:* Richard W. Leopold to Steven J. Harper, June 14, 1973, Harper papers.

176 *Later that summer, I received a handwritten letter from my freshman adviser:* Ruth Bonde to Steven J. Harper, July 17, 1973, Harper papers.

178 *The next day I received via university mail his letter to me:* Richard W. Leopold to Steven J. Harper, January 22, 1974, Harper papers.

179 *In the longest by far of the mid-quarter assessments I would ever receive from him:* Richard W. Leopold to Steven J. Harper, undated 1974 note, Harper papers.

179 *Noted journalist Georgie Anne Geyer ('56) would write years later:* Georgie Anne Geyer note in commemoration of the Richard W. Leopold Professorship, October 2006.

180 *As for the early meeting time, he later wrote:* Richard W. Leopold to Wayne S. Cole, October 22, 1992, Leopold papers.

180 *This echoed a similar comment he had written in a lengthy letter:* Richard W. Leopold to Richard H. Russell, August 10, 1982, Leopold papers.

181 *If a student did not own:* William Strunk and E. B. White, *The Elements of Style* (New York: Macmillan Publishing, 1959, 1972).

182 *Zarefsky once said that he would have taught:* David Zarefsky to Richard W. Leopold, October 2, 2006, Leopold papers.

183 *Dick sent us a wedding present:* Richard W. Leopold to Steven J. Harper, July 27, 1976, Harper papers.

183 *Dick's OAH presidential address reflected his continuing mission:* Richard W. Leopold, "The Historian and the Federal Government," *Journal of American History,* vol. 64 (June 1977), pp. 5–23.

184 *As his former student and preeminent historian John Morton Blum later wrote:* Blum, *A Life with History,* p. 154.

CHAPTER 22: THE TWILIGHT YEARS OF A BRILLIANT CAREER

190 *As he reflected in his 1982 letter to a former Harvard undergraduate:* Richard W. Leopold to Richard H. Russell, August 10, 1982, Leopold papers.

190 *He told the Northwestern Library Council in 1981:* Richard W. Leopold, "Aspirations Versus Achievements," remarks to Northwestern University Library Council (1981), p. 13, Leopold papers.

191 *He spent months identifying errors:* Alexander DeConde, ed., *Encyclopedia of American Foreign Policy: Studies of the Principal Movements and Ideas:* (New York: Charles Scribner's Sons, 1978).

191 *He then wrote a review detailing the mistakes:* Richard W. Leopold, "Historians and American Foreign Policy: An Encyclopedic Endeavor," *Pacific Historical Review,* vol. 50 (August 1983), pp. 339–50.

192 *Richard Dean Burns' Guide to American Foreign Relations since 1700 fared no better:* Richard Dean Burns, *Guide to American Foreign Relations since 1700* (Santa Barbara, Calif.: ABC-CLIO, 1983).

192 *In Dick's review, he wrote that in "the difficult area of finding aids":* Richard W. Leopold, "Historians and American Foreign Policy: A New Guide to the Field," *Diplomatic History,* vol. 8 (Summer 1984), pp. 273–85.

193 *When Bailey published:* Thomas A. Bailey, *The Pugnacious Presidents: White House Warriors on Parade* (New York: Collier Macmillan Publishers, 1980).

193 *In a 1985 article about the episode that followed, he described how his candor:* Richard W. Leopold, "Comments," *Diplomatic History,* vol. 9 (Fall 1985), pp. 326–27.

194 *"Retirement is akin to reading a book," he wrote:* Loeb autobiography, p. 44.

Chapter 23: Roll Call—Graduate Students

195 *By then, Kenneth E. Shewmaker had become a professor of history at Dartmouth College:* Kenneth E. Shewmaker to Richard W. Leopold, January 18, 1981, Leopold papers.

195 *Robert Moats Miller, professor of history at the University of North Carolina:* Robert Moats Miller to Richard W. Leopold, February 19, 1981, Leopold papers.

196 *The following year, he wrote, "How does one thank a mentor":* James C. Curtis to Richard W. Leopold, March 19, 1981, Leopold papers.

196 *Robert L. Tree of Iowa Wesleyan echoed the views of all:* Robert L. Tree to Lloyd E. Ambrosius, March 23, 1990, Leopold papers.

197 *Former senator and Democratic presidential candidate George S. McGovern reflected on Dick's significance to his life:* George S. McGovern to Benedict K. Zobrist, May 1, 1990, Leopold papers.

197 *Another early graduate student was Jack Blacksilver:* Jack Blacksilver to Lloyd E. Ambrosius, March 19, 1990, Leopold papers.

197 *In 1990, he wrote, "It is no exaggeration":* William Bruce Catton to Lloyd E. Ambrosius, March 24, 1990, Leopold papers.

197 *"In all the years I spent in graduate school I don't recall another faculty member who so struck me with the precision of his lectures":* Arnold Schrier to Lloyd E. Ambrosius, March 25, 1990, Leopold papers.

198 *"Of the numerous teachers of history whom I encountered":* Walter L. Arnstein to Lloyd E. Ambrosius, March 15, 1990, Leopold papers.

198 *"I remember Professor Leopold's lectures quite well":* Marc Raeff to Lloyd E. Ambrosius, March 28, 1990, Leopold papers.

199 *"His greatest contribution, I suspect, was in influencing graduate students like me":* Arthur M. Johnson to Lloyd E. Ambrosius, March 18, 1990, Leopold papers.

199 *"Leopold conveyed the ideals of rigorous, impartial scholarship":* Philip K. Lundeberg to Lloyd E. Ambrosius, March 26, 1990, Leopold papers.

199 *"Professor Leopold is unique . . . in the power of his teaching":* Philip C. F. Bankwitz to Lloyd E. Ambrosius, April 19, 1990, Leopold papers.

199 *Donald B. Cole wrote several books: Martin Van Buren and the American Political System* (Princeton, N.J.: Princeton University Press, 1984), *A Jackson Man: Amos Kendall and the Rise of American Democracy* (Baton Rouge: Louisiana State University Press, 2004), and *The Presidency of Andrew Jackson* (Lawrence: University Press of Kansas, 1993).

199 *Cole drew his inspiration to pursue a career in that profession in 1946:* Donald B. Cole to Lloyd E. Ambrosius, March 19, 1990, Leopold papers.

CHAPTER 24: A PRISONER OF HIS WHEELCHAIR

204 *In 1993, he acknowledged "the order of my current loyalties":* Richard W. Leopold to Ralph A. Bard, Jr., January 14, 1993, Leopold papers.

204 *As Zarefsky said at the time:* D. Shore, "Making History," *Northwestern Perspectives* (Winter 1991), p. 10.

205 *Dick was delighted to see his nephew:* Richard W. Leopold to Arthur W. Seligmann, March 15, 1995, Leopold papers.

206 *A month later, Dick lamented to Michael Barnhart:* Richard W. Leopold to Michael A. Barnhart, December 18, 1992, Leopold papers.

206 *In 1994, he wrote:* Richard W. Leopold to Robert B. Block, August 29, 1994, Leopold papers.

206 *In a letter to Edmund T. Delaney, he generally praised the author's manuscript:* Richard W. Leopold to Edmund T. Delaney, April 13, 1995, Leopold papers.

207 *He wrote a stirring letter of tribute to her son and daughter:* Richard W. Leopold to Penelope Demos Lawrence and John P. Demos, June 26, 1995, Leopold papers.

207 *On May 22, he wrote Arthur Link a letter:* Richard W. Leopold to Arthur S. Link, May 22, 1996, Leopold papers.

CHAPTER 25: NEARING THE FINAL STATION ON THE SCHEDULE

212 *Directly contrary to Dick's advice:* Leopold, *Growth*, p. 709.

214 *For as long as he could, he continued to review manuscripts of distinguished colleagues:* Blum, *A Life with History*, pp. 80–81, 125.

215 *Shortly after Dick's eighty-ninth birthday, someone typed up his reactions:* Richard W. Leopold to Arthur M. Schlesinger Jr., February 8, 2001, Leopold papers.

CHAPTER 26: THE MEASURE OF A MAN

220 *On April 13, 1995, Dick sent Edmund T. Delaney editorial comments:* Richard W. Leopold to Edmund T. Delaney, April 13, 1995, Leopold papers.

221 *Although Dick wrote in 1995, "I have no religion myself":* Richard W. Leopold to Edmund T. Delaney, March 7, 1995, Leopold papers.

222 *In it, he questioned whether he could make a career in history:* Richard W. Leopold to Ethel Leopold, January 6, 1933, Leopold papers.

222 *At the time, Dick did not know that the university's only Jewish tenured faculty member:* Shapiro, *A Time For Healing,* p. 16.

222 *He was unaware that only "western" applicants were eligible for the scholarships:* Blum, *A Life with History,* p. 22; Karabel, *The Chosen,* 175–78.

223 *But as Dick himself observed, Harvard "fumbled for six years over the field of diplomatic history":* Richard W. Leopold to Dr. Peter Carroll, November 22, 1989, Leopold papers.

223 *As he wrote to a college classmate in 1990:* Richard W. Leopold to Arthur M. Moody, February 27, 1990, Leopold papers.

223 *A similar distance from Judaism would accurately describe:* Loeb autobiography, p. 13.

223 *He, too, had no childhood connection to anything Jewish:* Blum, *A Life with History,* pp. 2, 4.

224 *In his 1938 inaugural address upon his ascent to the Yale presidency:* Shapiro, *We Are Many,* p. 135, citing Bradley J. Longfield, "'For God, for Country, and for Yale': Yale, Religion, and Higher Education between the World Wars" in *The Secularization of the Academy,* ed. George M. Marsden and Bradley J. Longfield (New York: Oxford University Press, 1992), pp. 151–58.

225 *Even as the war ended, Dartmouth's President Ernest M. Hopkins declared:* Shapiro, *We Are Many,* p. 97.

225 *In September 1945, John Blum heard directly from Elliot Perkins:* Blum, *A Life with History,* pp. 62–63.

225 *(Although, ironically, fellow Jews:* Blum, *A Life with History,* p. 213.

225 *The statistics prove that others must have had similar experiences:* Shapiro, *We Are Many,* p. 98, citing Stuart E. Rosenberg, *The New Jewish Identity in America* (New York: Hippocrene, 1985), pp. 252–56; Seymour Martin Lipset, "A Unique People in an Exceptional Country," in Seymour Martin Lipset, *American Pluralism and the Jewish Community* (New Brunswick, N.J.: Transaction, 1990), p. 4; Charles E. Silberman, *A Certain People: American Jews and Their Lives Today* (New York: Summit, 1985), p. 99; and Shapiro, *A Time for Healing,* p. 101, citing Everett Carll Ladd Jr. and Seymour Martin Lipset, *Divided Academy: Professors and Politics* (New York: McGraw-Hill, 1975), p. 150.

228 *In the most important lines on this topic in his autobiography, Pop wrote:* Loeb autobiography, pp. 31–32.

229 *In the postscript to his autobiography, he wrote:* Id., p. 63.

229 *When a would-be author on Northwestern's undergraduate life during the 1960s and 1970s asked:* Richard W. Leopold to Dr. Peter Carroll, November 22, 1989, Leopold papers.

231 *He grew up and lived in a time when men simply did not reveal emotional reactions; however, a 1933 letter to his mother is telling:* Richard W. Leopold to Ethel Leopold, January 6, 1933, Leopold papers.

231　*Twenty years later, he urged Arthur Link:* Richard W. Leopold to Arthur S. Link, February 6, 1955.

231　*Dick responded to the letter within twenty-four hours:* Richard W. Leopold to Richard H. Russell, August 10, 1982, Leopold papers.

232　*His 1995 letter to a former Exeter classmate who had become his mother's physician:* Richard W. Leopold to Dr. Arthur W. Seligmann, March 15, 1995.

233　*As Guthman once said, "We call ourselves Leopold people. We were adopted":* D. Shore, "Making History," *Northwestern Perspectives* (Winter 1991), p. 9.

233　*Returning to visit as often as he could:* Philip W. Stichter note in commemoration of the Richard W. Leopold Professorship, October 2006, Leopold papers.

233　*Mary Livingston Peterson ('62):* D. Shore, "Making History," *Northwestern Perspectives* (Winter 1991), p. 11.

233　*In a recent* Chicago Tribune *profile, a reporter asked Gordon: Chicago Tribune,* Business section (May 29, 2005), p. 3.

233　*As he later wrote:* Gordon Segal letter to Richard W. Leopold, October 12, 2006, Leopold papers.

233　*Entertainer Garry Marshall later noted:* Garry K. Marshall to Richard W. Leopold, October 2, 2006, Leopold papers.

Epilogue

242　*"Fair Harvard":* Samuel Gilman, Harvard class of 1811.

243　*"Non Sibi":* Words by H. S. Stuckey and music by F. N. Robinson; reprinted courtesy of the Phillips Exeter Academy Archives with thanks to Edouard L. Desrochers and Jacquelyn Thomas for their assistance in tracing the song's 1924 origins.

BOOKS, ARTICLES, AND PUBLISHED LETTERS BY RICHARD W. LEOPOLD

BOOKS

Leopold, Richard W. *Robert Dale Owen: A Biography*. Boston: Harvard University Press, 1940.

Leopold, Richard W. *Elihu Root and the Conservative Tradition*. Boston: Little, Brown, 1954.

Leopold, Richard W. *The Growth of American Foreign Policy: A History*. New York: Alfred A. Knopf, 1962.

Leopold, Richard W., and Arthur S. Link. *Problems in American History*. Englewood Cliffs, N.J.: Prentice-Hall, 1952.

Leopold, Richard W., and Arthur S. Link. *Problems in American History* (second edition). Englewood Cliffs, N.J.: Prentice-Hall, 1957.

Leopold, Richard W., Arthur S. Link, and Stanley S. Coben. *Problems in American History* (third edition). Englewood Cliffs, N.J.: Prentice-Hall, 1966.

Leopold, Richard W., Arthur S. Link, and Stanley S. Coben. *Problems in American History* (fourth edition). Englewood Cliffs, N.J.: Prentice-Hall, 1972.

Leopold, Richard W., and Dewey W. Grantham. *Final Report of the Joint AHA-OAH Ad Hoc Committee to Investigate the Charges against the Franklin D. Roosevelt Library and Related Matters*. Washington, D.C.: American Historical Association, 1970.

ARTICLES

History. *The American Year Book: a Record of Events and Progress. 1941*. (William M. Schuyler, ed.). New York: Thomas Nelson and Sons, 1942, pp. 856–61.

History. *The American Year Book: a Record of Events and Progress. 1946*. (William M. Schuyler, ed.). New York: Thomas Nelson and Sons, 1947, pp. 880–85.

History. *The American Year Book: a Record of Events and Progress. 1947*. (William M. Schuyler, ed.). New York: Thomas Nelson and Sons, 1948, pp. 900–905.

History. *The American Year Book: a Record of Events and Progress. 1948*. (William M. Schuyler, ed.). New York: Thomas Nelson and Sons, 1949, pp. 674–79.

History. *The American Year Book: a Record of Events and Progress. 1949*. (William M. Schuyler, ed.). New York: Thomas Nelson and Sons, 1950, pp. 694–99.

History. *The American Year Book: a Record of Events and Progress. 1950.* (S. Michaelis, ed.). New York: Thomas Nelson and Sons, 1951, pp. 696–702.

The Problem of American Intervention, 1917: An Historical Retrospect. *World Politics* (vol. 2, no. 3), April 1950, pp. 405–25.

The Mississippi Valley and American Foreign Policy, 1890–1941: An Assessment and an Appeal. *Mississippi Valley Historical Review* (vol. 37, no. 4), March 1951, pp. 625–42.

The Forty-Ninth Annual Meeting of the Mississippi Valley Historical Association. *Mississippi Valley Historical Review* (vol. 43, no. 2), September 1956, pp. 275–92.

The Foreign Relations Series: A Centennial Estimate. *Mississippi Valley Historical Review* (vol. 49, no. 4), March 1963, pp. 595–612.

The President and Foreign Policy: The Two Roosevelts. *Northwestern University Tri-Quarterly* (vol. 6), Fall 1963, pp. 3–9.

The Emergence of America as a World Power: Some Second Thoughts. *Change and Continuity in Twentieth-Century America* (John Braeman et al., eds.). Columbus: Ohio State University Press, 1964, pp. 3–34.

American Policy and China, 1937–1950: A Review. *Journal of Conflict Resolution* (vol. 8, no. 4), December 1964, pp. 505–10.

Report of Advisory Committee on "Foreign Relations," 1964. *American Journal of International Law* (vol. 59), October 1965, pp. 914–18.

The United States in World Affairs, 1941–1968. *Interpreting American History: Conversations with Historians* (John A. Garraty, ed.). New York: Macmillan, 1970.

A Crisis of Confidence: Foreign Policy Research and the Federal Government. *American Archivist* (vol. 34), April 1971, pp. 139–56.

A Crisis of Confidence: Foreign Policy Research and the Federal Government. *Society for Historians of American Foreign Relations Newsletter* (vol. 2), May 1971, pp. 1–14.

A Crisis of Confidence: Foreign Policy Research and the Federal Government. *Congressional Record,* June 23, 1971.

Viewpoint: George McGovern at NU. *The Daily Northwestern,* October 13, 1972, p. 7.

Historiographical Reflections. *Pearl Harbor as History: Japanese-American Relations, 1931–1941* (Dorothy Borg and Shumpei Okamoto, eds.). New York: Columbia University Press, 1973, pp. 1–23.

The *Foreign Relations* Series Revisited: One Hundred Plus Ten. *Journal of American History* (vol. 59, no. 4), March 1973, pp. 935–57.

Sarell Everett Gleason: A Memoir. *Massachusetts Historical Society Proceedings* (vol. 86), 1974, pp. 90–94.

Historical Advisory Committees: State, Defense, and Atomic Energy Commission ("Historians and the Federal Government"). *Pacific Historical Review* (vol. 44), August 1975, pp. 373–85.

Richard Hofstadter, The American Political Tradition and the Men Who Made It. *76 United Statesiana* (Edward Connery Latham, ed.). Washington, D.C.: Association of Research Libraries, 1976, p. 64.

The History of United States Foreign Policy: Past, Present, and Future. *The Future of History* (Charles F. Dalzell, ed.). Nashville, Tenn.: Vanderbilt University Press, 1977, pp. 231–46.

To the Editor (Presidential Libraries). *New York Times,* February 3, 1977.

The Historian and the Federal Government. *Journal of American History* (vol. 64, no. 1), June 1977, pp. 5–23.

The Korean War: The Historian's Task. *The Korean War: A 25-Year Perspective* (Francis H. Heller, ed.). Lawrence: Regents Press of Kansas, 1977, pp. 209–224.

The Future of History. *Essays in the Vanderbilt University Centennial Symposium.* Nashville, Tenn.: Vanderbilt University Press, 1977.

The Adventures of a Novice in Research: New Harmony and Indianapolis, 1935. *Indiana Magazine of History* (vol. 74), March 1978, pp. 1–22.

Frederick Merk: A Memoir. *American Historical Review* (vol. 83), October 1978, pp. 1152–53.

Report of the SHAFR Ad Hoc Committee on the *Foreign Relations* Series, May 8, 1979. *Society for Historians of American Foreign Relations Newsletter* (vol. 10), September 1979, pp. 19–23.

Reflections. *Northwestern University Syllabus, 1980,* February 9, 1980, pp. 110–113.

Historians and American Foreign Policy: An Encyclopedic Endeavor. Review essay of *Encyclopedia of American Foreign Policy: Studies of the Principal Movements and Ideas, 3* vols., Alexander DeConde, ed., Charles Scribner's Sons, 1978. *Pacific Historical Review* (vol. 50, no. 3), August 1981, pp. 339–50.

Ray Allen Billington: A Memoir. *Organization of American Historians Newsletter* (vol. 9), July 1981.

Ray Allen Billington: A Memoir. *Massachusetts Historical Society Proceedings* (vol. 93), 1981, pp. 119–22.

The Writings of a Teacher-Scholar: Aspirations versus Achievements. *Northwestern University Arts and Sciences* (vol. 4, Fall 1981), pp. 16–19.

Gray Cowan Boyce: A Memoir. *AHA Newsletter* (vol. 20), April 1982, p. 12.

American Diplomatic History: The Views of a Younger Generation. *Reviews in American History,* September 1982.

History over the Year: The MVHA and the OAH. *Organization of American Historians Newsletter* (vol. 11), February 1983, pp. 3–4.

Dudley W. Knox: Remarks at Dedication of Dudley Knox Center for Naval History. *A History of the Naval Historical Center and the Dudley Knox Center for Naval History.* Washington, D.C.: Naval Historical Foundation, 1983.

Elihu Root. *Biographical Dictionary of Internationalists* (Warren F. Kuehl, ed.). Westport, Conn.: Greenwood Press, 1983, pp. 634–36.

"Not Merely High Scholarship but High Character and Personality": The Harvard History Department a Half-Century Ago. *Massachusetts Historical Society Proceedings* (vol. 95), 1983, pp. 114–25.

Historians and American Foreign Policy: A New Guide to the Field. Review and Essay of *Guide to American Foreign Relations Since 1700,* Richard Dean Burns, ed., ABC-CLIO, 1983. *Diplomatic History* (vol. 8), Summer 1984, pp. 273–85.

Historians and American Foreign Policy: A New Guide to the Field. *Diplomatic History,* 1984.

Comments on Papers on Samuel F. Bemis, Thomas A. Bailey, and Fred Harvey Harrington at the Organization of American Historians. *Diplomatic History* (vol. 9), Fall 1985, pp. 321–27.

How a Big Ship Was Sunk. *Fortitudine,* Summer 1986.

A Primer for Statesmen. Review essay of *Thinking in Time: The Uses of History for Decision-Makers,* Richard E. Neustadt and Ernest R. May, Free Press, 1986. *Reviews in American History* (vol. 15, no. 4), December 1987, pp. 527–32.

A History of the Department of History, Northwestern University, 1885–1960. *Department of History Newsletter, July 1984–June 1985,* 1985, pp. 10–18.

Ibid., *July 1985–June 1986,* 1986, pp. 18–26.

Ibid., *July 1986–June 1987,* 1987, pp. 13–28.

Ibid., *July 1987–June 1988,* 1988, pp. 10–31.

The Second World War Revisited. Review essay of *Commander in Chief: Franklin Delano Roosevelt, His Lieutenants, and Their War,* Eric Larrabee, Harper and Row, 1987. *Reviews in American History* (vol. 16, no. 1), March 1988, pp. 110–14.

Warren F. Kuehl: In Memoriam. *Society for Historians of American Foreign Relations Newsletter* (vol. 19), March 1988, pp. 1–5.

W. Ernest Gillespie: A Memoir. *Phillips Exeter Bulletin,* Winter 1989–1990, p. 26.

422 Davis Street. Before We Were Here: Part One. *Georgian Newsletter,* October 1990.

422 Davis Street. Before We Were Here: Part Two. *Georgian Newsletter,* January 1991.

Arthur S. Link at Northwestern: The Maturing of a Scholar. *The Wilson Years: Essays in Honor of Arthur S. Link* (John Milton Cooper Jr. and Charles E. Neu, eds.). Harland Davidson, 1991, pp. 30–51.

The January Congressional Debate in Historical Perspective. *Georgian Newsletter,* March 1991.

422 Davis Street: From Hotel to Retirement Residence. *Georgian Newsletter,* May 1991.

422 Davis Street: The Road to an Independent Retirement Residence. *Georgian Newsletter,* June 1991.

Memories of the Princeton History Department, 1929–1933. [*Princeton University*] *Class of 1933 Summer Newsletter,* August 1991, pp. 27–29.

Contribution to *Fairbank Remembered* (compiled by Paul A. Cohen and Merle Goldman). Cambridge, Mass.: John K. Fairbank Center for East Asian Research, distributed by Harvard University Press, 1992.

An Early Boon from the Mather Foundation. *Georgian Newsletter,* April 1993.

Franklin D. Scott. *Northwestern University Department of History Newsletter,* September 1993–November 1994.

Mather Has Been a Good Neighbor. *Evanston Round Table,* March 10, 2004.

Letter to the Editor, *PAW* [*Princeton Alumni Weekly*] Online, www.princeton .edu/~paw/archive_new/PAW05-06/14-0607/letters.html, June 7, 2006.

INDEX

THE AUTHOR

Steven J. Harper has been a litigation partner in the international law firm of Kirkland & Ellis LLP for more than twenty years. He joined the firm upon graduation from Harvard Law School, having completed his undergraduate work in economics at Northwestern University. Currently, he is an adjunct professor of trial advocacy at Northwestern's School of Law and a fellow of the American College of Trial Lawyers. He is the author of *Crossing Hoffa: A Teamster's Story* (2007). More information is available at: www.stevenjharper.com.